RUIN

HENRIKE NAUMANN
SUNG TIEU

61ST International Art Exhibition
La Biennale di Venezia
German Pavilion 2026

61. Internationale Kunstausstellung
La Biennale di Venezia
Deutscher Pavillon 2026

ON WHAT REMAINS—
AND CONTINUES TO HAVE AN IMPACT

Germany's participation in the Venice Biennale is more than just an exhibition: it is an opportunity for self-examination in a historically charged building that is far removed from the assumed neutrality of the conventional white cube. The architecture of the German Pavilion in the Giardini, which was erected in 1909 and rebuilt in 1938 to conform to the representational aesthetics of National Socialism, is itself part of the history explored here. Those who exhibit in the pavilion always operate both with and within its political form.

ifa – Institut für Auslandsbeziehungen (Institute for Foreign Cultural Relations) has managed the German Pavilion on behalf of the Federal Foreign Office since 1971. In each edition, it establishes the framework for one or more independent artistic positions and helps bring about an internationally relevant exchange that also resonates with national debates. Exhibitions from Germany have been awarded the Golden Lion seven times to date. These awards not only recognize individual outstanding achievements, but also the continuity of a diverse arts scene in Germany, sustained by artists, institutions, and patrons.

For the 2026 Venice Biennale, Sung Tieu and Henrike Naumann have transformed the pavilion. Titled *RUIN*, their contribution layers architectural, social, and emotional landscapes of destruction to create a multifaceted reflection on the past and present. Their work exemplifies a practice that combines research, an understanding of material, and political sensitivity to explore the relationship between personal memory and societal power structures with precision.

The concept behind *RUIN* conceives of ruins not merely as remnants or an aesthetic motif, but as the outcome of multiple processes. It understands ruin as a historical and social phenomenon, as the remaining traces of political decisions, economic dynamics, and societal shifts. Ruin is seen here as an active process, because systems establish orders, generate exclusions, and leave behind ruptures. In this sense, the exhibition asks what remains of political systems and what continues to exert an effect from their fissures. It reminds us that history is not finished, but continues to be written in material, institutional, and social structures. And it invites us to understand the German Pavilion not as a static monument, but as a mutable place in dialogue with the present.

Kathleen Reinhardt is responsible for the curatorial concept behind the 2026 German Pavilion. She understands her curatorial practice as a form of research, a way of working with history, its gaps, and its repercussions in the present. Her exhibitions link artistic positions with historical material, archives, and social contexts, creating spaces in which diverse perspectives converge. Again and again, Reinhardt focuses on stories that have long been marginalized in art historical and national narratives. Against this backdrop, she brings together two artistic positions in the German Pavilion that engage with the material and social legacies of political systems in different ways. Sung Tieu and Henrike Naumann belong to a generation that reflects on the upheavals of recent German history from a historical perspective; they question these upheavals in terms of their own biographical experience. Each of their works addresses these questions from their own perspective, bringing them into a shared dialogue in the pavilion.

To our deepest regret, Henrike Naumann will not present her work at this year's Biennale herself. Following a brief and serious illness, she passed away on February 14, 2026. At ifa, we are deeply saddened for her family and all who were close to her, and at the same time filled with admiration for her. Henrike Naumann nonetheless completed the concept for her contribution, which is carried out in close collaboration with her studio and realized as a collaborative effort in keeping with her artistic vision.

ifa has supported Henrike Naumann for many years; one of her projects was the touring exhibition *EVROVIZION*. Her work demonstrates a precise understanding of historical and social contexts and creates the framework for an international perspective on contemporary Germany. With her contribution to the Venice Biennale, her artistic vision retains a presence in the pavilion beyond her death, continuing its influence and demonstrating how art can forge connections across time and place.

Biennials are places where international artistic, political, and social discourses converge. In this sense, they often act as a seismograph for contemporary developments. It's precisely for this reason that the Biennale is of particular importance to Germany's cultural relations and education policy. For over five decades, ifa has provided a framework for artistic contributions from Germany that incorporate international perspectives while reflecting social debates. This work is based on the conviction that freedom of art and freedom of expression are essential prerequisites for an open international exchange and that art can act as a catalyst for strengthening democracy by bringing into dialogue different experiences, histories, and interpretations of the present. The Biennale offers a unique setting for this, where encounters and dialogue become possible. Hence, the German Pavilion becomes a place where art transcends national borders; where it becomes apparent how cultural exchange can contribute to mutual understanding. In this sense, the German Pavilion also represents ifa's mission to fortify international relations through art and culture and to enable an open, differentiated view of Germany in a global context.

Germany's cultural relations and education policy, as the Foreign Office puts it, aims to build strong networks in times of geopolitical upheaval. The Venice Biennale demonstrates what networks like these can achieve: people, ideas, and artistic perspectives come together to create new platforms for understanding. The German Pavilion is part of this network of international connections. In the future, too, it is set to contribute to keeping these connections alive and furthering the exchange on art and society.

Daniela Schwarzer
President

Gitte Zschoch
Secretary General

ifa – Institut für Auslandsbeziehungen

ÜBER DAS, WAS BLEIBT – UND WEITERWIRKT

Die Beteiligung Deutschlands an der Venedig Biennale ist mehr als eine Ausstellungsteilnahme: Sie ist die Möglichkeit einer Selbstbefragung in einem historisch aufgeladenen Gebäude, fernab einer vermeintlichen Neutralität des konventionellen White Cube. Die Architektur des Deutschen Pavillons in den Giardini, der 1909 errichtet und 1938 im Geist nationalsozialistischer Repräsentationsästhetik umgebaut wurde, ist selbst Teil der Geschichte, die hier verhandelt wird. Wer ihn bespielt, arbeitet immer zugleich mit und in seiner politischen Gestalt.

Das ifa – Institut für Auslandsbeziehungen trägt seit 1971 die Verantwortung für den Deutschen Pavillon im Auftrag des Auswärtigen Amts. In jeder Edition schafft es die Rahmenbedingungen für eine oder mehrere freie künstlerischen Positionen und ermöglicht eine international anschlussfähige Auseinandersetzung, die zugleich zurück in nationale Debatten wirkt. Künstlerische Beiträge aus Deutschland wurden bisher sieben Mal mit dem Goldenen Löwen ausgezeichnet. Diese Auszeichnungen stehen nicht nur für einzelne herausragende Positionen, sondern auch für die Kontinuität einer vielfältigen Kunstlandschaft in Deutschland, getragen von Kunstschaffenden, Institutionen und Förderinnen und Förderer.

Für die Biennale 2026 haben Sung Tieu und Henrike Naumann den Pavillon transformiert. Unter dem Titel *RUIN* vernetzen sie architektonische, soziale und emotionale Trümmerlandschaften zu einer vielschichtigen Reflexion über Gegenwart und Vergangenheit. Ihre Arbeiten stehen für eine Praxis, die Recherche, Materialbewusstsein und politische Sensibilität miteinander verbindet und die das Verhältnis von persönlicher Erinnerung und gesellschaftlichen Machtverhältnissen präzise auslotet.

Das Konzept *RUIN* begreift die Ruine nicht allein als Überrest oder ästhetisches Motiv, sondern als Ergebnis von Prozessen. Es versteht Ruinierung als historisches und gesellschaftliches Geschehen, als Spur politischer Entscheidungen, ökonomischer Dynamiken und gesellschaftlicher Verschiebungen. Ruinierung erscheint hier als aktiver Vorgang, denn Systeme errichten Ordnungen, produzieren Ausschlüsse, hinterlassen Brüche. So fragt die Ausstellung, was von politischen Systemen bleibt und was in ihren Rissen weiterwirkt. Sie erinnert daran, dass Geschichte nicht abgeschlossen ist, sondern in materiellen, institutionellen und gesellschaftlichen Strukturen fortgeschrieben wird. Und sie lädt dazu ein, den Deutschen Pavillon nicht als statisches Monument, sondern als einen wandelbaren Ort im Dialog mit der Gegenwart zu begreifen.

Die kuratorische Konzeption des Deutschen Pavillons 2026 liegt bei Kathleen Reinhardt. Ihre Arbeit versteht kuratorische Praxis als eine Form der Recherche, als ein Arbeiten mit Geschichte, ihren Leerstellen und ihren Nachwirkungen in der Gegenwart. In ihren Ausstellungen verbindet sie künstlerische Positionen mit historischen Materialien, Archiven und gesellschaftlichen Kontexten und schafft Räume, in denen unterschiedliche Perspektiven aufeinandertreffen. Immer wieder richtet sie den Blick auf Geschichten, die in kunsthistorischen oder nationalen Erzählungen lange marginalisiert waren. Vor diesem Hintergrund bringt Reinhardt im Deutschen Pavillon zwei künstlerische Positionen zusammen, die sich auf unterschiedliche Weise mit den materiellen und sozialen Hinterlassenschaften politischer Systeme auseinandersetzen. Sung Tieu und Henrike Naumann gehören einer Generation an, die die Umbrüche der jüngeren deutschen Geschichte nicht nur historisch reflektiert, sondern aus eigenen biografischen Erfahrungen heraus befragt. Ihre Arbeiten greifen diese Fragen jeweils aus einer eigenen Perspektive auf und führen sie im Pavillon in einen gemeinsamen Dialog.

Zu unserem großen Bedauern kann Henrike Naumann ihr Werk auf der diesjährigen Biennale nicht selbst präsentieren. Nach kurzer und schwerer Krankheit ist sie am 14. Februar 2026 gestorben. Wir sind voller Mitgefühl für ihre Familie und alle, die ihr nahestanden, und voller Bewunderung für sie. Henrike Naumann hat die Konzeption ihres Beitrags für den Deutschen Pavillon noch selbst vollendet. Die Realisierung der Installation in Venedig erfolgt in enger Zusammenarbeit mit ihrem Studio und wird im Sinne ihrer künstlerischen Vision als Gemeinschaftsarbeit umgesetzt.

Das ifa begleitete Henrike Naumann über viele Jahre, unter anderem im Rahmen der Tourneeausstellung *EVROVIZION*. Ihre Arbeiten zeigen ein präzises Gespür für historische und gesellschaftliche Zusammenhänge und eröffnen internationale Perspektiven auf deutsche Gegenwart. Mit dem Beitrag auf der Venedig Biennale bleibt ihre künstlerische Vision auch über ihren Tod hinaus im Pavillon präsent, wirkt weiter und zeigt, wie Kunst Verbindungen über Zeit und Ort hinweg schaffen kann.

Biennalen sind Orte, an denen sich internationale künstlerische, politische und gesellschaftliche Diskurse verdichten. In diesem Sinne wirken sie oft wie ein Seismograf für Entwicklungen der Gegenwart. Gerade deshalb ist die Biennale auch für die auswärtige Kultur- und Bildungspolitik Deutschlands von besonderer Bedeutung. Das ifa schafft hier seit über fünf Jahrzehnten den Rahmen für künstlerische Beiträge aus Deutschland, die internationale Perspektiven einbeziehen und zugleich gesellschaftliche Debatten widerspiegeln. Grundlage dieser Arbeit ist die Überzeugung, dass Kunst- sowie Meinungsfreiheit zentrale Voraussetzungen für einen offenen internationalen Austausch sind und dass Kunst als Impulsgeber für die Stärkung von Demokratie wirken kann, indem unterschiedliche Erfahrungen, Geschichten und Gegenwartsdeutungen miteinander in Beziehung gesetzt werden. Die Biennale bietet dafür einen einzigartigen Rahmen, in dem Begegnung und Dialog möglich werden. Der Deutsche Pavillon wird so zu einem Ort, an dem Kunst über nationale Grenzen hinaus wirkt und an dem sichtbar wird, wie kultureller Austausch zum gegenseitigen Verständnis beitragen kann. In diesem Sinne steht der Deutsche Pavillon auch für das Anliegen des ifa, internationale Beziehungen durch Kunst und Kultur zu stärken und einen offenen, differenzierten Blick auf Deutschland im globalen Kontext zu ermöglichen.

Die aktuelle auswärtige Kultur- und Bildungspolitik verfolgt das Ziel, so beschreibt es das Auswärtige Amt, starke Netzwerke in Zeiten geopolitischer Umbrüche aufzubauen. Die Biennale von Venedig zeigt, was solche Netzwerke leisten können: Menschen, Ideen und künstlerische Perspektiven treten in Beziehung und eröffnen neue Verständigungsräume. Der Deutsche Pavillon ist Teil dieses Geflechts internationaler Netzwerke. Auch in Zukunft soll er dazu beitragen, diese Verbindungen lebendig zu halten und den Austausch über Kunst und Gesellschaft weiterzuführen.

Daniela Schwarzer
Präsidentin

Gitte Zschoch
Generalsekretärin

ifa – Institut für Auslandsbeziehungen

THE HIEROGLYPHS OF HENRIKE NAUMANN

Bakri Bakhit and Clemens Villinger

Henrike Naumann was open-minded and curious, but she was also determined. She knew she wanted to create good art that was uncomplicated, but discerning: inviting and accessible to as many people as possible, yet deeply researched and thought-provoking. Naumann's art focuses on places and materials, effortlessly drawing connections between the farmhouse living rooms (Bauernstuben) and hieroglyphs of the Erzgebirge region with a post-war divided Germany. There were no limits to her associations, yet they were never random. All over the world, from Tokyo to Kinshasa and Port-au-Prince, she connected with people who understood and appreciated her art as well as her way of producing it: clear, determined, uncompromising, inclusive, and in solidarity. Henrike Naumann's exhibition in the German Pavilion is no exception to this; despite her physical absence, it is typical of her working method—because while her artistic vision acted as a guide, she was never alone in creating her works. Her art has always been collaborative, with Henrike Naumann as its author.

For fifteen years, Naumann worked indefatigably towards exhibiting her art in the German Pavilion. Shortly before she died, she was still selecting objects, ordering furniture, deciding on colors, and honing her concept. Deconstructing the National Socialist pavilion was not on her mind. Instead, she reassembled it, decorated it, and painted it green, the color of the Soviet barracks. Her approach stands in contrast with previous artistic interventions that enlisted destruction in an attempt to grapple with the loaded history of the German Pavilion. The "worst destruction," she said, seems to be "making oneself comfortable. Not constantly digging up all the filth, while shaking your head in disbelief and feeling rattled, but saying: This is the normality we grew up with, the reality that has shaped this country and will continue to shape it. We make ourselves comfortable in the German Pavilion, and feel at every juncture that there's no such thing as comfortable here."

The pavilion's atmosphere is now uncomfortable, in that the *inner front* runs between inside and out; yesterday, today, and tomorrow. Front lines are dynamic, and it's the perspective that decides who is standing on what side. The reliefs, hieroglyphs, and living rooms in the German Pavilion function as legible and illegible maps of this *inner front*, offering viewers orientation while simultaneously leading them astray. The visitor hopes for a clear direction and a clarifying debate that fail to materialize. Henrike Naumann's work examines how history and community were and continue to be constructed; she investigates the power relations in these attempts at order and how they express themselves. She saw herself not as a neutral observer of these negotiation processes, but as a powerful actor fully aware of her responsibility. She implemented furniture and objects as a reference system to render visible how people react to change and make themselves at home within it. "And we seek shelter between shot-up curtains and battered wall units, but we can only progress by fleeing forward, where the front awaits us." (Henrike Naumann)

At the same time, the way she took on space has increasingly changed in her recent works: in lieu of large-scale, expansive works, they have become more and more reduced. "In Venice, her formerly three-dimensional spatial installations have flattened into wall reliefs that became at the same time highly condensed," as Henrike Naumann herself formulated it in a concept text. The result: spaces of signification in which lines of meaning are disrupted and what was believed to be certain is called into question.

Naumann distilled the archaeological aspects of her practice for her contribution to the pavilion. To her, digging in the true sense of the word, research without respite has always been a necessity for understanding, or attempting to understand, the horrors of the present. While the accessible furniture and objects provide an easy entry point for viewers, they simultaneously defy any clear interpretation; instead, one's own engagement becomes uncomfortable and even disturbing. In this way, the relevance of Naumann's work in the pavilion is made clear through her working method. The radical here is not what's obvious, but what challenges us.

"The space can be read like a text whose beginning we think we know and whose end we're afraid to read. Between the beginning and end, we, in the present, are uncertain about our ability to influence the course of events. But we are the front line. Just as we can be sent to a front at any moment, the front is also dependent on us. What we want to fight for, or against. Whether or not we fight. Or radically love, let go, be vulnerable. Give up all hardness. Or fight out of love, twice as fierce, hardcore." (Henrike Naumann)

DIE HIEROGLYPHEN DER HENRIKE NAUMANN

Bakri Bakhit und Clemens Villinger

Trotz ihrer Aufgeschlossenheit und Neugier war Henrike Naumann zielstrebig, sie wusste, was sie wollte: gute Kunst machen, unkompliziert, aber anspruchsvoll. Einladend und für möglichst viele Menschen zu verstehen und gleichzeitig tiefgründig recherchiert und zum Weiterdenken provozierend. Mit ihrer auf Orte und Materialitäten bezogenen Kunst verknüpfte sie mühelos erzgebirgische Bauernstuben und Hieroglyphen mit der deutsch-deutschen Nachkriegszeit. Ihren Assoziationen waren keine Grenzen gesetzt, aber zufällig waren sie nie. Überall auf der Welt, von Tokio über Kinshasa bis nach Port-au-Prince, konnte sie sich mit Menschen verbinden, die nicht nur ihre Kunst verstanden und schätzten, sondern auch ihre Art, Kunst zu produzieren. Klar, bestimmt, kompromisslos, inklusiv und solidarisch. Henrike Naumanns Ausstellung im Deutschen Pavillon ist keine Ausnahme, sondern trotz ihrer körperlichen Abwesenheit typisch für ihre Arbeitsweise: Sie leitete mit ihrer künstlerischen Vision an, aber alleine war sie beim Produzieren ihrer Arbeiten nie. Alle ihre Kunstwerke sind Gemeinschaftswerke, deren Autorin Henrike Naumann ist.

Um ihre Kunst im Deutschen Pavillon auszustellen, hat sie 15 Jahre unermüdlich gearbeitet. Noch bis kurz vor ihrem Tod hat sie Objekte ausgewählt, Möbel bestellt, Farben festgelegt und ihr Konzept präzisiert. Den nationalsozialistischen Pavillon zu dekonstruieren, lag ihr fern. Stattdessen hat sie ihn neu zusammengesetzt, dekoriert und im Grünton sowjetischer Kasernen angestrichen. Bisherigen künstlerischen Versuchen, der aufgeladenen Geschichte des Deutschen Pavillons durch Zerstörungen beizukommen, setzt Henrike Naumann einen anderen Ansatz entgegen: Die „schlimmste Vernichtung" scheint die zu sein, „es sich gemütlich zu machen. Den ganzen Dreck nicht immer wieder wundernd und kopfschüttelnd auszugraben und erschüttert zu sein, sondern zu sagen: Das ist die Normalität, mit der wir aufgewachsen sind, und die Realität, die dieses Land geprägt hat und weiter prägen wird. Wir machen es uns im Deutschen Pavillon gemütlich, und spüren an allen Ecken und Kanten, dass es gemütlich hier nicht gibt" (Henrike Naumann).

Im Pavillon ist es ungemütlich geworden, denn die *Innere Front* verläuft zwischen Innen und Außen, Gestern, Heute und Morgen. Frontverläufe sind dynamisch und wer auf welcher Seite steht, ist abhängig von der Perspektive. Die Reliefs, Hieroglyphen und Stuben im Deutschen Pavillon funktionieren als lesbare und unlesbare Karten der *Inneren Front*, die den Betrachtenden Orientierung geben und dabei vom Weg abkommen lassen. Man hofft auf eine klare Ausrichtung und klärende Auseinandersetzung, die nicht eintritt. Henrike Naumann untersucht in ihrer Arbeit, wie Geschichte und Gemeinschaft hergestellt wurden und werden und welche Machtverhältnisse sich wie in diesen Ordnungsversuchen ausdrücken. Sie selbst hat sich in diesen Aushandlungsprozessen nicht als neutrale Beobachterin verstanden, sondern als machtvolle und verantwortungsbewusste Akteurin. Sie setzte Möbel und Objekte als ein Referenzsystem ein, um sichtbar zu machen, wie Menschen mit Wandel umgehen und sich darin einrichten. „Und zwischen zerschossenen Gardinen und verletzten Schrankwänden suchen wir Schutz, doch nur durch die Flucht nach vorn kommen wir weiter, wo uns die Front erwartet" (Henrike Naumann). Gleichzeitig veränderte sich ihre Raumeinnehmung in den letzten Arbeiten immer mehr: Statt großformatiger, sich ausbreitender Arbeiten, entwickelten sich diese reduziert. „Ihre vormals dreidimensionalen Rauminstallationen haben sich in Venedig zu Wandreliefs verflacht und zugleich verdichtet", so formulierte es Henrike Naumann selbst in einem Konzeptpapier. Es entstanden Zeichenräume, in denen Bedeutungslinien aufgebrochen und Sichergeglaubtes infrage gestellt wurde.

Für den Beitrag im Pavillon konzentrierte sie die archäologischen Elemente ihrer Praxis. Unermüdlich tief graben und recherchieren, das war für sie, im Wortsinn, immer eine Notwendigkeit, um die Schrecken der Gegenwart (versuchen) zu verstehen. Der für die Betrachtenden leichte Einstieg über zugängliche Möbel und Objekte verweigert gleichzeitig eine klare Lesart, vielmehr wird die eigene Auseinandersetzung ungemütlich und mitunter verstörend. Die Relevanz ihres Pavillonbeitrags macht ihre Arbeitsweise so deutlich. Das Radikale ist nicht das Offensichtliche, sondern das Herausfordernde.

„Der Raum lässt sich lesen wie ein Text, dessen Anfang wir zu kennen meinen und dessen Ende wir uns fürchten zu lesen. Zwischen Anfang und Ende sind wir, die Gegenwart, unsicher, welche Möglichkeiten wir haben, auf den Lauf der Dinge Einfluss zu nehmen. Doch die Front sind wir. So wie wir jederzeit an eine Front geschickt werden können, so ist sie auch abhängig von uns. Wofür wir kämpfen wollen, oder wogegen. Ob wir kämpfen. Oder radikal lieben, loslassen, schutzlos sein. Alles Harte aufgeben. Oder aus Liebe kämpfen, doppelt so hart, hardcore." (Henrike Naumann)

RUIN
HENRIKE NAUMANN AND SUNG TIEU AT THE 2026 GERMAN PAVILION

Kathleen Reinhardt

> ...the secret prohibitions, the observation, the suspicion, the fear, the isolation and exclusion, the branding and silencing of those who don't conform—that will come back, believe me. Institutions will be created that work much more effectively, much more finely than the Stasi. The constant lying will also return, the disinformation, the fog in which everything loses its contours.
> —Bärbel Bohley, 1991

Sung Tieu and Henrike Naumann's deeply personal, research-based practices evince an urgent search for form and meaning amidst the fog of constant wars, hyperreactive public discourse, historical amnesia, algorithmic manipulations, the return of patriarchal power claims, and countless other markers of a turbulent contemporary existence.

With their understanding of art and aesthetics as resonant political realms, their skillful interweaving of times and spaces, and their rigorous intellectual examination of everyday materialities and processes, Tieu and Naumann occupy the German Pavilion of the 2026 Venice Biennale. Among other works, the exhibition pairs a large-scale mosaic depicting the ruin of a socialist housing complex in East Berlin with an immersive relief of discarded things, forming a mediation on the persistent presence of material ruins. The ruin motif has accrued multiple, often overlapping meanings across history and occupies a singular place in German self-mythologizing.[1] In this charged terrain, the artists' works engage with immaterial forms of ruin, unfolding across art historical, psychological, sociological, and allegorical registers.

In 2019, the subtitle of Natascha Sadr Haghighian's presentation at the German Pavilion addressed "surviving in the ruinous ruins" of the present—today, in a new global era, we might ask what this survival entails. With formal vocabularies spanning minimalist clarity and maximalist opulence, Naumann and Tieu actively grapple with the imposing fascist architecture of the German Pavilion, using it as an ambiguous mirror for contemporary dynamics. In doing so, they foreground the layered traces of presences and absences, a focus encapsulated in the exhibition's title. *Ruin* is a space in which the polychronic traces of physical and social structures, German ideologies, and lives once lived remain materially present. The title riffs on the term's

1) Kevin Bücking, *Ruinen-Ästhetik: Über die Spuren der Zeit im Raum der Gegenwart,* Bielefeld: transcript, 2023; Éva Kocziszky, ed., *Ruinen in der Moderne: Archäologie und die Künste,* Berlin: Reimer, 2011; Norbert Bolz and Willem van Reijen, eds., *Ruinen des Denkens: Denken in Ruinen,* Frankfurt am Main: Suhrkamp, 1996.

semantic plasticity, encompassing not only how it describes the decay of physical structures and objects, but also gestures toward bankruptcy—whether financial, political, or moral. The works presented at the pavilion thus address not a past that has passed, but one that is perhaps even more present and tangible today.

In their newly created works, the artists disrupt what anthropologist and historian Ann Laura Stoler described as a "facile distinction between political history and poetic form urging us to think differently about both the language we use to capture the tenacious hold of imperial effects and their tangible if elusive forms."[2] In this vein, the distinct artistic vocabularies of Henrike Naumann and Sung Tieu dare visitors to surpass viewing "ruins" as (n)ostalgic and fixed aesthetic realms, and instead reconfigure them as active, violent, and "ruin-producing" political forces. While Stoler applies this conceptual frame to the ruins and debris of colonial regimes, significantly expanding the realms of ruin theory, the artists' interventions in the pavilion can be read alongside this, transforming its architecture and historical resonances into sites of reflection and resistance.

THE DIVIDED HEAVEN

Sung Tieu envelops the pavilion's monumental, neoclassical façade in an all-over trompe-l'œil mosaic, obscuring the historically charged "Germania" lettering above the portal. The mosaic forms a pixelated image of the skeletal remains of a prefabricated apartment block covered in graffiti and overgrown with vegetation. Located on Gehrenseestrasse in Berlin-Hohenschönhausen, the building was the artist's childhood home and one of the largest housing complexes for Vietnamese contract workers in East Germany, later inhabited by various migrant communities after reunification. Over three million miniature mosaic marble tiles simulate the image and textures of an architectural form once conceived as one of the most equalizing structures in socialism.[3] Tieu's metabolization of the 1938 German Pavilion architecture also evokes the erased history of state socialism in Germany in perhaps its most obvious form: the demolition of the GDR's former parliament building, the Palace of the Republic, to make way for the resurrection of the Prussian castle that stood on the site before it was destroyed in World War II.[4] By transposing the image of a highly personal space onto the pavilion façade—one largely absent from grand historical narratives—Sung Tieu makes clear that this history of ideological erasure and historic denial goes far beyond official accounts.

2) Ann Laura Stoler, ed., *Imperial Debris: On Ruins and Ruination,* Durham: Duke University Press, 2013, p. 2.

3) In the nascent post-World War II GDR, prefabricated housing, stemming from 1920s industrialized building methods, was continuously redeveloped. By the 1970s, it was applied en masse to construct functional, modern, and equal living spaces for the working population. Residential units were assembled from prefabricated panels, often flexible within predefined geometric constructions, forming large complexes with stores, kindergartens, playgrounds, policlinics, and access to public transport. After reunification, these neighborhoods were often considered the epitome of flawed urban planning—as their original function to pragmatically serve the working population became obsolete with a wave of unemployment hitting East Germany after its people-owned industries were sold and closed down. For more on socialist housing complexes and their role in art, please see Kito Nedo and Kevin Hanschke, eds., *Wohnkomplex,* Berlin: Distanz, 2025. For a sociological examination, please see: Steffen Mau, *Lütten Klein: Leben in der ostdeutschen Transformationsgesellschaft,* Berlin: Suhrkamp, 2019.

4) The castle was severely damaged by bombing during World War II. Thereafter, the GDR demolished and cleared away its ruin and reconceptualized the area according to an East-modern vision of urban planning. Today, the reconstructed castle also houses many of the collections created in colonial times.

She further highlights these ambivalences in her detailed timeline of the Gehrenseestrasse areal included in this publication, tracing its use since its construction in the GDR era, the transition period of the 1990s while she lived there, and its subsequent incarnation as an object of investment and speculation. By foregrounding the history of her childhood apartment block through the mosaic and accompanying timeline, Tieu's intervention illustrates not only the lingering effects of what political philosopher Susan Buck-Morss described as the collapse of socialist dreamworlds and their transformative aftermath, but also the inherent flaws of any state or ideological system—its anti-human and exclusionary structures of control and discipline, which disproportionately affect the most vulnerable.[5]

While the political structure of a reunified Germany in the 1990s was shaped by a West German desire for continuity, profound social and aesthetic transformations took place in the East, which Henrike Naumann aptly describes as "Secondhand-Re-Education." Parallel to the political and economic changes, which left many without jobs for years to come, East Germans also implemented an aesthetic transformation within their own four walls. Within these multiple processes of reorganization, people adapted, radicalized, or retreated from the public. Both Tieu's and Naumann's works make the interactions between individuals and the structural forces surrounding them hauntingly palpable. While Naumann spatially translates these dynamics in her interior installations, Tieu grapples with the shadows of these reforms in her critical reflections on systemic oppression and the wave of right-wing extremist violence against former contract workers and refugees, showing how they continue to shape the lives and identities of diasporic communities to this day.

In earlier works, Sung Tieu had already begun to address the living conditions of Vietnamese contract workers[6] before and after 1989, who have experienced firsthand the realities of a "socialism of difference"[7] in the face of an uncritical *white* internationalist consciousness. This approach, which mobilized "race without racism,"[8] was unable to unlearn racism or prevent racist acts of violence. From the 1990s onward, it veered toward extreme right-wing violence, directly targeting migrant communities, while also becoming firmly established in a *white*-majority society in the East in its search for new coordinates. Dramaturge Heiner Müller analyzed these dynamics of the immediate post-reunification period:

> The botched attack on the Intershops resulted in kowtowing to the goods. From the heroic city of Leipzig to the terror of Rostock. The scars cry out for wounds: the

5) Tieu's work examines the interplay of socialist utopias (as embodied in the idea of prefabricated housing), neoliberal dystopia (the ruin of investment schemes), and the resilience of the people who lived there.

6) Around 70,000 Vietnamese contract workers (Vertragsarbeiter) and trainees were employed in the GDR between 1980 and 1990 following intergovernmental agreements as part of socialist solidarity pacts, making them the largest foreign workforce group of the GDR. These workers primarily worked in state-owned enterprises (VEB) in manufacturing, textiles, and electronics to address labor shortages. Their strict contracts regulated the length of their stay under highly restrictive conditions. They lived in segregated housing and were often subjected to surveillance, undermining any contact with the GDR population outside the work setting.

7) Peggy Piesche, "Making African Diasporic Pasts Possible: A Retrospective View of the GDR and its Black (Step-) Children," in *Remapping Black Germany: New Perspectives on Afro-German History*, ed. Sara Lennox, Amherst/Boston: University of Massachusetts Press, 2016, p. 229.

8) Quinn Slobodian, "Socialist Chromatism: Race, Racism, and the Racial Rainbow in East Germany," in *Comrades of Color: East Germany in the Cold War World*, ed. Quinn Slobodian, New York/Oxford: Berghahn Books, 2015, p. 23.

repressed potential for violence—no revolution/emancipation without violence against the oppressor—breaks through in attacks on the weaker members of society: asylum seekers and (poor) foreigners, the poor against the poorest, no real estate sharks, no matter the nationality, shall come to any harm. The reaction to the economic war on housing rights is a war on those without homes. A trip through Mecklenburg: at every gas station, the victory banners of the oil companies; in every village, instead of the usual stationery stores, Mc Paper & Co. In a sea of foreign influence, being German is the last illusion of identity, the last island. But what is that: German?[9]

This central question, omnipresent in the German Pavilion, is present in how both artists interrogate power relations and collective memorialization—as well as their quest to exit linear narratives that reserve only marginalized spaces for such inquiries. Naumann's early film installation *Triangular Stories* (2012) is based on her research into the NSU complex. Active in the 2000s, this right-wing terrorist group hid close to her grandmother's house in Zwickau for years, where they planned a murder spree of migrants across Germany with substantial support from police networks.[10] In 1992, the first pogroms after World War II took place in Rostock-Lichtenhagen, a housing complex erected between the late 1970s and early 1980s. In 1979, artist Reinhard Dietrich created a large-scale tile mosaic of sunflowers that covered the entire side façade of one block, giving the Sonnenblumenhaus (Sunflower House) its name. In the vein of producing uplifting public art for the socialist masses, artists were commissioned to adorn the buildings, create playgrounds, or design fountains. On August 24, 1992, a mob of neo-Nazis, residents, and bystanders attacked the complex, which housed former contract workers and asylum seekers. Local police deliberately refrained from intervening, allowing mob rule for four days and nights, during which they attacked the building with Molotov cocktails, speech choirs, and other violent means. This highly traumatizing episode in recent German history still awaits proper official memorialization.[11] Hans Haacke's 1993 German Pavillion work also referenced this historical event, but Tieu now takes up this symbol of one of the darkest periods for post-reunification Germany, translating it into a contemporary form of pixelization. By enshrouding the German Pavilion's façade with a potent visual reference to her personal history and the history of contract workers in Germany, Tieu expands the narratives of national identity and enables new ways of critical and self-reflexive remembering in a diverse German society.

9) Heiner Müller, "Die Küste der Barbaren," *Frankfurter Rundschau*, September 25, 1992.

10) Between the years 2000 and 2007, the Nationalsozialistischer Untergrund (NSU) committed ten murders. Nine of the victims were small business owners with immigrant backgrounds. German authorities failed to link the murders to right-wing terrorism for many years, focusing instead on the victims' families and communities.

11) A heated public debate on immigration preceded the incident, and afterwards, the Bundestag restricted the fundamental right to asylum, also falling back on the precarious status of the East German Vietnamese communities. See Angelika Nguyen, "Film ohne Auftrag—Perspektiven, die ausgegrenzt und unterschlagen wurden," Bundeszentrale für politische Bildung, https://www.bpb.de/themen/deutschlandarchiv/512249/film-ohne-auftrag-perspektiven-die-ausgegrenzt-und-unterschlagen-wurden/ (accessed February 13, 2026); Esther Dischereit, "Vor aller Augen: Pogrome und der untätige Staat," Bundeszentrale für politische Bildung, https://www.bpb.de/themen/deutschlandarchiv/505377/vor-aller-augen-pogrome-und-der-untaetige-staat/ (accessed February 13, 2026); see also the film by Burhan Qurbani, *Wir sind jung. Wir sind stark* (2014).

Henrike Naumann's immersive readymade object installation takes a different approach to narratives of national identity, fusing metaphorical references to the postwar period in both Germanys, Socialist Realist paintings, and the East German "baseball bat years" of the 1990s—epitomized by the Rostock-Lichtenhagen pogroms—into what the artist terms an "archaeological prehistory of the present." One wall is dedicated to a sort of "sign system" for the entire installation. In its function as an alphabet of "hieroglyphs," as the artist calls them, this display functions like a glossary that explains the work's cosmos through associations and references, representing her method of archaeological research. In her practice, Naumann often reflects on socio-political issues through interior design, exploring the friction between opposing political opinions in relation to taste and personal everyday aesthetics. Working in her signature medium—furniture and decorative consumer objects—the artist composes a multi-part, large-scale relief of objects partly damaged by holes and cuts, set against a mint-green background. The installation's upper level displays a gallery of chairs and curtains, deepening a central artistic theme for Naumann: homeyness as a parallel-operating emotional space. Her employment of the form of a history painting assemblage, citing the work of her grandfather Karl Heinz Jakob, a socialist-realist painter in the GDR, allegorically resurrects different episodes of FRG and West German history diametrically opposed to GDR and East German history.[12] Setting them in a haunted space of folkloric traditions adds another layer to the "disturbances" arising from lost or erased places, broken time, and political systems rendered obsolete. Working with the set pieces of a past that will not pass, as seen in the current resurrections of post-World War II political desires, remnants of Cold War orders, and a return to "traditions" of various kinds, Naumann offers a glimpse into a future-past that can become a present reality much sooner than expected. Her work proposes a hieroglyphic realm where "folkic art," different phases of Socialist Realism, and a retrospective "self-folklorization" of the East converge, unsettling easy references to modernism's centralization of folklore and primitivism, while also serving as a vehicle to conjure "authentic ideals"—and with them lost futures. This also evokes what Jacques Derrida, and later Mark Fisher drawing on Derrida, described as hauntology: the persistence of past aesthetics as a structuring presence in the present. The mass of outdated home decor objects, her uncanny citation of the wall color of former Soviet army barracks in the GDR as a backdrop, and the traces of damage

12) The mural *The Mechanization of Agriculture* (1960) by Karl Heinz Jakob had already served as a reference for Naumann in her performance *Hard Style* (2024) at the Pochen Biennale in Chemnitz. The mural, which was covered with drywall in the early 2000s, is uncovered again in the German Pavilion and re-staged with her artistic vocabulary.

within this complex panorama of an other German history render East Germany, for the artist, an "inner front"—a border that will not disappear.

"THE FUTURE IS CERTAIN, IT'S THE PAST WHICH IS UNPREDICTABLE"

In past works, Naumann has reflected on Albert Speer's Ruinenwerttheorie (theory of ruin value), in which the architect of the Third Reich retrospectively theorized his monumental constructions not only in their intended glory, but also in their projected state of ruin, anticipating how they might be perceived after a German 1000 year rule.[13] Read alongside what Boris Groys once described as the time-lapse experienced by socialist subjects—who had lived in an ideal socialist future and then, after the collapse of state socialisms, were transported back to an already overcome past to enter outdated political models under capitalism—the temporalities explored in and on the pavilion propose yet another dimension of time and space. The relief and the mosaic take on specific meanings in this context: both forms stem from Greco-Roman traditions, entered Christian visual culture, and were subsequently developed as realms that sought to balance traditional form, accessible figurative representation, and new uplifting visual programs under socialism. Resonating with both artists' skepticism toward linear readings of time and their use of archaic forms such as relief and mosaic, their works fuse notions of circular time and temporal compression. In doing so, they disrupt fantasies of continuity and notions of progress—embodied, for example, in the idea of reunification as a means to overcome the past, eliminate the brief socialist interlude, and continue writing a German success story. They instead emphasize the many parallel realities that compose this history.

Returning to Stoler's theoretical proposition about imperial ruins, the artists break down the distinction between political histories and artistic form through their tactile methodologies, offering precise artistic vocabularies to show how and where these past traces are present today.[14] In this sense, their practices do not necessarily mobilize ruin as a noun, but as a verb: referring to the ongoing processes of ruination triggered by current political endeavors to silence how history is told from the margins. While Henrike Naumann reenvisions our immediate future through her use of historical traces and materials, Sung Tieu approaches figurative form and conceptual abstraction as reflexive, non-opposing media to craft narratives around visibility and invisibility, desire, and refusal.

13) Speer's theory of ruin value can be interpreted as a distorted ideological appropriation of an older German appreciation of ruins, articulated perhaps most fully during the era of German Romanticism in the late eighteenth and early nineteenth centuries, when ruins became powerful symbols of emotion and spirituality—as seen in the crumbling monasteries and overgrown abbeys of Caspar David Friedrich. For Naumann's employment of Speer's theory see, Henrike Naumann, Angela Schönberger, and Andreas Brandolini, *Tumbling Ruins*, Berlin: DISTANZ Verlag, 2021.

14) Stoler 2013

Henrike Naumann's material aesthetic cosmos draws on postmodern traditions, notably through her use of the cheap, mass-produced 1990s copies of designs associated with the Italian Alchimia movement and the New German Design (Neues Deutsches Design) of the 1970s and 1980s, establishing a complex analysis of taste and class across cultural and temporal realms. In the vein of a horizontal art history for East and Central European practices as proposed by Piotr Piotrowski, Naumann employs a notion of postmodernism as situated knowledge with a non-universal claim in an anti-modernist and anti-art history sense.[15] Extending this approach, in the performative element of her installation, Naumann invited dancers from the vertical dance group Il Posto, who started a distinctively Venetian contemporary tradition of façade dance. Suspended by ropes that enable them to use house façades as their dancefloor, they perform on and in-between Naumann's reliefs and assemblages in the pavilion. In this work, she foregrounds the ephemeral and the discarded, unsettling the distinction between vertical, continuity-driven narratives and the horizontal art histories of the East, the margins, and beyond.

Sung Tieu's personal, emotionally inflected minimalism equally disrupts conventional, linear art historical narratives. Shifting between multiple layers of history, Tieu picks up the thread from her Gehrenseestrasse façade in the side wings of the pavilion. Set against a titanium white background, her minimal wall sculptures show aluminium bars measuring the bodily proportions of the artist's mother.[16] For this series of works, Tieu researched Albrecht Dürer's *Four Books on Human Proportion* (1528), which contain an approach to the measurement of the human form that, as scholar Noam Andrews notes, "articulates a dynamic vision of bodily difference—one that avoids moral or medical judgment yet would be reinterpreted through exclusionary frameworks of physiognomic classification in the following centuries."[17] By pursuing an open approach to proportionality that accommodates difference within a flexible framework, Tieu resists the dehumanizing frameworks of bodily measurement, in line with her ongoing critique of rigid systems and control mechanisms that enforce classification and obedience by leaving no space for variation. Visually, her practice often insists on aesthetics as a sober means of clarification, while actively resisting discourses that attempt to reduce her work to an expression of pain or confine it to questions of identity. While Tieu enforces rigorous clarity in the left wing of the pavilion, she opens an emotional space in the right wing, for example, with her new glass works. Glass is a fragile

15) See Piotr Piotrowski, *In the Shadow of Yalta: Art and the Avant-garde in Eastern Europe, 1945–1989*, London: Reaktion Books, 2011. See also Piotr Piotrowski, "Toward a Horizontal History of the European Avant-Garde," in *Europa! Europa?: The Avant-Garde, Modernism and the Fate of a Continent*, eds. Sascha Bru, Jan Baetens, Benedikt Hjartarson, Peter Nicholls, Tania Ørum, and Hubert van den Berg, Berlin: De Gruyter, 2009, pp. 49–58; Agata Jakubowska, Magdalena Radomska, eds., *Horizontal Art History and Beyond: Revising Peripheral Critical Practices*, New York/London: Routledge, 2023.

16) This work is not the first time that Tieu has measured bodies in her works. To create the series *Exposure to Havana Syndrome* (2020–ongoing), Tieu reconstructed an alleged sonic attack that induced inexplicable bouts of nausea, memory loss, dizziness, and vertigo in CIA operatives staying in a Havana hotel. After exposing herself to the influence of sonic weaponry, Tieu had MRI captures of her brain engraved onto metal plates.

17) Noam Andrews, "Dürer on Difference," *Nuncius. Journal of the Material and Visual History of Science*, vol. 40, no. 3, 2025, https://doi.org/10.1163/18253911-bja10154.

yet resistant materiality, while also evoking the liminality between tangible form and invisibility. The glass hands of the artist's mother Vũ Thị Hạnh are marked by decades of labor, which is quite literally imprinted upon the body. In *The Cultural Politics of Emotion* (2004), scholar Sara Ahmed examines how emotional impressions are formed, writing:

> Forming an impression also depends on how objects impress upon us. An impression can be an effect on the subject's feelings ("she made an impression"). It can be a belief ("to be under an impression"). It can be an imitation or an image ("to create an impression"). Or it can be a mark on the surface ("to leave an impression"). We need to remember the "press" in an impression. It allows us to associate the experience of having an emotion with the very affect of one surface upon another, an affect that leaves its mark or trace.[18]

Ahmed goes on to propose that the constant repetition of these impressions results in "stickiness as an effect of the histories of contact between bodies, objects, and signs."[19] What is often mistaken for emotion originating from within does not in fact come from inside. Instead, it is shaped through interaction and exists in zones of contact. Its "stickiness therefore is an effect" that stems from "histories of contact"—arising from repeated exchanges that result in an "accumulation of affective value."[20] Tieu's cast glass, cut-metal objects and small ladybird sculptures, along with her pixelated façade, evoking the close-up/far effects of Impressionist paintings,[21] capture a fragmented world in which emotion—often misread as intrinsic and natural—is instead produced through relational and perceptual encounters.

RISEN FROM RUINS

The Giardini, and the German Pavilion in particular, operate as a political topography, where the display and interpretation of art reveal the historical and contemporary intersections of history, politics, and societal values. With their layered formal, political, social, and historical implications, the works of Tieu and Naumann contribute to the main exhibition's choruses in "minor keys," consistently stimulating polyphonically conceived pasts, presents, and futures. It is precisely in the art of Sung Tieu and Henrike Naumann—which responds to the aftermath of the infamously proclaimed "end of history," with its triumphant narrative exposing the failures of "realistic socialism" (shaped internally by oppressive mechanisms and manipulations, as Bärbel Bohley's opening quote reflects, and later externally by forces that profited from this failure, monetarily

18) Sara Ahmed, *The Cultural Politics of Emotion*, New York/ London: Routledge, 2004, p. 6.

19) Ibid, p. 90.

20) Ibid, p. 92.

21) See Richard Shiff, "Marks of Low Resolution: Impressionism's Artistic Language," in *Impressionism: The Art of Landscape*, eds. Ortrud Westheider, Michael Philipp, exh. cat. Museum Barberini, Potsdam, Munich/London/ New York: Prestel, 2017. I would like to thank Daniel Milnes for sharing this reference with me.

or ideologically)—that the complications and ruinations of German narratives can be found.

Patriarchal constructs—in their realities of disciplining, violence, and war—always speak a clear language, but it is art that recognizes the truth within and can bring it to expression. Henrike Naumann and Sung Tieu describe, in ruinous and urgent yet poetic form, the stickiness of transitions, memory, and affect. And beyond the current rewriting of history, the degradation of debate, and the reality of wars, it is their art that insists on creating new truths.

RUIN
HENRIKE NAUMANN UND SUNG TIEU IM DEUTSCHEN PAVILLON 2026

Kathleen Reinhardt

> Die geheimen Verbote, das Beobachten, der Argwohn, die Angst, das Isolieren und Ausgrenzen, das Brandmarken und Mundtotmachen derer, die sich nicht anpassen – das wird wiederkommen, glaubt mir. Man wird Einrichtungen schaffen, die viel effektiver arbeiten, viel feiner als die Stasi. Auch das ständige Lügen wird wiederkommen, die Desinformation, der Nebel, in dem alles seine Kontur verliert.
> – Bärbel Bohley, 1991

Inmitten des Nebels ständiger Kriege, hyperreaktiver öffentlicher Diskurse, historischer Amnesie, algorithmischer Manipulationen, der Rückkehr patriarchalischer Machtansprüche und zahlloser anderer Merkmale einer unruhigen zeitgenössischen Existenz machen die sehr persönlichen, recherchebasierten Praktiken von Sung Tieu und Henrike Naumann eine dringliche Suche nach Form und Bedeutung erfahrbar.

Tieu und Naumann besetzen den Deutschen Pavillon der Venedig Biennale 2026 mit ihrem erweiterten Verständnis von Kunst und Ästhetik als widerhallende politische Sphären, ihrem gekonnten Verweben von Zeit und Raum und ihrer rigorosen intellektuellen Untersuchung alltäglicher Materialien und Prozesse. Neben anderen Arbeiten bringt die Ausstellung ein großformatiges Mosaik, das die Ruine eines sozialistischen Wohnkomplexes in Ost-Berlin zeigt, mit einem mehrteiligen immersiven Relief ausrangierter Objekte zusammen und leitet so eine Untersuchung zur anhaltenden Gegenwart materiellen Verfalls ein. Das Ruinenmotiv hat im Laufe der Geschichte vielfältige, sich oft überschneidende Bedeutungen angenommen und besitzt in der deutschen Selbstmythologisierung einen einzigartigen Platz.[1] In diesem aufgeladenen Terrain beschäftigen sich die Werke der Künstlerinnen ebenso mit immateriellen Formen von Verfall, die sich über kunsthistorische, psychologische, soziologische und allegorische Register erstrecken.

Im Jahr 2019 thematisierte der Untertitel von Natascha Sadr Haghighians Präsentation im Deutschen Pavillon den Versuch, in der ruinösen Ruine der Gegenwart zu überleben („surviving in the ruinous ruin") – heute, in einer neuen globalen Ära, könnten wir fragen, was dieses Überleben ausmacht. Mit einem formalen Vokabular von minimalisti-

1) Kevin Bücking, *Ruinen-Ästhetik. Über die Spuren der Zeit im Raum der Gegenwart*, Bielefeld: transcript, 2023; Éva Kocziszky (Hg.), *Ruinen in der Moderne. Archäologie und die Künste*, Berlin: Reimer, 2011; Norbert Bolz, Willem van Reijen (Hg.), *Ruinen des Denkens – Denken in Ruinen*, Frankfurt am Main: Suhrkamp, 1996.

scher Klarheit bis zu maximal(istisch)er Opulenz setzen sich Naumann und Tieu aktiv mit der imposanten faschistischen Architektur des Deutschen Pavillons auseinander und nutzen ihn als vieldeutigen Spiegel für zeitgenössische Dynamiken. So stellen sie übereinander gelagerte Spuren von An- und Abwesenheiten in den Vordergrund, wie es der Ausstellungstitel impliziert. *Ruin* ist ein Raum, in dem polychrome Spuren physischer und sozialer Strukturen, deutscher Ideologien und einst gelebter Leben materiell präsent bleiben. Der Titel spielt mit der semantischen Plastizität des Begriffs, indem er nicht nur den Verfall physischer Strukturen und Objekte umfasst, sondern auch auf Bankrott weist – sei es finanziell, politisch oder moralisch. Die im Pavillon präsentierten Arbeiten adressieren so keine Vergangenheit, die vergangen ist, sondern eine, die heute vielleicht sogar noch gegenwärtiger und greifbarer geworden ist.

In ihren neu geschaffenen Arbeiten brechen die Künstlerinnen mit dem, was die Anthropologin und Historikerin Ann Laura Stoler als eine „simple Unterscheidung zwischen politischer Geschichte und poetischer Form" bezeichnet, „die uns dazu drängt, über die Sprache, die wir benutzen, anders zu denken, um den beharrlichen Einfluss imperialer Effekte sowie deren schwer greifbare Formen zu erfassen".[2] In diesem Sinne fordert das höchst eigenständige künstlerische Vokabular von Henrike Naumann und Sung Tieu die Besucher*innen auf, über die Sichtweise auf „Ruinen" als (n)ostalgische und festgefügte ästhetische Bereiche hinauszugehen und sie stattdessen als aktive, gewaltsame und „ruin(en)-produzierende" politische Kräfte neu zu konfigurieren. Während Stoler diesen konzeptuellen Rahmen auf die Ruinen und Trümmer kolonialer Regime anwendet und damit das Feld der Ruinentheorie signifikant erweitert, können die Interventionen der Künstlerinnen am und im Pavillon als Transformation von dessen Architektur und dessen historischer Resonanzen zu Stätten der Reflexion und des Widerstands gelesen werden.

DER GETEILTE HIMMEL

Sung Tieu verhüllt die monumentale, neoklassizistische Fassade des Pavillons mit einem Trompe-l'œil-Mosaik, das auch den geschichtlich aufgeladenen Schriftzug „Germania" über dem Portal verdeckt. Das Mosaik zeigt das verpixelte Bild eines mit Graffiti überzogenen und von Vegetation überwucherten, stehen gebliebenen Skeletts eines Plattenbaus. Das Gebäude in der Gehrenseestraße in Berlin-Hohenschönhausen war das Haus, in dem die Künstlerin einen Teil ihrer Kindheit verbrachte und einer der größten Wohnkomplexe

2) Ann Laura Stoler (Hg.), *Imperial Debris: On Ruins and Ruination*, Durham: Duke University Press, 2013, S. 2.

für vietnamesische Vertragsarbeiter*innen in Ostdeutschland. Nach der Wiedervereinigung wurde es von verschiedenen migrantischen Gemeinschaften bewohnt. Mehr als drei Millionen kleiner Marmormosaikplättchen simulieren das Bild und die Texturen einer architektonischen Form, die im Sozialismus einst als höchst egalisierende Struktur konzipiert worden war.[3] Tieus Metabolisierung der Architektur des Deutschen Pavillons von 1938 erinnert auch an die ausgelöschte Geschichte des Staatssozialismus in Deutschland in ihrer vielleicht deutlichsten Form: den Abriss des ehemaligen Parlamentsgebäudes der DDR, des Palastes der Republik, um Platz zu schaffen für die Wiedererrichtung des preußischen Schlosses, das vor seiner Zerstörung im Zweiten Weltkrieg dort stand.[4] Durch die Übertragung des Bildes eines sehr persönlichen – in großen historischen Narrativen weitgehend abwesenden – Ortes auf die Pavillonfassade zeigt Sung Tieu, dass diese Geschichte ideologischer Auslöschung und geschichtlicher Leugnung weit über offizielle Darstellungen hinausgeht. Sie verdeutlicht diese Ambivalenzen darüber hinaus in ihrer detaillierten Chronik zum Areal der Gehrenseestraße, die in dieser Publikation enthalten ist, und zeichnet dessen Nutzung seit Baubeginn in der DDR-Zeit, in der Transformationszeit der 1990er-Jahre, als sie dort lebte, sowie dessen spätere Wandlung in ein Investitions- und Spekulationsobjekt nach. Indem sie die Geschichte des Plattenbaus ihrer Kindheit durch das Mosaik und die dazugehörige Chronik in den Vordergrund rückt, veranschaulicht Tieu nicht nur die anhaltenden Auswirkungen dessen, was die politische Philosophin Susan Buck-Morss als Zusammenbruch sozialistischer Traumwelten und deren transformative Nachwirkungen bezeichnet hat, sondern auch die inhärenten Fehlstellen eines jeden Staates oder ideologischen Systems – seine menschenverachtenden und ausgrenzenden Kontroll- und Disziplinierungsstrukturen, die die Schwächsten unverhältnismäßig stark treffen.[5]

Während die politische Struktur des wiedervereinigten Deutschlands in den 1990er-Jahren vom westdeutschen Wunsch nach Kontinuität geprägt war, fanden im Osten tiefgreifende soziale und ästhetische Veränderungen statt, die Henrike Naumann treffend als „Secondhand-Re-Education" beschreibt. Parallel zu den politischen und wirtschaftlichen Veränderungen, die viele auf Jahre hinaus arbeitslos machten, vollzogen die Ostdeutschen auch innerhalb ihrer eigenen vier Wände einen ästhetischen Wandel. In diesen vielfältigen Umstrukturierungsprozessen passten sich die Menschen an, radikalisierten sich oder zogen sich aus der Öffentlichkeit zurück. Sowohl Tieus als auch Naumanns

3) In der nach dem Zweiten Weltkrieg entstandenen DDR wurden Fertigteilbauten, die aus den industrialisierten Bauweisen der 1920er-Jahre hervorgingen, kontinuierlich weiterentwickelt. In den 1970er-Jahren wurden sie massenhaft eingesetzt, um funktionale, moderne und gleichwertige Wohnräume für die arbeitende Bevölkerung zu schaffen. Wohneinheiten, die innerhalb vorgegebener geometrischer Konstruktionen oft flexibel waren, wurden aus vorfabrizierten Platten zusammengesetzt; angeschlossen an öffentliche Verkehrsmittel, bildeten sie große Komplexe mit Läden, Kindergärten, Spielplätzen und Polikliniken. Nach der Wiedervereinigung galten diese Wohngebiete oft als Inbegriff verfehlter Stadtpolitik, da ihre eigentliche Funktion, der arbeitenden Bevölkerung pragmatisch zu dienen, obsolet geworden war, als Ostdeutschland nach dem Verkauf und der Abwicklung volkseigener Betriebe von einer Welle der Arbeitslosigkeit erfasst wurde. Weitere Informationen zu sozialistischen Wohnkomplexen und deren Rolle in der Kunst finden sich bei Kito Nedo, Kevin Hanschke (Hg.), *Wohnkomplex*, Berlin: Distanz, 2025. Für eine soziologische Untersuchung siehe: Steffen Mau, *Lütten Klein. Leben in der ostdeutschen Transformationsgesellschaft*, Berlin: Suhrkamp, 2019.

4) Im Zweiten Weltkrieg wurde das Schloss durch Bombenangriffe schwer beschädigt. In den 1950er-Jahren wurde die Ruine gesprengt und das Areal gemäß einer ostmodernen stadtplanerischen Vision umgestaltet. Heute beherbergt das wiederaufgebaute Schloss viele Sammlungen, die in der Kolonialzeit entstanden sind.

5) Tieus Werk untersucht das Zusammenspiel aus sozialistischen Utopien (verkörpert in der Idee des Plattenbaus), neoliberaler Dystopie (dem Scheitern von Investitionsprogrammen) und der Resilienz der Menschen, die dort lebten.

Arbeiten machen die Interaktionen zwischen Individuen und den sie umgebenden strukturellen Kräften auf eindringliche Weise greifbar. Während Naumann diese Dynamik in ihre Innenrauminstallationen übersetzt, beschäftigt sich Tieu in ihren kritischen Überlegungen zu systemischer Unterdrückung und der Welle rechtsextremer Gewalt gegen ehemalige Vertragsarbeiter*innen und Geflüchtete mit den Schatten dieser Reformen und zeigt, wie diese bis zum heutigen Tag das Leben und die Identität von Diasporagemeinschaften prägen.

In früheren Werken setzte sich Sung Tieu bereits mit den Lebensbedingungen vietnamesischer Vertragsarbeiter*innen[6] vor und nach 1989 auseinander, die die Realitäten eines „Differenzsozialismus"[7] angesichts eines unkritischen *weißen* internationalistischen Bewusstseins am eigenen Leib erfahren hatten. Dieser Ansatz, der „Rasse ohne Rassismus"[8] in Umlauf brachte, war nicht in der Lage, Rassismus zu verlernen („unlearn") oder rassistische Gewalttaten zu verhindern. Ab den 1990er-Jahren schlug er in rechtsextreme Gewalt um, die direkt auf Migrant*innengemeinschaften zielte, und etablierte sich im Osten gleichzeitig fest in einer mehrheitlich *weißen* Gesellschaft, die auf der Suche nach neuen Koordinaten war. Der Dramatiker Heiner Müller analysierte diese Dynamik der unmittelbaren Nachwendezeit:

> Der versäumte Angriff auf die Intershops mündete in den Kotau vor der Ware. Von der Heldenstadt Leipzig zum Terror von Rostock. Die Narben schrein nach Wunden: das unterdrückte Gewaltpotential, keine Revolution/Emanzipation ohne Gewalt gegen die Unterdrücker, bricht sich Bahn im Angriff auf die Schwächeren: Asylanten und (arme) Ausländer, der Armen gegen die Ärmsten, keinem Immobilienhai, gleich welcher Nation, wird ein Haar gekrümmt. Die Reaktion auf den Wirtschaftskrieg gegen das Wohnrecht ist der Krieg gegen die Wohnungslosen. Eine Fahrt durch Mecklenburg: an jeder Tankstelle die Siegesbanner der Ölkonzerne, in jedem Dorf statt der gewohnten Schreibwaren McPaper & Co. Im Meer der Überfremdung ist Deutschsein die letzte Illusion von Identität, die letzte Insel. Aber was ist das: deutsch.[9]

Diese im Deutschen Pavillon allgegenwärtige zentrale Frage zeigt sich darin, wie beide Künstlerinnen Machtverhältnisse und kollektive Erinnerung hinterfragen – sowie in ihrem Streben, aus linearen Narrativen herauszutreten, die solchen Fragestellungen nur marginale Räume vorbehalten. Naumanns frühe Filminstallation *Triangular Stories* (2012) basiert auf ihren Recherchen zum NSU-Komplex. Die in den

6) Zwischen 1980 und 1990 waren etwa 70 000 vietnamesische Vertragsarbeiter*innen und Auszubildende im Rahmen zwischenstaatlicher Vereinbarungen als Teil sozialistischer Solidaritätsverträge in der DDR angestellt, was sie zur größten ausländischen Arbeitsnehmer*innengruppe DDR machte. Diese Arbeiter*innen waren vor allem in volkseigenen Betrieben in den Bereichen Fertigung, Textil und Elektronik tätig, um den Arbeitskräftemangel auszugleichen. Ihre strengen Verträge regelten ihre Aufenthaltsdauer unter äußerst restriktiven Bedingungen. Sie lebten in segregierten Unterkünften und standen oft unter Beobachtung, was jeglichen Kontakt mit der DDR-Bevölkerung außerhalb des Arbeitsumfelds unterband.

7) Peggy Piesche, „Making African Diasporic Pasts Possible: A Retrospective View of the GDR and its Black (Step-)Children", in: *Remapping Black Germany: New Perspectives on Afro-German History*, hg. von. Sara Lennox, Amherst/Boston: University of Massachusetts Press, 2016, S. 229.

8) Quinn Slobodian, „Socialist Chromatism: Race, Racism, and the Racial Rainbow in East Germany", in: *Comrades of Color: East Germany in the Cold War World*, hg. von Quinn Slobodian, New York/Oxford: Berghahn Books, 2015, S. 23.

9) Heiner Müller, „Die Küste der Barbaren", *Frankfurter Rundschau*, 25. September 1992.

2000er-Jahren aktive rechtsextreme Terrorgruppe versteckte sich in der Nähe des Hauses von Naumanns Großmutter in Zwickau, wo sie mit erheblicher Unterstützung von Polizeinetzwerken eine Mordserie an Migrant*innen in ganz Deutschland plante.[10] 1992 fanden in Rostock-Lichtenhagen, einer zeitgleich zur Gehrenseestraße errichteten Plattenbau-Wohnsiedlung, die ersten Pogrome in Deutschland nach dem Zweiten Weltkrieg statt. Im Jahr 1979 schuf der Künstler Reinhard Dietrich ein großflächiges Fliesenmosaik mit Sonnenblumen, das die gesamte Seitenfassade eines Gebäudeblocks einnahm und dem Sonnenblumenhaus seinen Namen gab. Im Sinne der Schaffung erbaulicher öffentlicher Kunst für die sozialistischen Massen waren Künstler*innen beauftragt, Gebäude und Spielplätze zu gestalten oder Brunnen zu entwerfen. Am 24. August 1992 attackierte ein Mob aus Neonazis, Anwohner*innen und Beistehenden den Komplex, in dem ehemalige Vertragsarbeiter*innen und Asylsuchende untergebracht waren. Die örtliche Polizei schritt bewusst nicht ein und ließ vier Tage und Nächte lang, in denen das Gebäude mit Molotow-Cocktails, Sprechchören und anderen gewaltsamen Mitteln angegriffen wurde, den Mob gewähren. Dieses zutiefst traumatisierende Ereignis der jüngeren deutschen Geschichte wartet noch immer auf eine angemessene offizielle Erinnerung.[11] Auch Hans Haackes Arbeit für den Deutschen Pavillon 1993 bezieht sich auf dieses historische Ereignis, Tieu aber greift dieses Symbol einer der dunkelsten Perioden der deutschen Nachwende-Zeit auf und übersetzt sie in eine zeitgenössische Form der Verpixelung. Indem sie die Fassade des Deutschen Pavillons mit einem starken visuellen Verweis auf ihre persönliche Geschichte und der Vertragsarbeiter*innen in Deutschland verhüllt, erweitert Tieu die Narrative von nationaler Identität und ermöglicht neue Wege des kritischen und selbstreflexiven Erinnerns in einer diversen deutschen Gesellschaft.

Henrike Naumanns immersive Readymade-Objektinstallation verfolgt einen unterschiedlichen Ansatz im Hinblick auf Narrative nationaler Identität und verbindet metaphorische Bezüge zur Nachkriegszeit in beiden deutschen Staaten mit Gemälden des Sozialistischen Realismus und mit Referenzen zu den ostdeutschen „Baseballschläger-Jahren" der 1990er – verkörpert durch die Pogrome von Rostock-Lichtenhagen –, zu dem, was die Künstlerin als „archäologische Vorgeschichte der Gegenwart" bezeichnet hat. Eine Wand ist einer Art Zeichensystem für die gesamte Installation gewidmet, das in seiner Funktion als Alphabet von „Hieroglyphen", wie die Künstlerin sie nennt, für bestimmte Aspekte des Werks steht und wie ein Glossar

10) Zwischen 2000 und 2007 verübte der Nationalsozialistische Untergrund (NSU) zehn Morde. Neun der Opfer waren Kleinunternehmer mit Migrationshintergrund. Die deutschen Behörden wollten die Morde viele Jahre lang nicht mit Rechtsterrorismus in Verbindung bringen und konzentrierten sich stattdessen auf die Familien und Gemeinschaften der Opfer.

11) Dem Vorfall ging eine hitzige öffentliche Debatte über Einwanderung voraus, und anschließend schränkte der Bundestag das Grundrecht auf Asyl ein, was auch den prekären Status der ostdeutschen vietnamesischen Gemeinschaften betraf. Vgl. Angelika Nguyen, „Film ohne Auftrag – Perspektiven, die ausgegrenzt und unterschlagen wurden", Bundeszentrale für politische Bildung, https://www.bpb.de/themen/deutschlandarchiv/512249/film-ohne-auftrag-perspektiven-die-ausgegrenzt-und-unterschlagen-wurden, letzter Zugriff am 13.2.2026; Esther Dischereit, „Vor aller Augen: Pogrome und der untätige Staat", Bundeszentrale für politische Bildung, https://www.bpb.de/themen/deutschlandarchiv/505377/vor-aller-augen-pogrome-und-der-untaetige-staat, letzter Zugriff am 13.2.2026; siehe auch Burhan Qurbani, *Wir sind jung. Wir sind stark* (2014).

funktioniert, um den Kosmos des Werks durch Assoziationen und Verweise zu erklären und ihre Methode der archäologischen Forschung darzustellen. In ihrer Praxis reflektiert Naumann häufig gesellschaftspolitische Aspekte durch Innenarchitektur und untersucht dabei die Spannungen zwischen entgegengesetzten politischen Ansichten in Bezug auf Geschmack und Alltagsästhetik. In der Arbeit mit ihrem charakteristischen Medium der Möbel und dekorativen Konsumgegenstände komponiert die Künstlerin ein mehrteiliges großformatiges Relief auf mintgrünem Hintergrund, bei dem die Objekte teilweise Beschädigungen in Form von Löchern und Schnitten aufweisen. Die obere Ebene der Installation zeigt eine Galerie aus Stühlen und Vorhängen, die ein zentrales künstlerisches Thema von Naumann vertiefen: heimische Gemütlichkeit als parallel operierender emotionaler Raum. In Anlehnung an ein Werk ihres Großvaters Karl Heinz Jakob, eines Malers des Sozialistischen Realismus in der DDR, verwendet sie die Form eines Assemblage-Historiengemäldes und lässt verschiedene Episoden der DDR- und ostdeutschen Geschichte im Gegensatz zur BRD und westdeutschen Geschichte allegorisch wiederaufleben.[12] Dies in einem von volkstümlichen Traditionen heimgesuchten Raum zu zeigen, fügt den „Störungen“, die durch verlorene oder ausgelöschte Orte, gebrochene Zeitlichkeit und überholte politische Systeme entstehen, eine weitere Ebene hinzu. Durch die Arbeit mit Versatzstücken einer Vergangenheit, die nicht vergeht, wie sich in der aktuellen Wiederbelebung politischer Bestrebungen der Nachkriegszeit, den Überresten der Ordnung des Kalten Krieges und einer Rückkehr zu „Traditionen“ verschiedenster Art zeigt, bietet Naumann Einblick in eine Zukunft in der Vergangenheit, die viel früher als erwartet gegenwärtige Realität werden kann. Ihre Arbeit entwirft einen hieroglyphischen Raum, in dem Volkskunst, „Volkstümlichkeit“, verschiedene Phasen des Sozialistischen Realismus und eine retrospektive „Selbstfolklorisierung“ des Ostens zusammenfließen. Damit hinterfragt sie vereinfachte Deutungen des Zusammenspiels von Folklore und Primitivismus in der Moderne, während diese gleichzeitig als Mittel dienen, um authentische Ideale heraufzubeschwören – und mit ihnen verlorene Zukünfte. Dies verweist auch darauf, was Jacques Derrida und später Mark Fisher in Anlehnung an Derrida als Hauntologie bezeichnet haben: das Fortbestehen vergangener Ästhetiken als strukturierende Präsenz in der Gegenwart. Die Menge an veralteten Einrichtungsgegenständen, ihre unheimliche Anspielung auf die Wandfarbe ehemaliger sowjetischer Kasernen in der DDR als Hintergrund und die Spuren der Zerstörung innerhalb dieses

12) Das Wandbild *Die Mechanisierung der Landwirtschaft* (1960) von Karl Heinz Jakob war bereits in der Vergangenheit Referenz für Naumann in ihrer Performance *Hard Style* (2024) auf der Pochen Biennale in Chemnitz. Das in den frühen 2000er-Jahren mit einer Trockenbauwand verkleidete Wandbild wird im Deutschen Pavillon wieder freigelegt und mit Naumanns künstlerischem Vokabular neu inszeniert.

komplexen Panoramas einer anderen deutschen Geschichte machen Ostdeutschland für die Künstlerin zu einer *Inneren Front* – einer Grenze, die nicht verschwinden wird.

„DIE ZUKUNFT IST SICHER, NUR DIE VERGANGENHEIT IST UNVORHERSEHBAR"

In früheren Arbeiten hat sich Naumann mit Albert Speers Ruinenwerttheorie auseinandergesetzt, in welcher der Architekt des Dritten Reiches rückblickend seine monumentalen Bauwerke nicht nur in ihrer beabsichtigten Pracht, sondern auch in ihrem prognostizierten Ruinenzustand imaginierte und dabei vorwegnahm, wie sie nach tausendjähriger deutscher Herrschaft wahrgenommen werden könnten.[13] Zusammengelesen mit dem, was Boris Groys einmal als Zeitraffer beschrieben hat, den die in einer idealen sozialistischen Zukunft lebenden und dann, nach dem Zusammenbruch des Staatssozialismus, in eine bereits überwundene Vergangenheit zurückversetzten sozialistischen Subjekte erfahren haben, um im Kapitalismus in veraltete politische Modelle einzutreten, eröffnen die im und am Pavillon erforschten Zeitlichkeiten noch eine weitere Dimension von Zeit und Raum. Das Relief und das Mosaik erhalten in diesem Kontext eine besondere Bedeutung: Beide Formen entstammen der griechisch-römischen Tradition, fanden Eingang in die christliche Bildkultur und wurden später als Bereiche weiterentwickelt, die ein Gleichgewicht zwischen traditioneller Form, zugänglicher figurativer Darstellung und neuen, erhebenden Bildprogrammen im Sozialismus anstrebten. Die Skepsis beider Künstlerinnen gegenüber linearen Zeitauffassungen und ihr Einsatz archaischer Formen wie Relief und Mosaik lassen in ihren Arbeiten Vorstellungen von zirkulärer Zeit und zeitlicher Verdichtung verschmelzen. Dadurch brechen sie mit Kontinuitätsfantasien und Fortschrittsvorstellungen – verkörpert beispielsweise in der Idee der Wiedervereinigung als Mittel, die Vergangenheit zu überwinden, das kurze sozialistische Intermezzo auszulöschen und die deutsche Erfolgsgeschichte fortzuschreiben – und betonen stattdessen die vielen parallelen Realitäten, aus denen sich diese Geschichte zusammensetzt.

Im Rückgriff auf Stolers theoretischen Ansatz zu imperialen Ruinen heben die Künstlerinnen durch ihre taktilen Methoden die Unterscheidung zwischen politischer Geschichte und künstlerischer Form auf und bieten präzise künstlerische Vokabularien, um zu zeigen, wie und wo diese Vergangenheitsspuren heute präsent sind.[14] In diesem Sinne setzen ihre Praktiken „Ruin" nicht unbedingt als Substantiv ein, sondern als Verb: Sie beziehen sich auf die fortlaufenden Prozesse

13) Speers Theorie des Ruinenwerts kann als verzerrte ideologische Aneignung der deutschen Beschäftigung mit Ruinen interpretiert werden, die vielleicht am deutlichsten in der Zeit der deutschen Romantik im späten 18. und frühen 19. Jahrhundert zum Ausdruck kam, als Ruinen zu starken Symbolen für Emotionen und Spiritualität wurden – wie an den zerfallenden Klöstern und überwucherten Abteien von Caspar David Friedrich vielleicht am deutlichsten zu sehen ist. Zu Naumanns Beschäftigung mit Speers Theorie siehe: Henrike Naumann, Angela Schönberger, Andreas Brandolini, *Einstürzende Reichsbauten*, Berlin: DISTANZ Verlag, 2021.

14) Stoler 2013.

des Ruinierens, die durch aktuelle politische Bestrebungen ausgelöst werden, um eine Geschichtsschreibung des Marginalen und an den Rand gedrängten zum Schweigen zu bringen. Während Henrike Naumann unsere unmittelbare Zukunft durch ihren Einsatz historischer Spuren und Materialien neu interpretiert, nähert sich Sung Tieu figurativen Formen und konzeptueller Abstraktion als reflexiven, nicht gegensätzlichen Medien, um Narrative rund um Sichtbarkeit und Unsichtbarkeit, Begehren und Ablehnung zu schaffen.

Henrike Naumanns materieller ästhetischer Kosmos knüpft an postmoderne Traditionen an, insbesondere durch ihre Verwendung billiger, massenproduzierter Kopien von Designs aus den 1990er-Jahren, die mit der italienischen Alchimia-Bewegung und des Neuen Deutschen Designs der 1970er- und 1980er-Jahre in Verbindung stehen, und stellt so eine komplexe Analyse von Geschmack und Klasse über kulturelle und zeitliche Grenzen hinweg dar. In Anlehnung an eine horizontale Kunstgeschichtsschreibung Mittel- und Osteuropas, wie sie Piotr Piotrowski vorschlug, verwendet Naumann einen Ansatz der Postmoderne als situiertes Wissen mit einem nicht-universellen Anspruch im antimodernistischen und anti-kunsthistorischen Sinne.[15] Darüber hinaus lud Naumann für den performativen Teil ihrer Installation Tänzer*innen der Vertikaltanzgruppe Il Posto ein, die eine venezianische zeitgenössische Tradition des Fassadentanzes begründet haben. An Seilen hängend, was es ihnen erlaubt, Hausfassaden als Tanzfläche zu nutzen, performen sie im Pavillon auf und zwischen Naumanns Reliefs und Assemblagen. In dieser Arbeit rückt sie das Vergängliche und Verworfene in den Vordergrund und hebt die Unterscheidung zwischen vertikalen, auf Kontinuität ausgerichteten Narrativen und den horizontalen Kunstgeschichten des Ostens, des Marginalen und des damit Assoziierten auf.

Sung Tieus persönlicher, und zugleich emotional geprägter Minimalismus bricht gleichermaßen mit konventionellen, linearen kunsthistorischen Narrativen. Im Wechsel zwischen multiplen Ebenen von Geschichte knüpft Tieu in den Seitenflügeln des Pavillons an ihre Fassade aus der Gehrenseestraße an. Vor einem Titanium-weißen Hintergrund zeigen minimalistische Wandskulpturen aus Aluminiumstäben die körperlichen Proportionen ihrer Mutter auf.[16] Für diese Werkserie untersuchte die Künstlerin Albrecht Dürers *Vier Bücher von menschlicher Proportion* (1528), die einen Ansatz zur Vermessung der menschlichen Gestalt enthalten, der, wie der Wissenschaftler Noam Andrews feststellt, „eine dynamische Vision körperlicher Unterschiede zum Ausdruck bringt – eine Vision, die moralische oder medizinische Urteile vermeidet,

15) Vgl. Piotr Piotrowski, *In the Shadow of Yalta: Art and the Avant-garde in Eastern Europe, 1945–1989*, London: Reaktion Books, 2011. Siehe auch: Piotr Piotrowski, „Toward a Horizontal History of the European Avant-Garde“, in: *Europa! Europa?: The Avant-Garde, Modernism and the Fate of a Continent*, hg. von Sascha Bru u. a., Berlin: De Gruyter, 2009, S. 49–58; Agata Jakubowska, Magdalena Radomska (Hg.), *Horizontal Art History and Beyond: Revising Peripheral Critical Practices*, New York/London: Routledge, 2023.

16) Dies ist nicht das erste Mal, dass Tieu Körper in ihren Werken vermessen hat. Für die Serie *Exposure to Havana Syndrome* (2020–fortlaufend) rekonstruierte Tieu einen angeblichen Schallangriff, der bei CIA-Agenten, die in einem Hotel in Havanna übernachteten, unerklärliche Übelkeit, Gedächtnisverlust, Schwindel und Gleichgewichtsstörungen auslöste. Nachdem sie sich dem Einfluss von Schallwaffen ausgesetzt hatte, ließ Tieu MRT-Aufnahmen ihres Gehirns auf Metallplatten gravieren.

jedoch in den folgenden Jahrhunderten durch ausgrenzende Rahmenwerke physiognomischer Klassifizierung neu interpretiert werden sollte"[17]. Durch ihren offenen Ansatz zur Proportionalität, der Unterschieden in einem flexiblen Rahmen Platz bietet, widersetzt sich Tieu den entmenschlichenden Rahmenwerken körperlicher Vermessungen in Weiterführung ihrer fortwährenden Kritik an starren Systemen und Kontrollmechanismen, die Klassifizierung und Gehorsam erzwingen, indem sie keinen Raum für Abweichungen lassen. Zugleich macht Tieu ihre Mutter zur Muse, die im Deutschen Pavillon ihre Würdigung erfährt. Visuell insistiert ihre Praxis auf einer nüchternen Ästhetik als Mittel der Klarstellung, während sie sich zugleich jenen Diskursen entzieht, die versuchen, ihre Arbeit allein als Ausdruck von Schmerz zu erfassen und auf Identität zu verengen. Während Tieu in dem linken Flügel des Pavillons stringente Klarheit forciert, eröffnet sie im rechten Flügel einen emotionalen Raum, beispielsweise mit ihren neuen Glasarbeiten. Glas ist ein zerbrechliches und dennoch widerstandsfähiges Material, das gleichzeitig die Schwelle zwischen berührbarer Form und Unsichtbarkeit evoziert. Die gläsernen Hände der Mutter der Künstlerin, Vũ Thị Hạnh, sind von jahrzehntelanger Arbeit gezeichnet, die sich buchstäblich in ihren Körper eingeprägt hat. In *The Cultural Politics of Emotion* untersucht die Wissenschaftlerin Sara Ahmed, wie emotionale Eindrücke entstehen, und schreibt:

> Die Entstehung eines Eindrucks hängt auch davon ab, wie Objekte auf uns einwirken. Ein Eindruck kann eine Wirkung auf die Gefühle des Subjekts sein („sie hat Eindruck gemacht"). Es kann eine Überzeugung sein („unter einem Eindruck stehen"). Es kann sich um eine Nachahmung oder ein Bild handeln („einen Eindruck erwecken"). Oder es kann eine Markierung auf der Oberfläche sein („einen Eindruck hinterlassen"). Wir müssen uns an den „Druck" in einem Eindruck erinnern. Das ermöglicht uns, die Erfahrung, eine Emotion zu haben, mit eben der Wirkung einer Oberfläche auf eine andere zu verbinden, einer Wirkung, die ihre Spuren hinterlässt.[18]

Ahmed fährt fort und schlägt vor, dass die ständige Wiederholung dieser Eindrücke zu einer „Klebrigkeit als Folge der Geschichte der Berührungen zwischen Körpern, Objekten und Zeichen"[19] führe. Was oft irrtümlich für ein aus dem Inneren herrührendes Gefühl gehalten wird, kommt tatsächlich nicht von innen. Stattdessen wird es durch Interaktion geformt und existiert in Kontaktzonen. Seine „Klebrigkeit ist daher ein Effekt", der aus „Kontaktgeschichten" stammt – entstanden aus wiederholten Austauschprozessen, die zu einer „Anhäufung affektiver Werte" führen.[20] Tieus Objekte

17) Noam Andrews, „Dürer on Difference", *Nuncius. Journal of the Material and Visual History of Science*, Bd. 40, Nr. 3, 2025, https://doi.org/10.1163/18253911-bja10154.

18) Sara Ahmed, *The Cultural Politics of Emotion*, New York: Routledge, 2004, S. 6.

19) Ebd., S. 90.

20) Ebd., S. 92.

aus Gussglas, Metallschnitt und kleinen Maikäfer-Skulpturen sowie ihre verpixelte Fassade, die an die Nah- und Fernwirkungen impressionistischer Gemälde erinnert,[21] fangen eine fragmentierte Welt ein, in der Emotionen – oft fälschlicherweise als intrinsisch und natürlich missgedeutet – vielmehr durch relationale und wahrnehmungsbezogene Begegnungen hervorgerufen werden.

AUFERSTANDEN AUS RUINEN

Die Giardini, insbesondere der Deutsche Pavillon, wirken als politische Topografie, in der die Präsentation und Interpretation von Kunst die historischen und zeitgenössischen Überschneidungen von Geschichte, Politik und gesellschaftlichen Werten offenlegen. Mit ihren sich überlagernden formalen, politischen, sozialen und historischen Implikationen stimmen die Werke der Künstlerinnen in „Moll-Tonart" in den Refrain der diesjährigen Hauptausstellung der Biennale ein und stimulieren so als polyphon zu verstehende Vergangenheiten, Gegenwarten und Zukünfte. Die Kunst von Sung Tieu und Henrike Naumann kann als Verkomplikation und Ruinierung deutscher Narrative verstanden werden, reagieren sie doch auf das Nachspiel des infam behaupteten „Endes der Geschichte" mit seiner triumphalen Erzählung, die das Versagen des „realistischen Sozialismus" herausstellt. Dabei wurde dieses intern geformt durch Mechanismen der Unterdrückung und der Manipulation sowie später extern durch Kräfte, die von diesem Versagen monetär oder ideologisch profitierten, um heute wieder genau diese Mechanismen anzuwenden, wie im Eingangszitat von Bärbel Bohley vorhergesagt.

Patriarchale Konstrukte mit ihrer Realität aus Disziplinierung, Gewalt und Krieg sprechen immer eine klare Sprache, aber es ist die Kunst, die die Wahrheit darin erkennt und zum Ausdruck bringen kann. Henrike Naumann und Sung Tieu beschreiben in ruinöser und dringlicher, aber poetischer Weise die Klebrigkeit von Transformation, Erinnerung und Affekt. Und jenseits der aktuellen Umschreibung der Geschichte, der Verrohung der Debatten und der Realität der Kriege ist es ihre Kunst, die darauf besteht, neue Wahrheiten zu schaffen.

21) Vgl. Richard Shiff, „Fragmentierung der Welt. Die künstlerische Handschrift im Impressionismus", in: *Impressionismus – die Kunst der Landschaft*, hg. von Ortrud Westheider, Michael Philipp, Ausst.-Kat. Museum Barberini, 2017, München/London/New York: Prestel, 2017. Ich danke Daniel Milnes für diesen Hinweis.

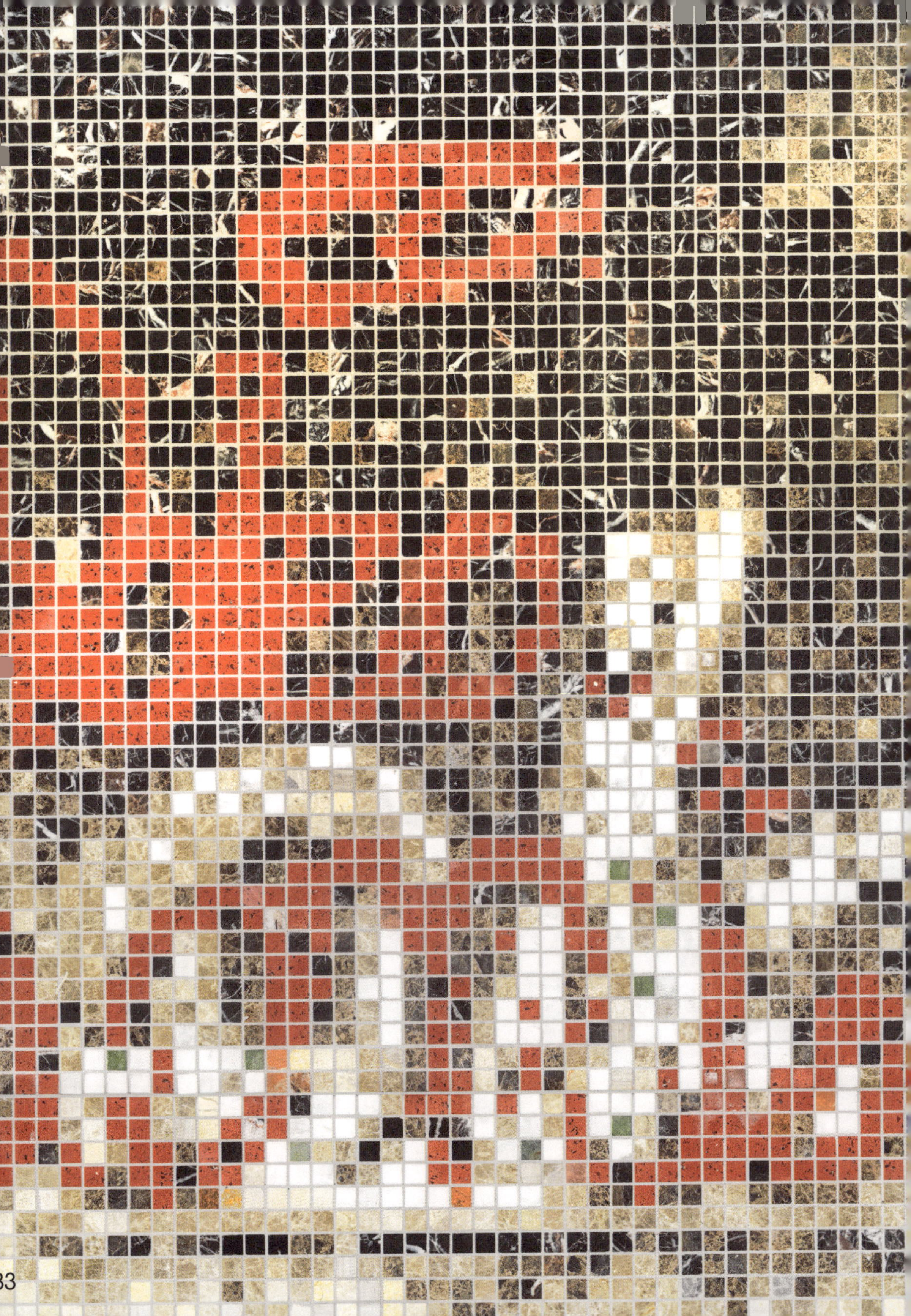

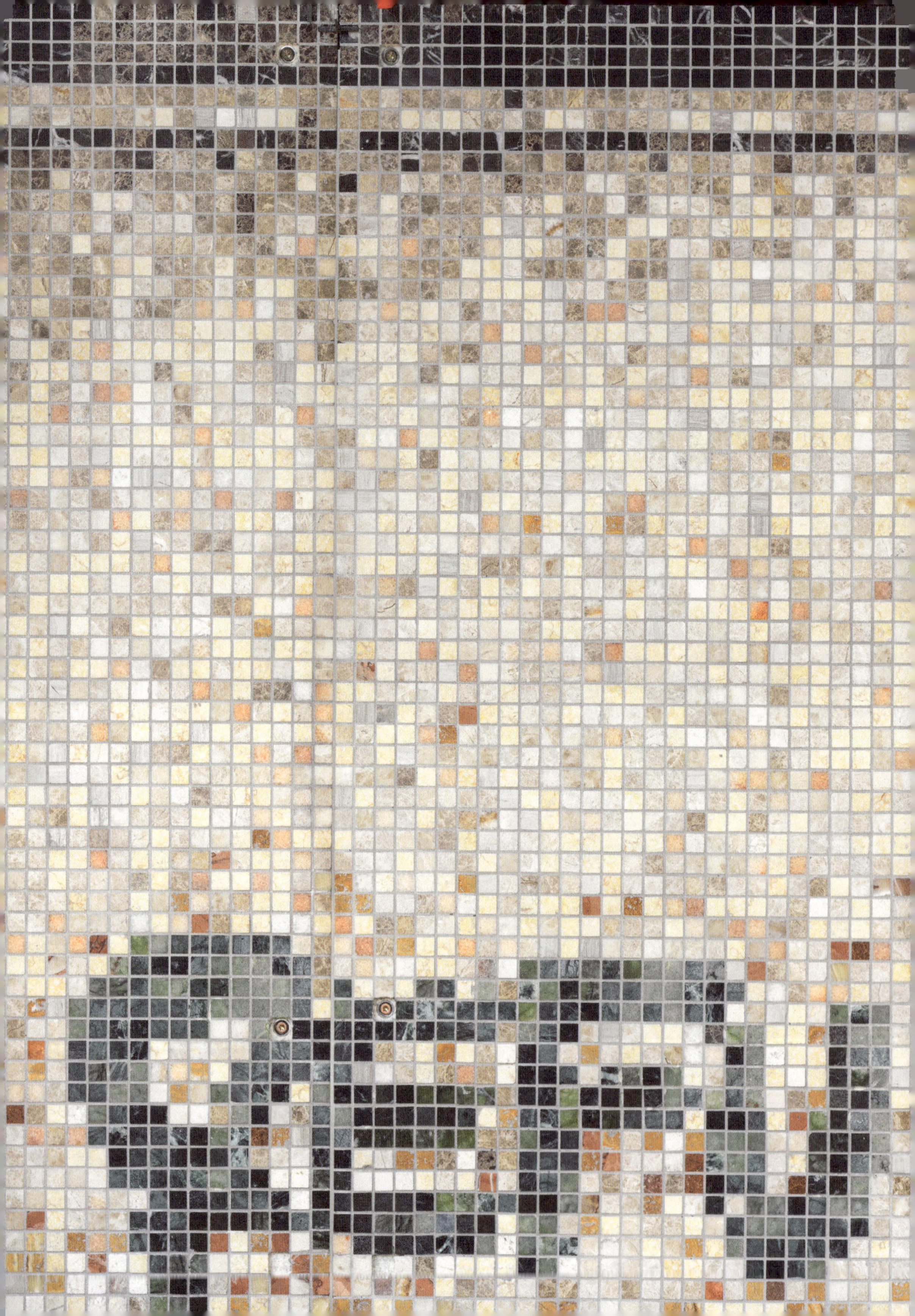

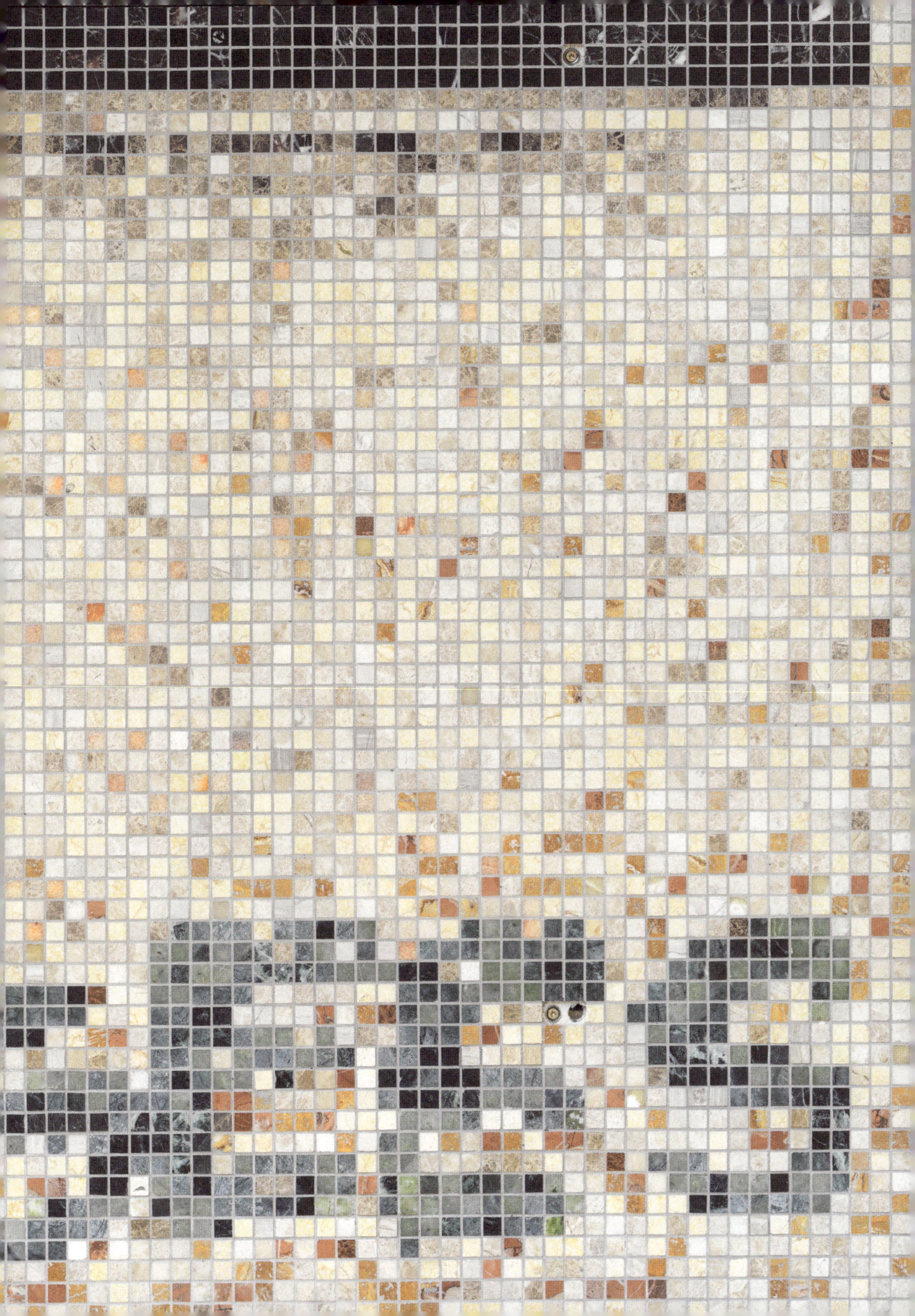

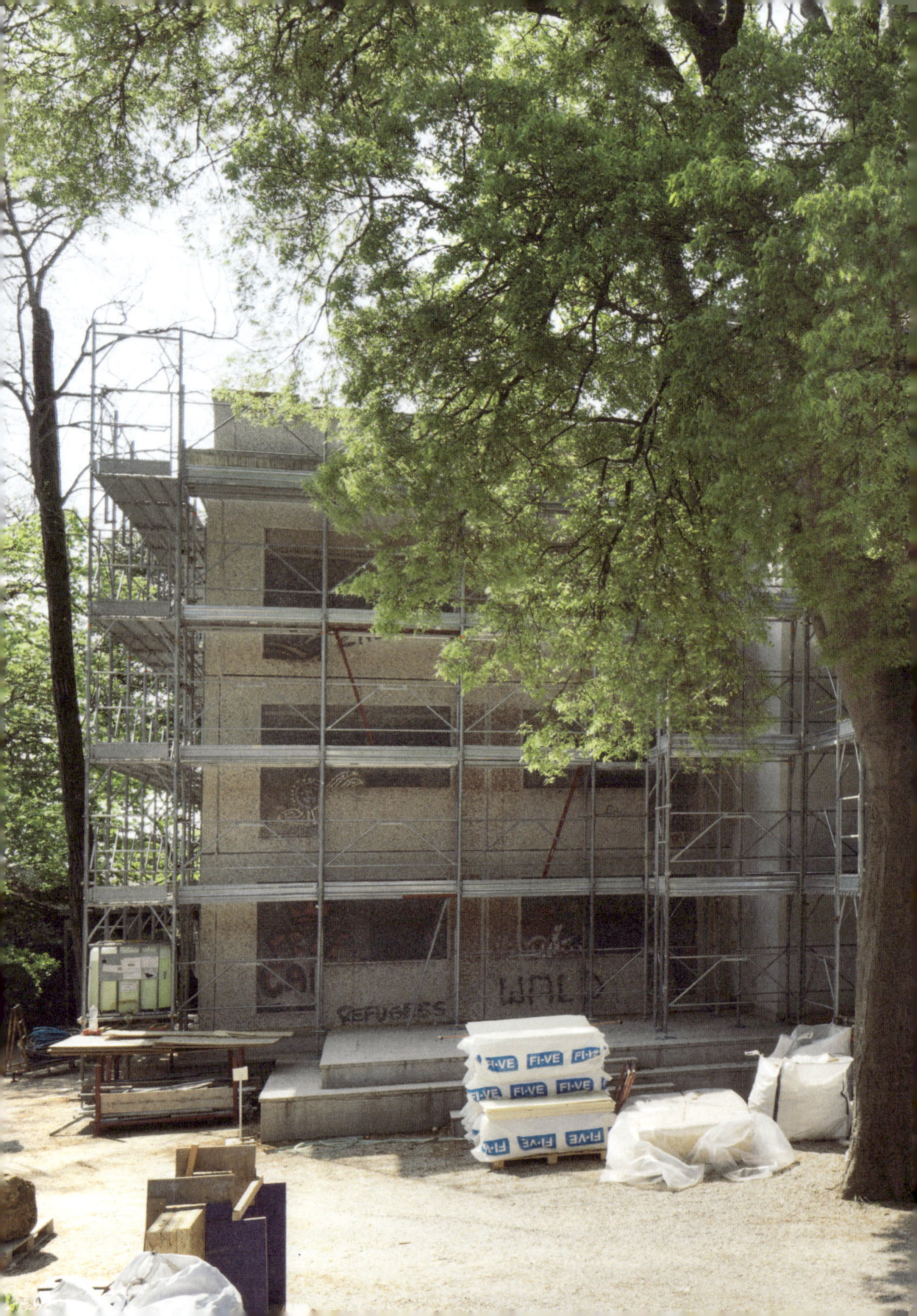
FI-VE

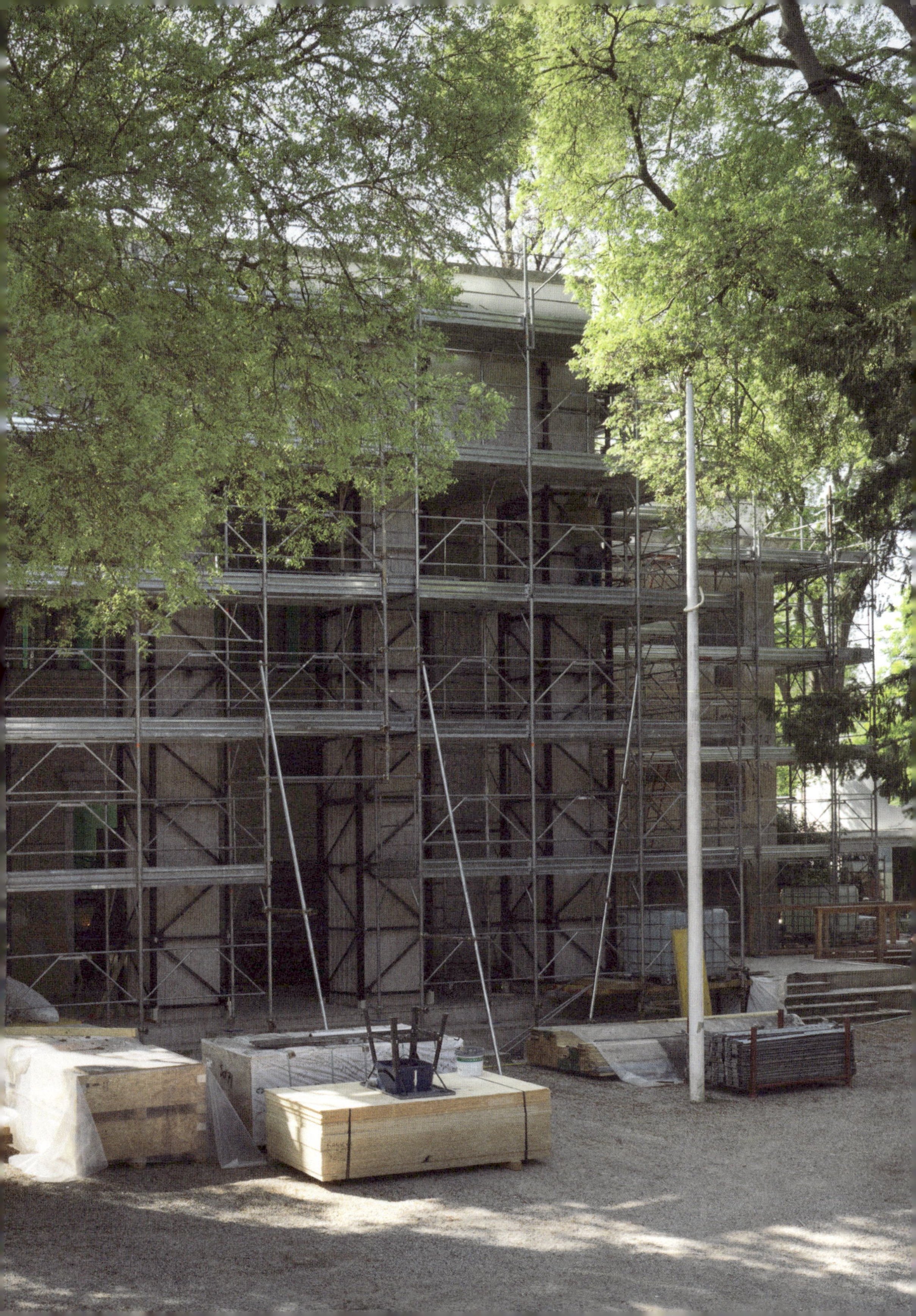

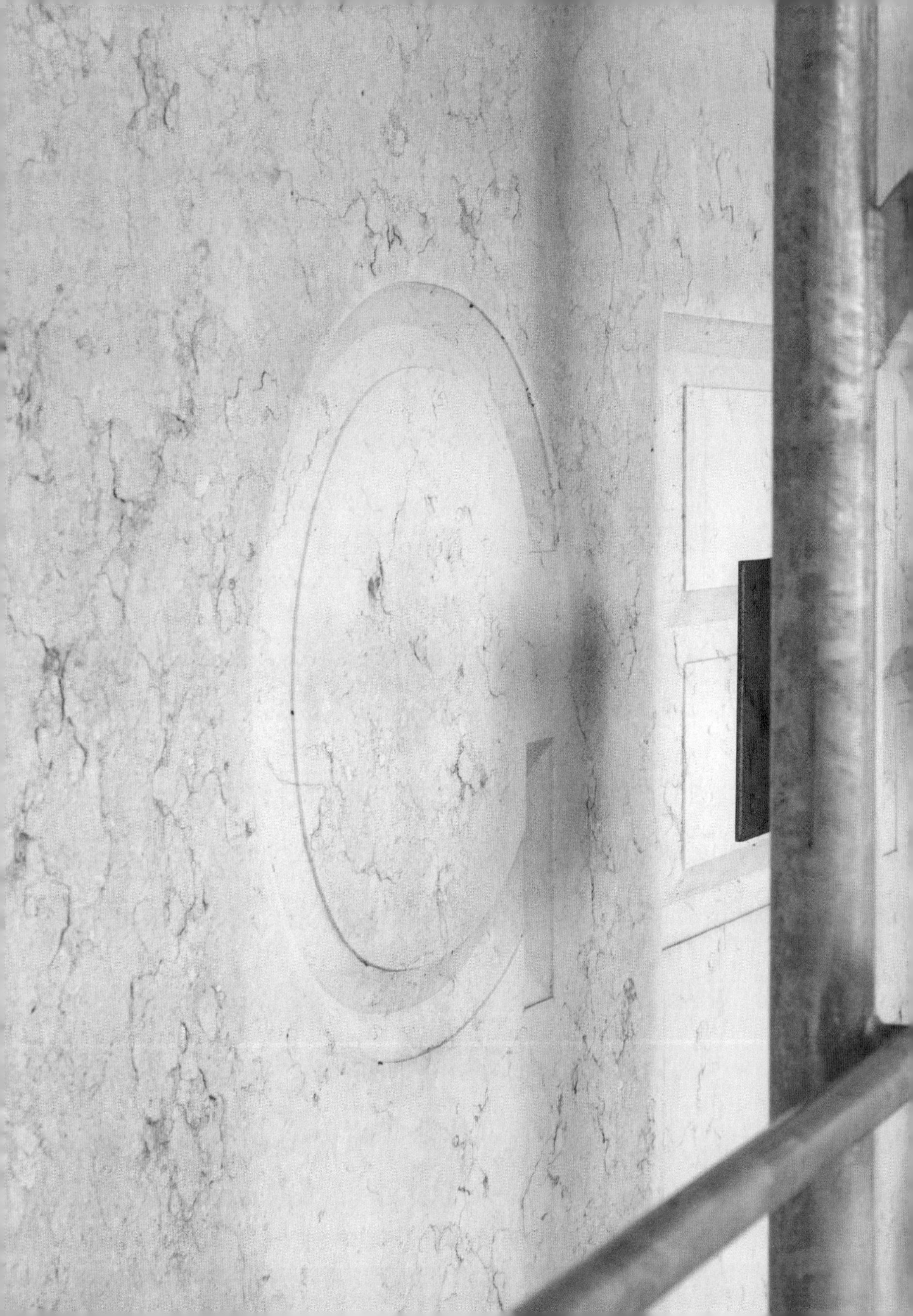

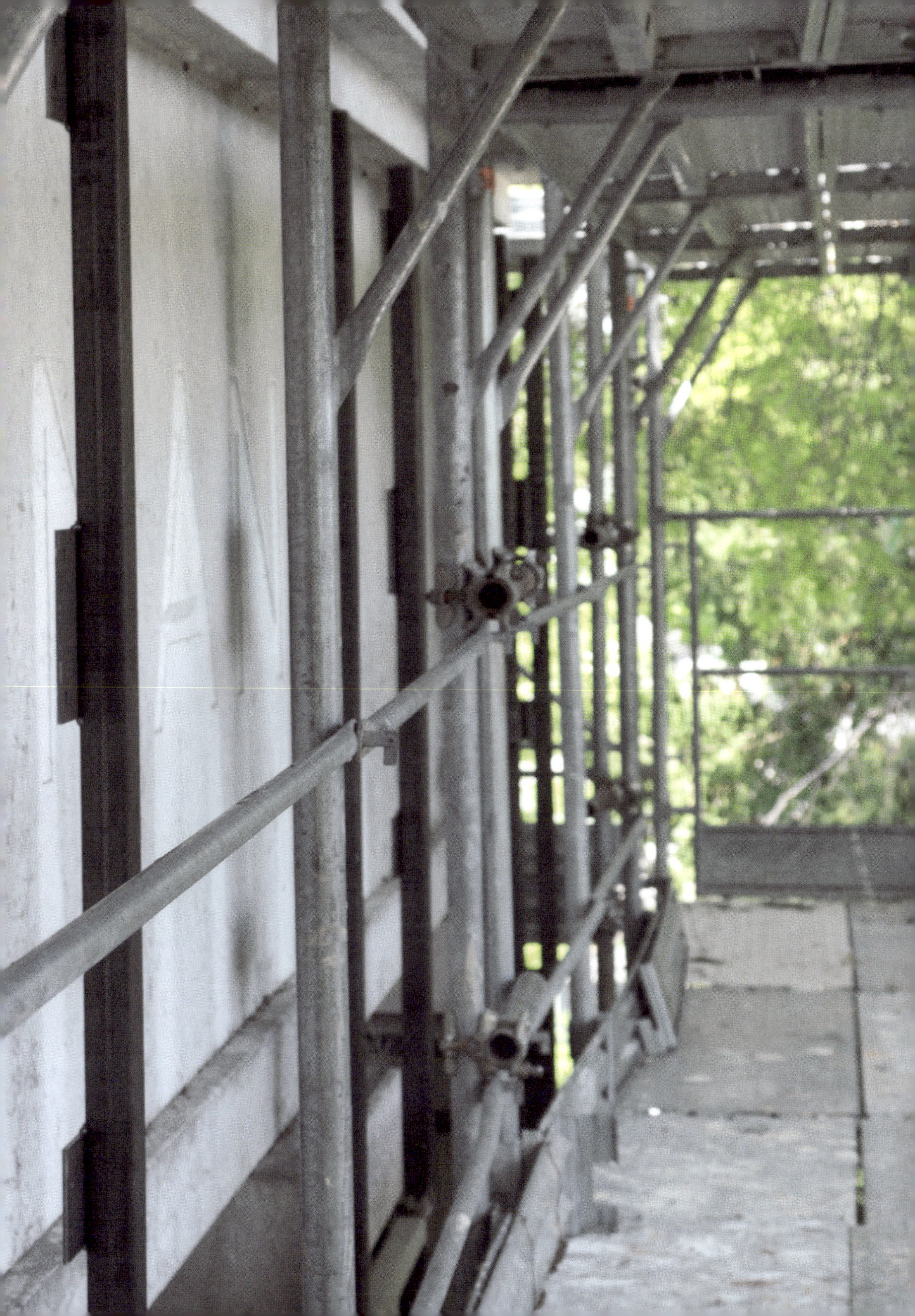

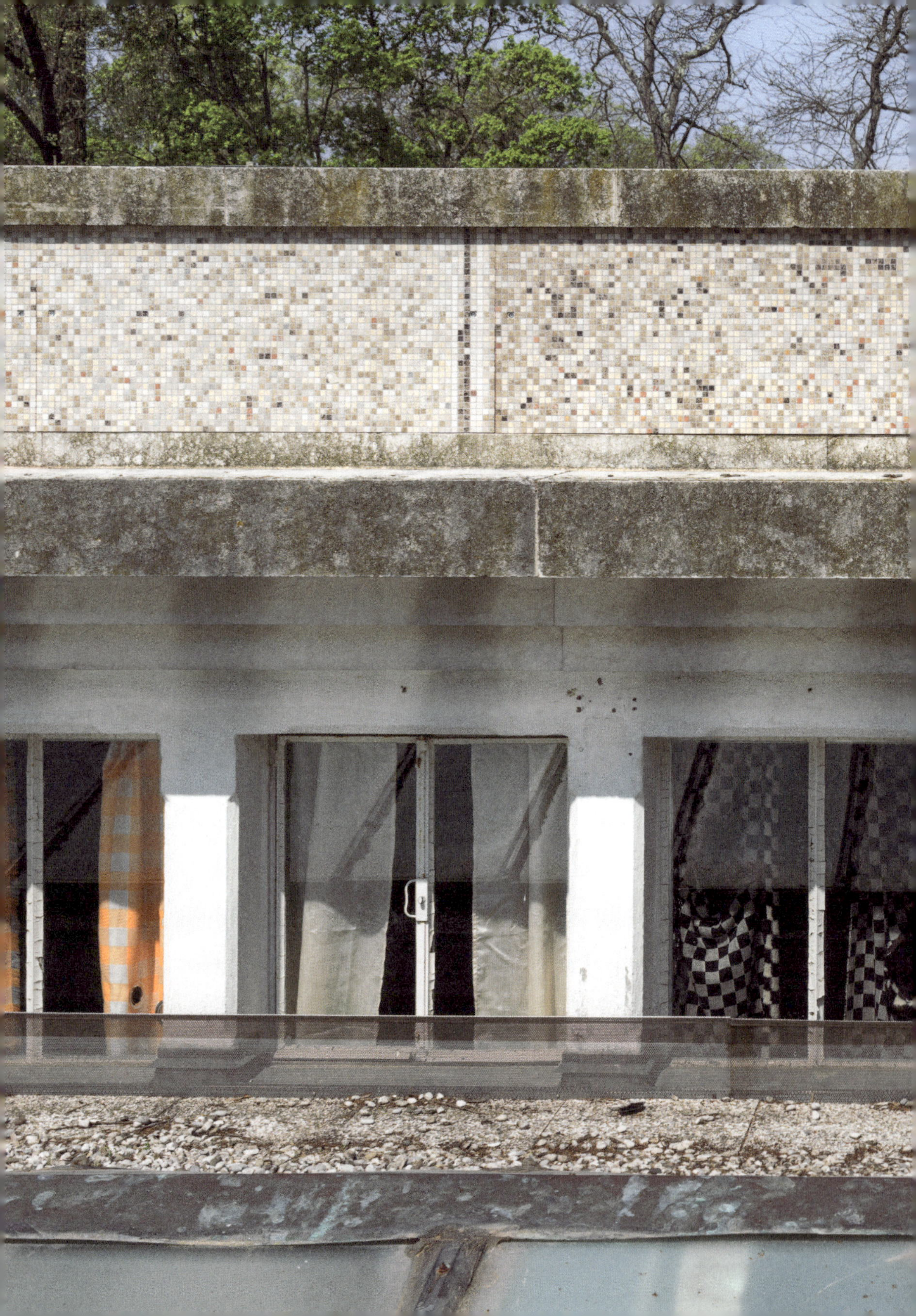

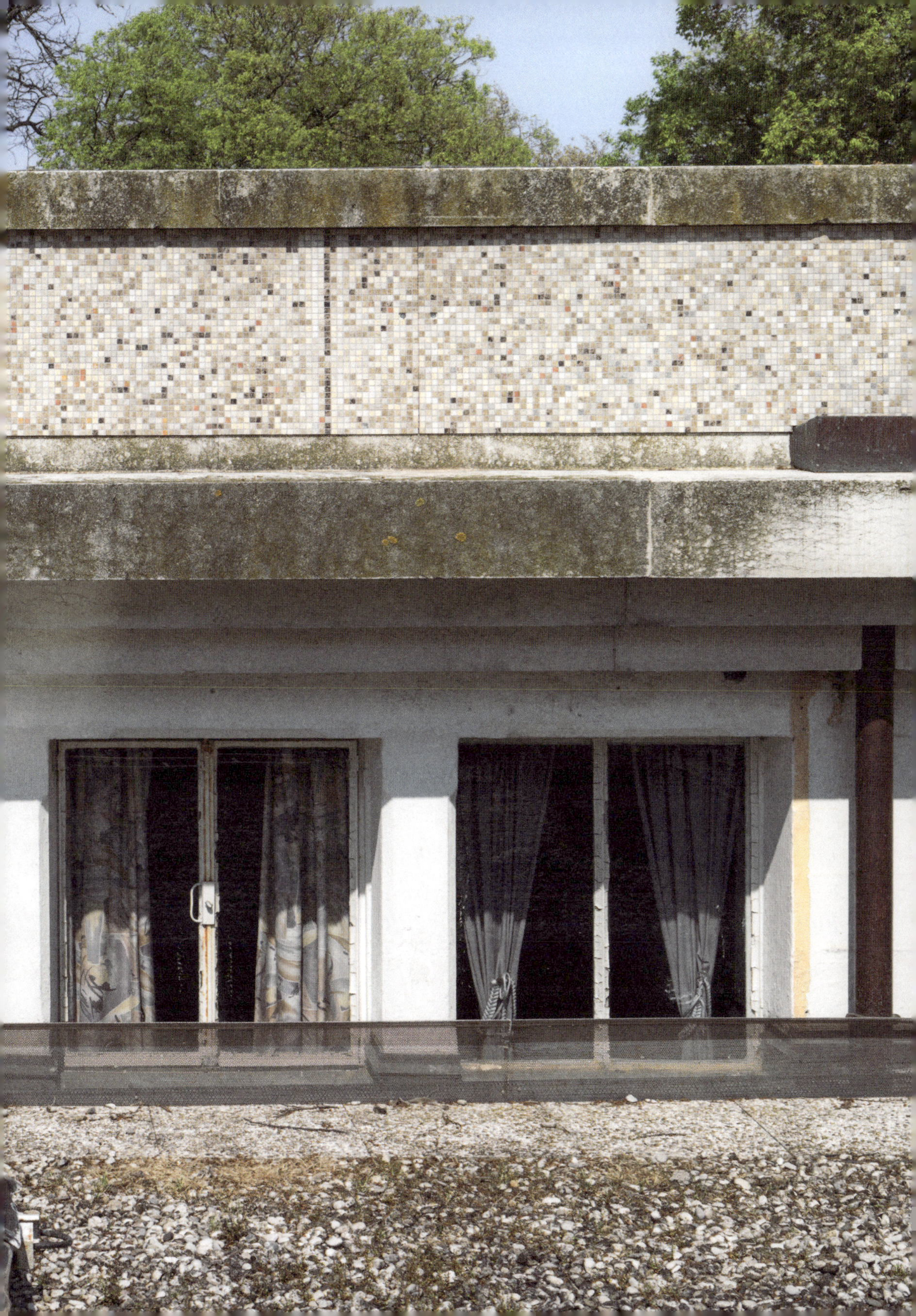

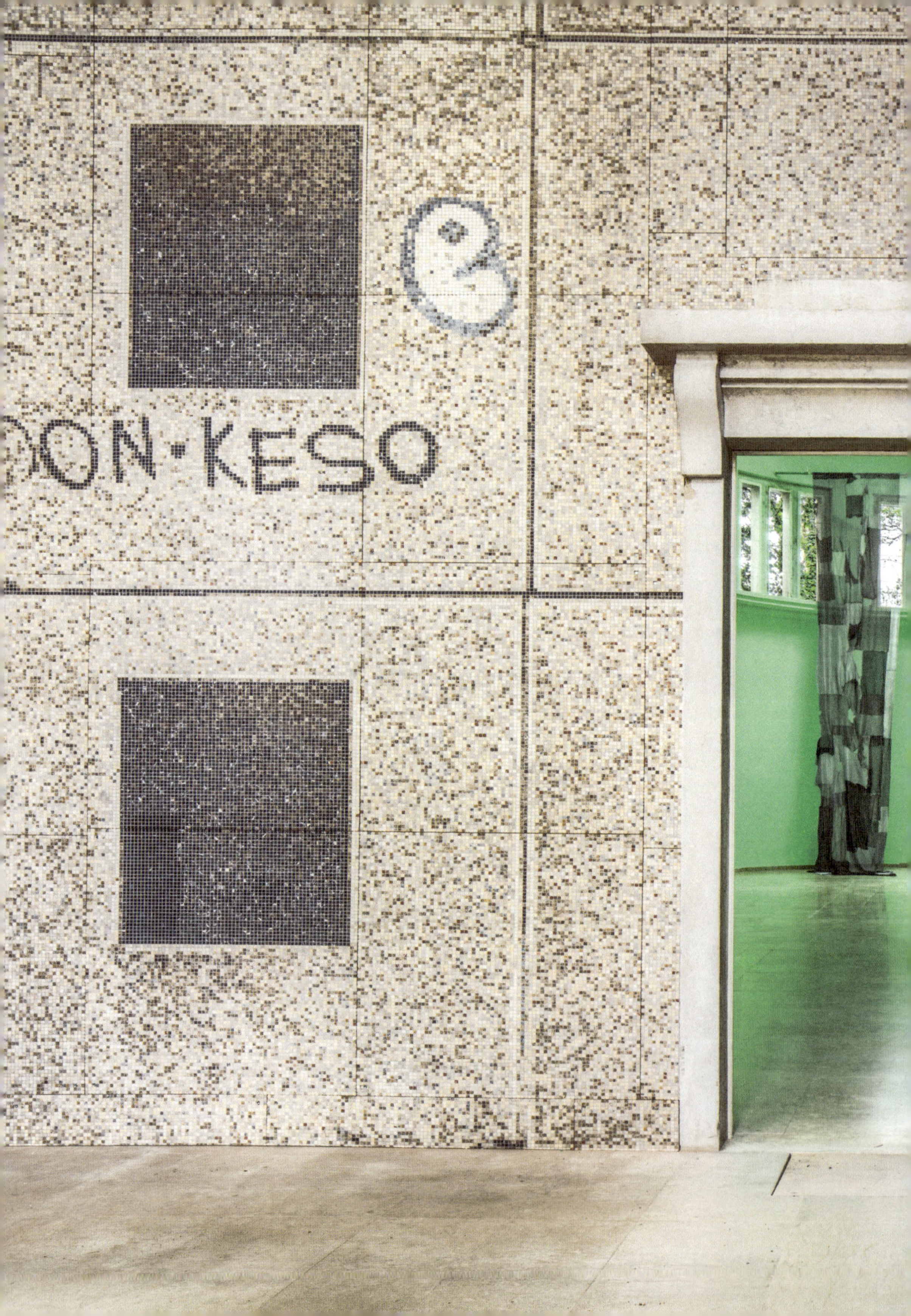
DON·KESO

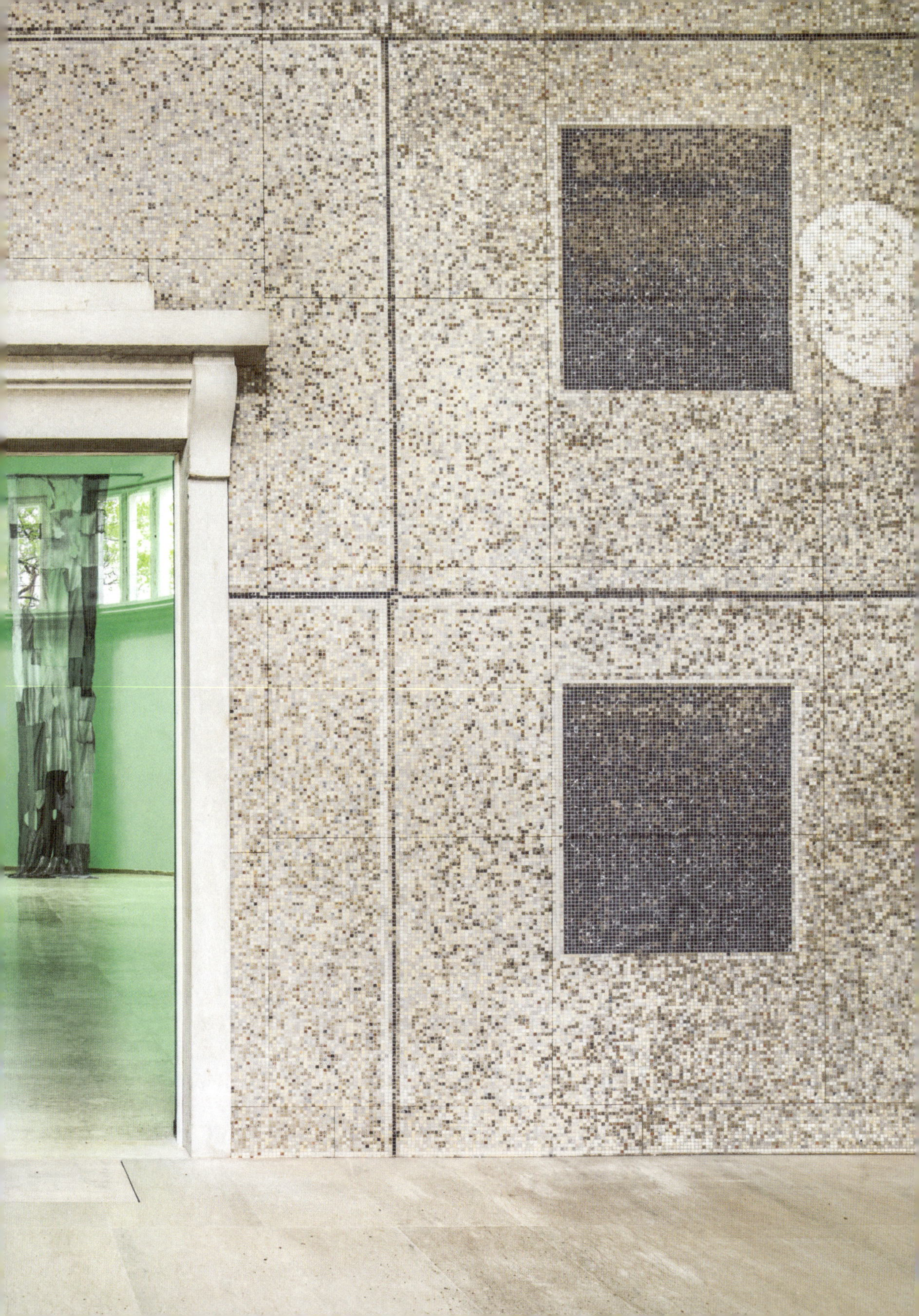

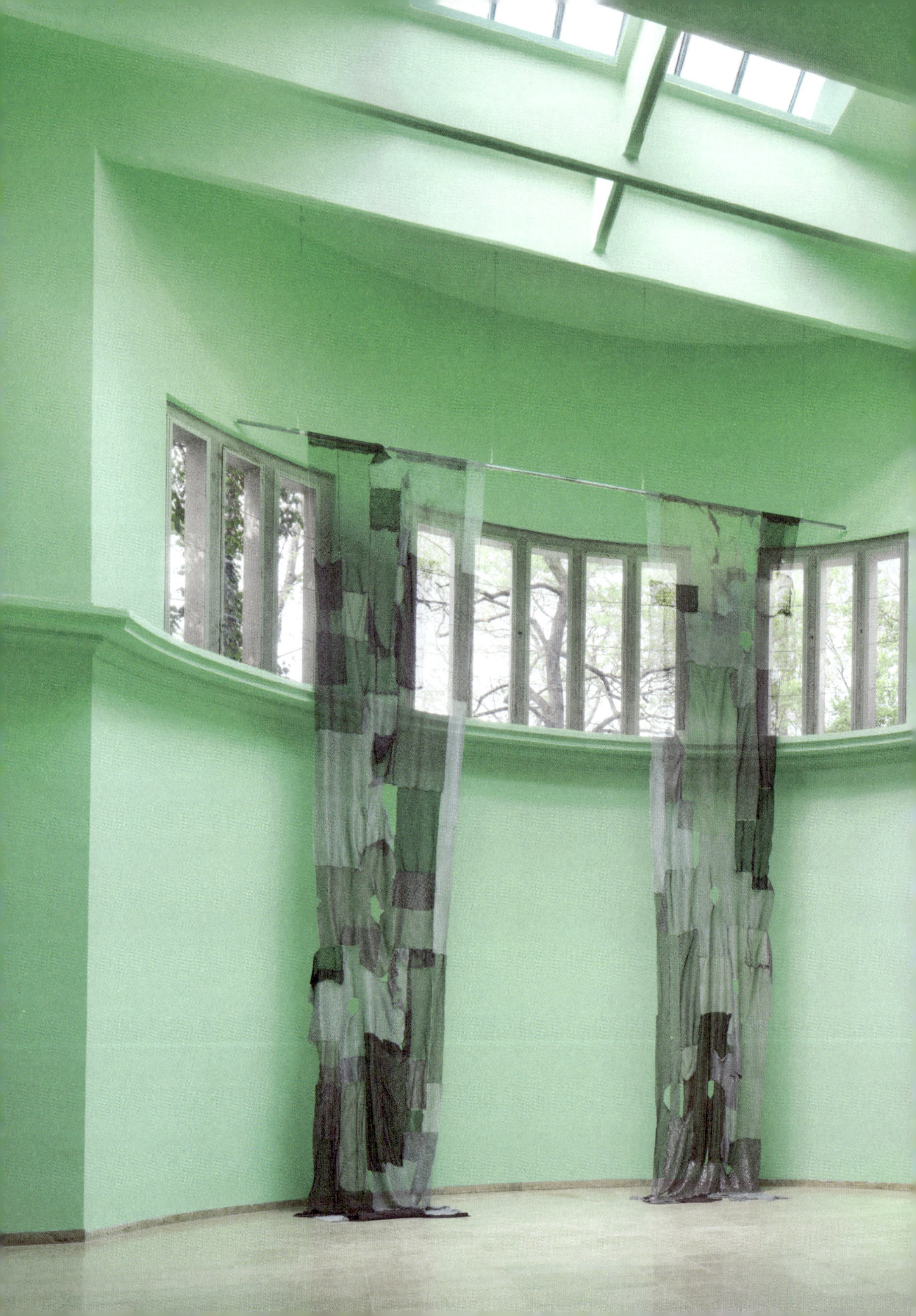

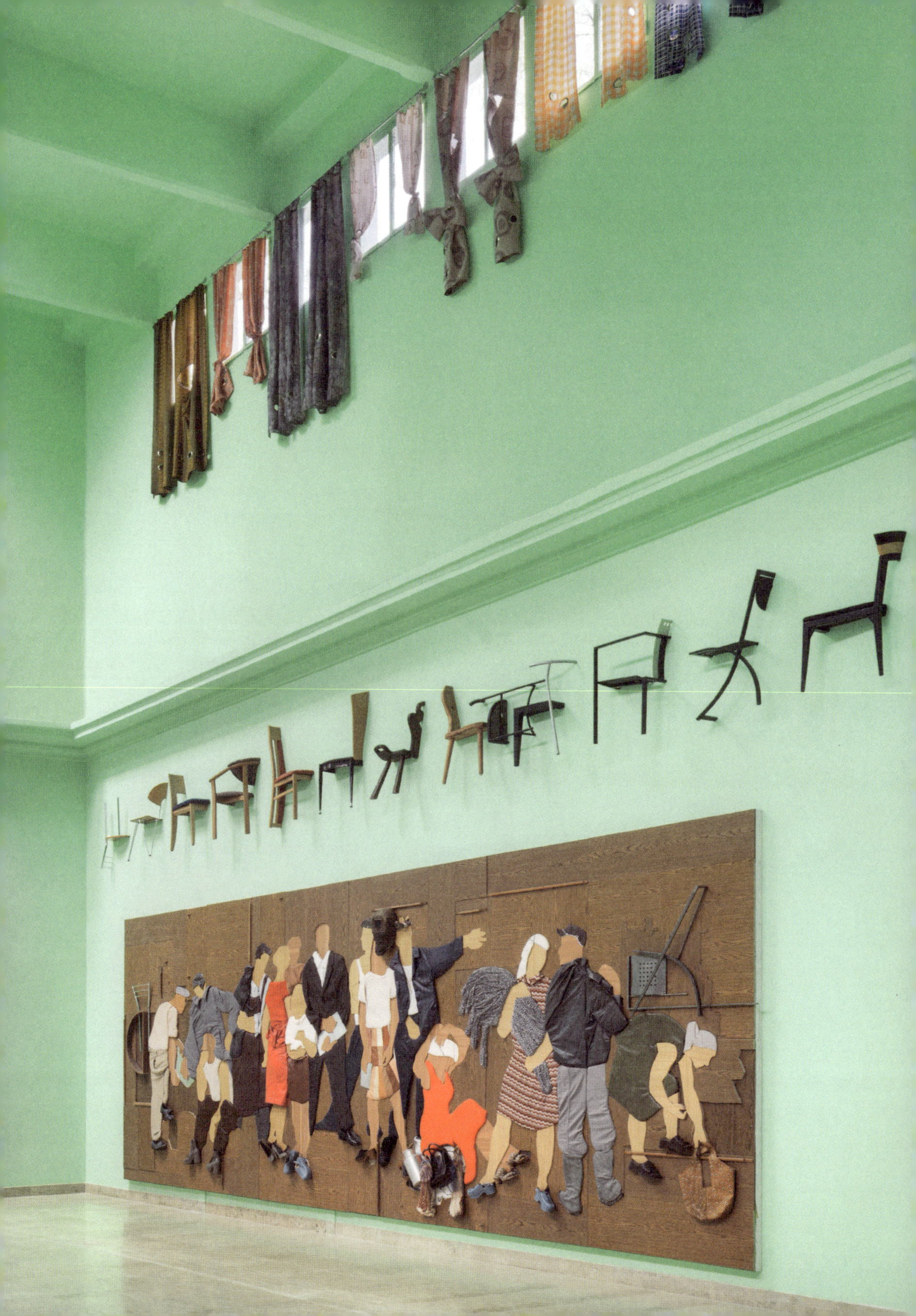

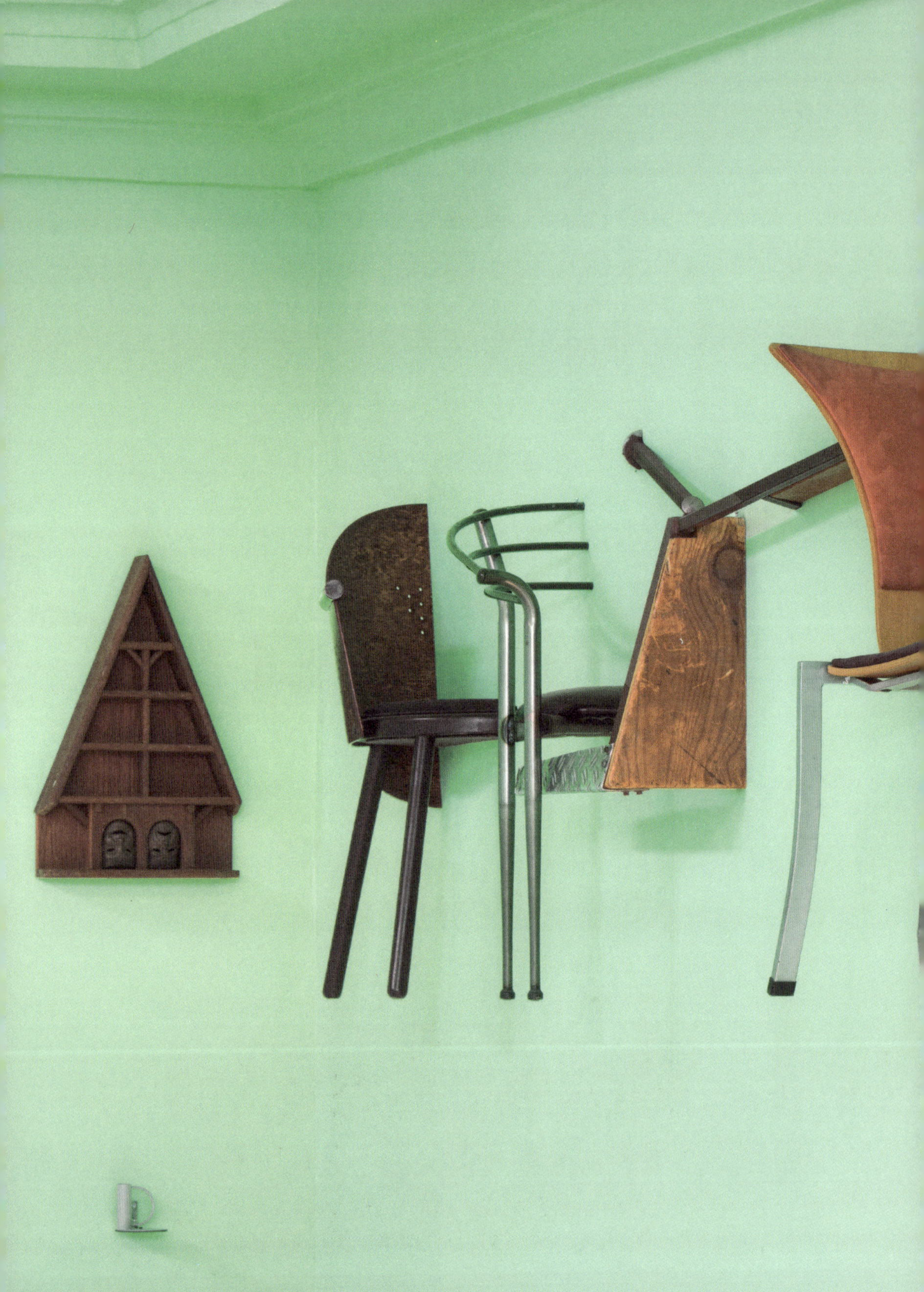

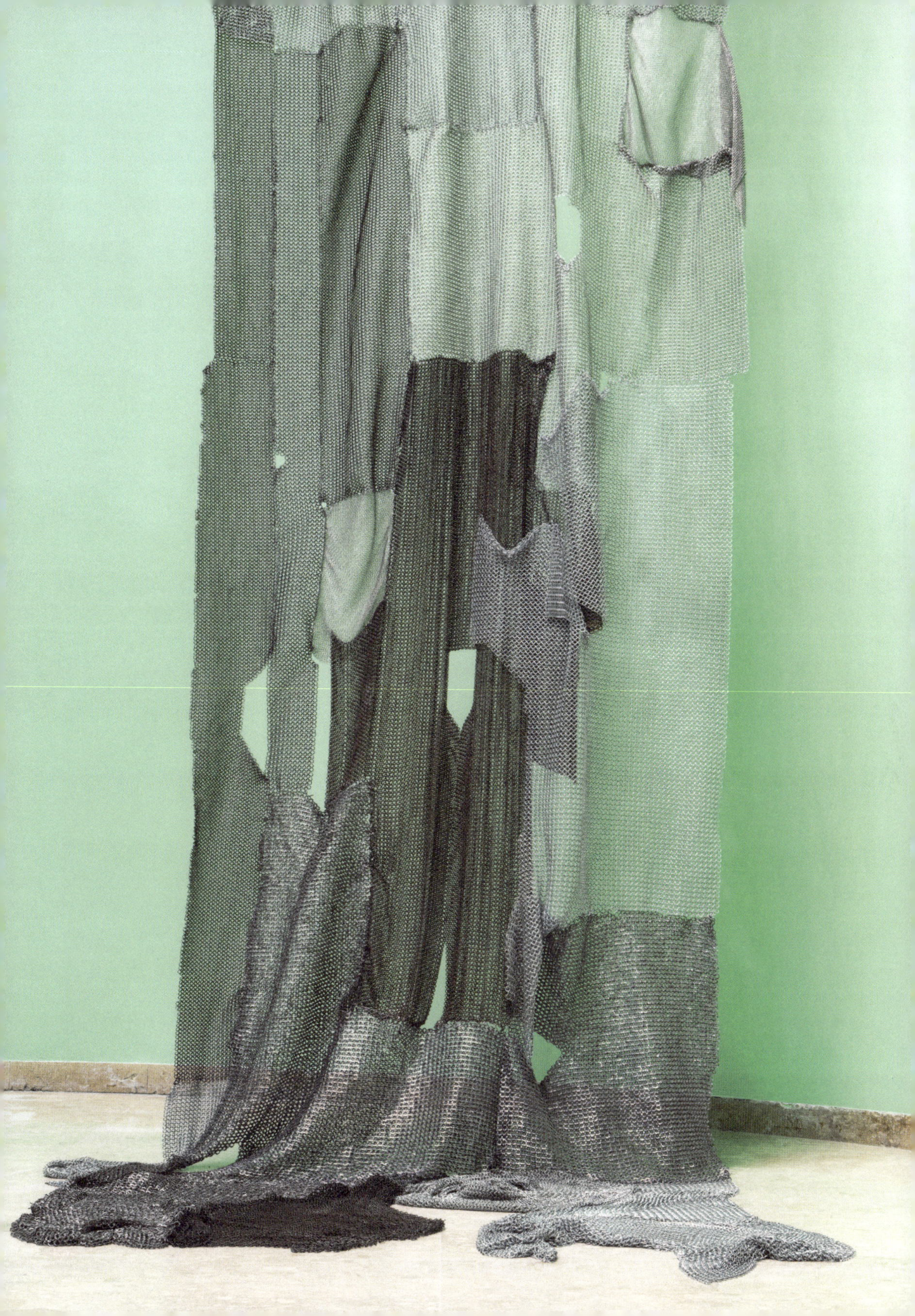

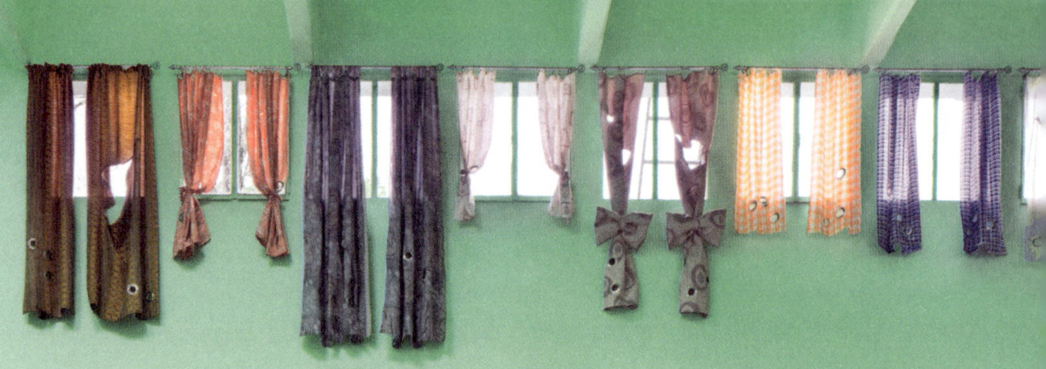

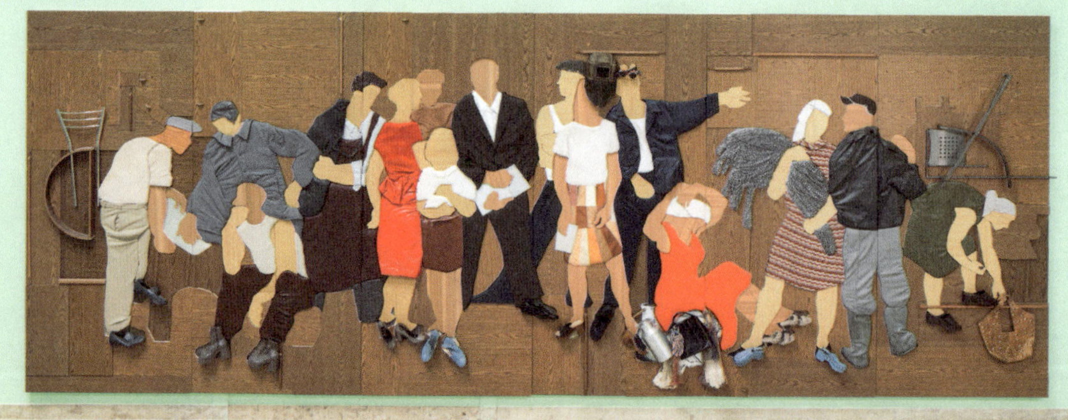

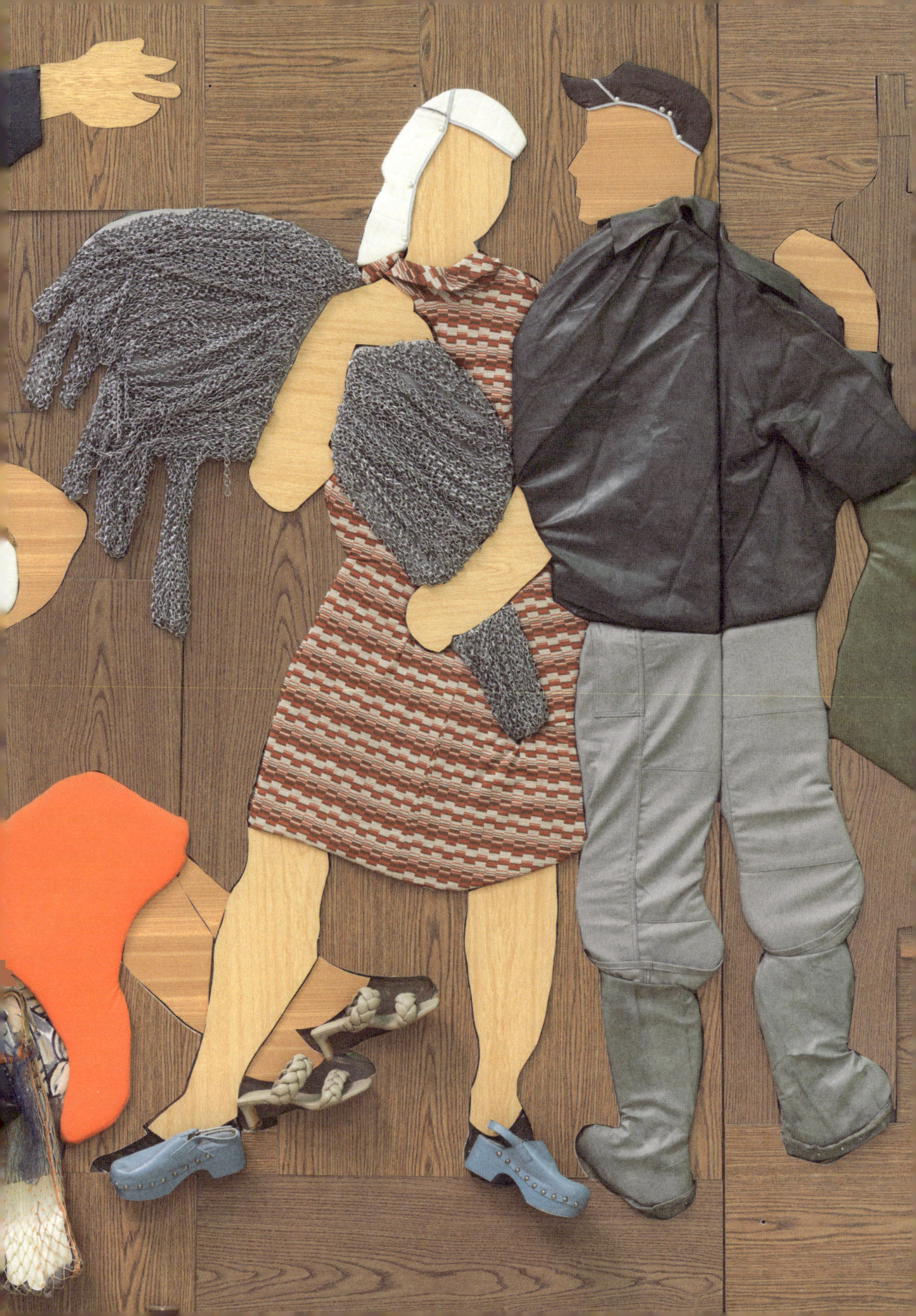

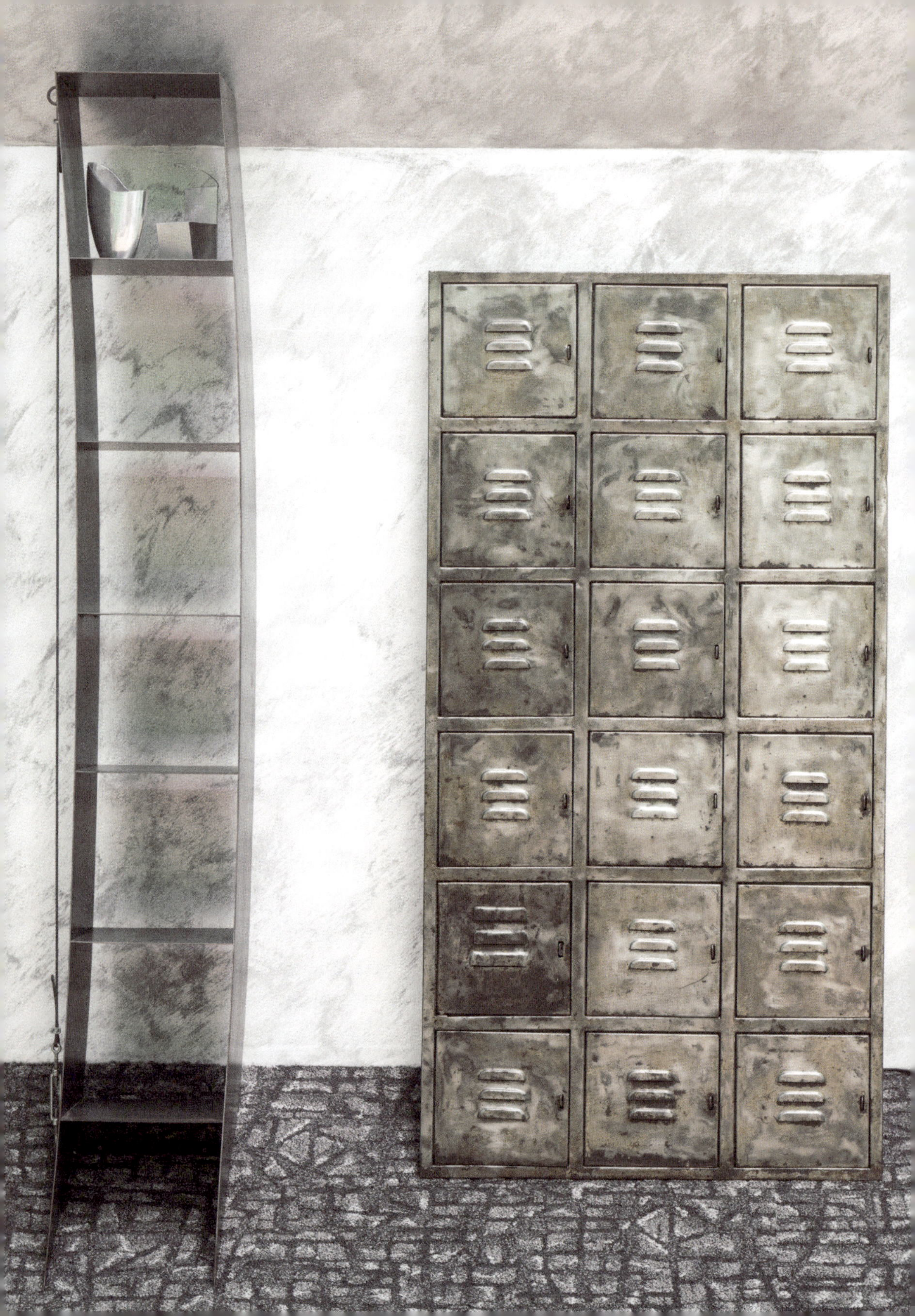

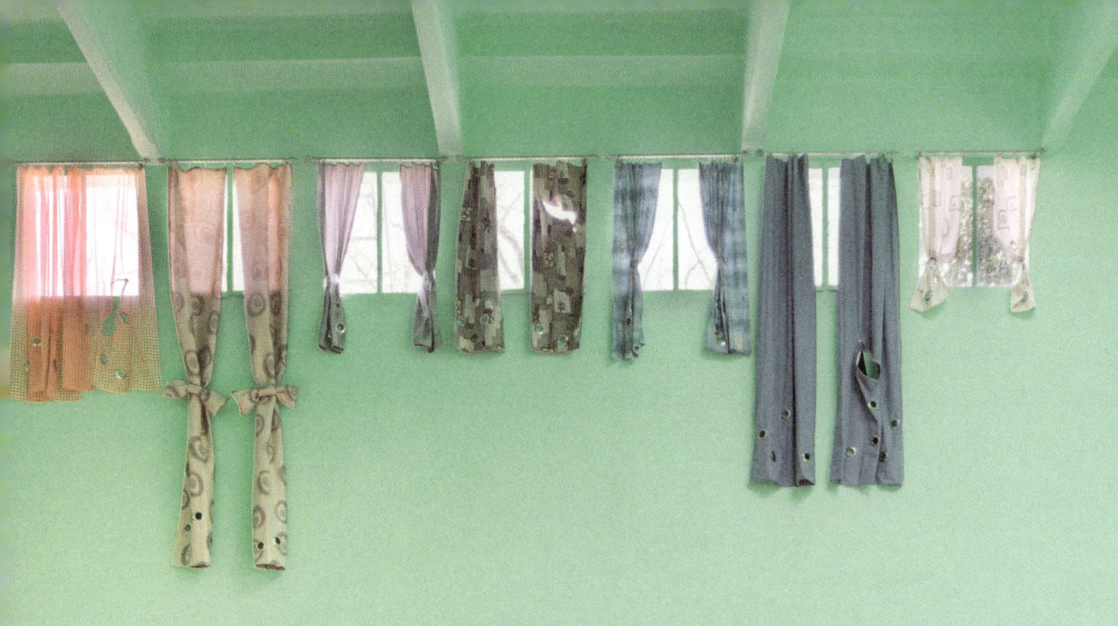
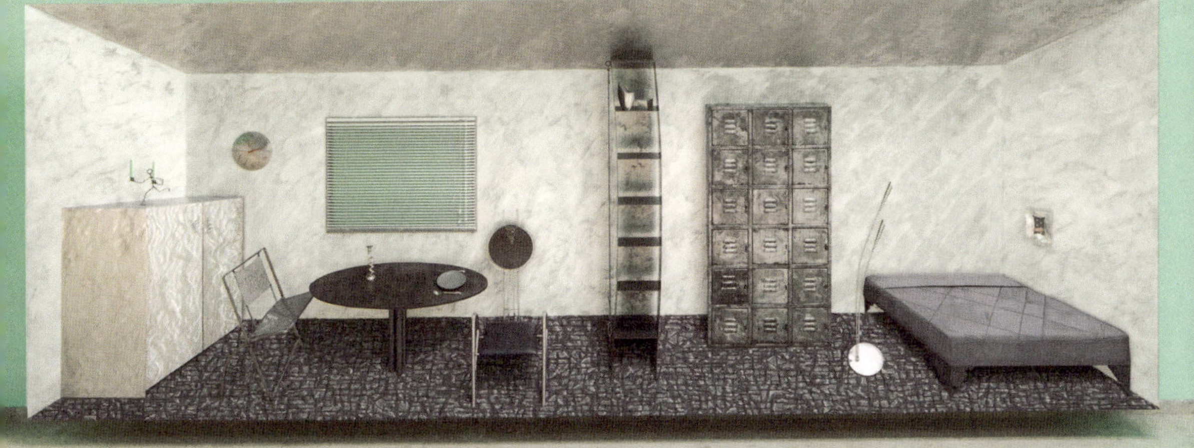

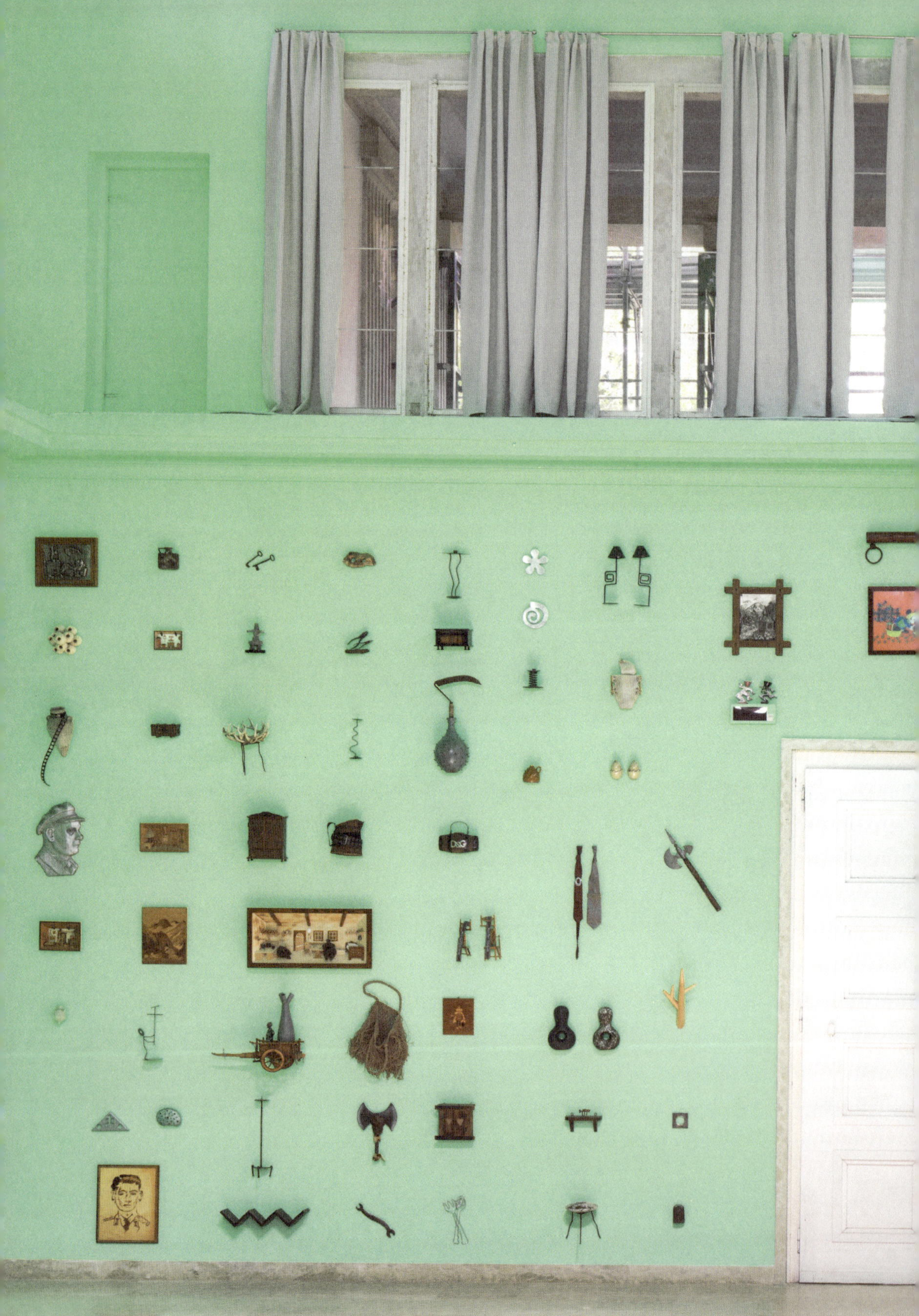

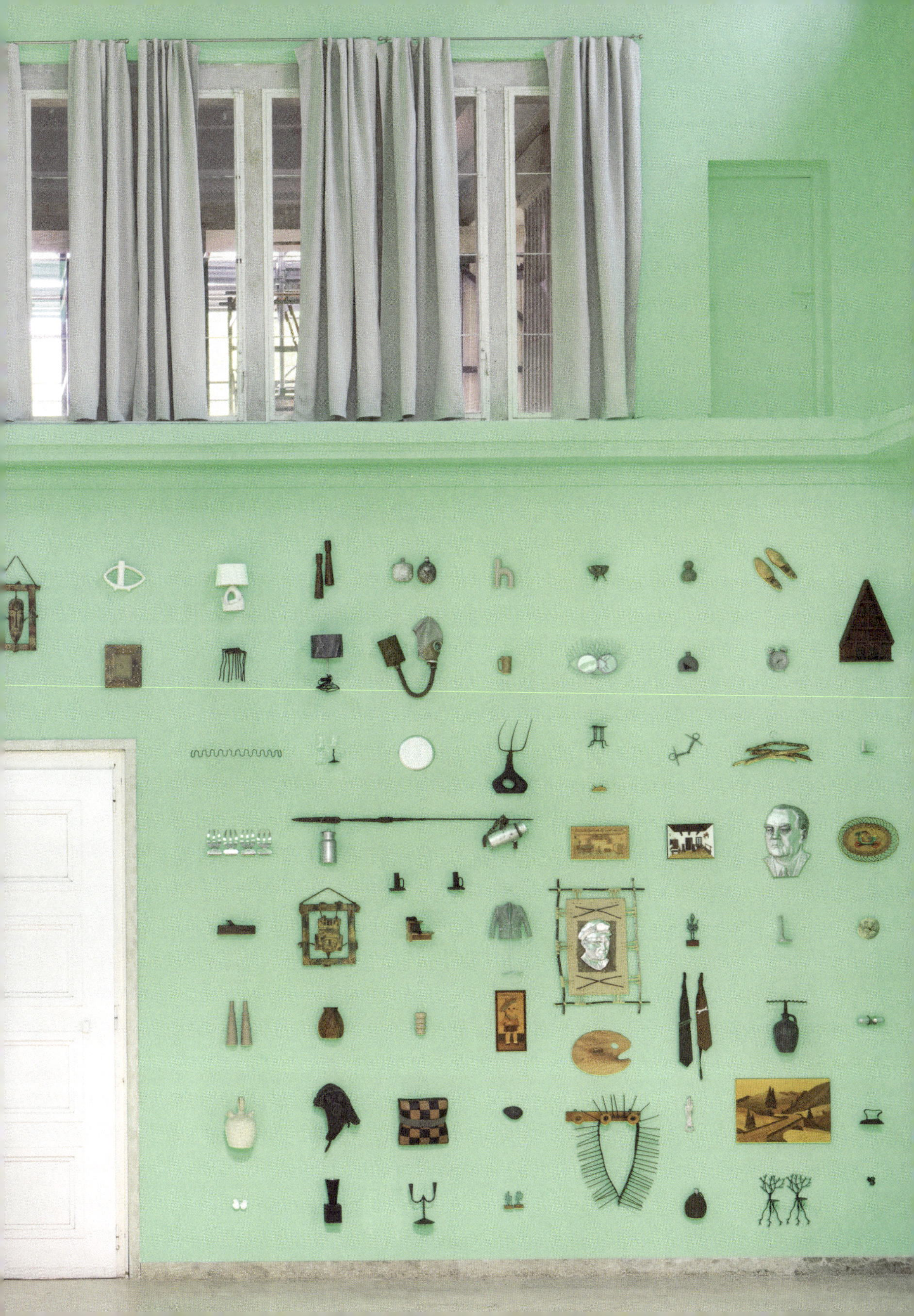

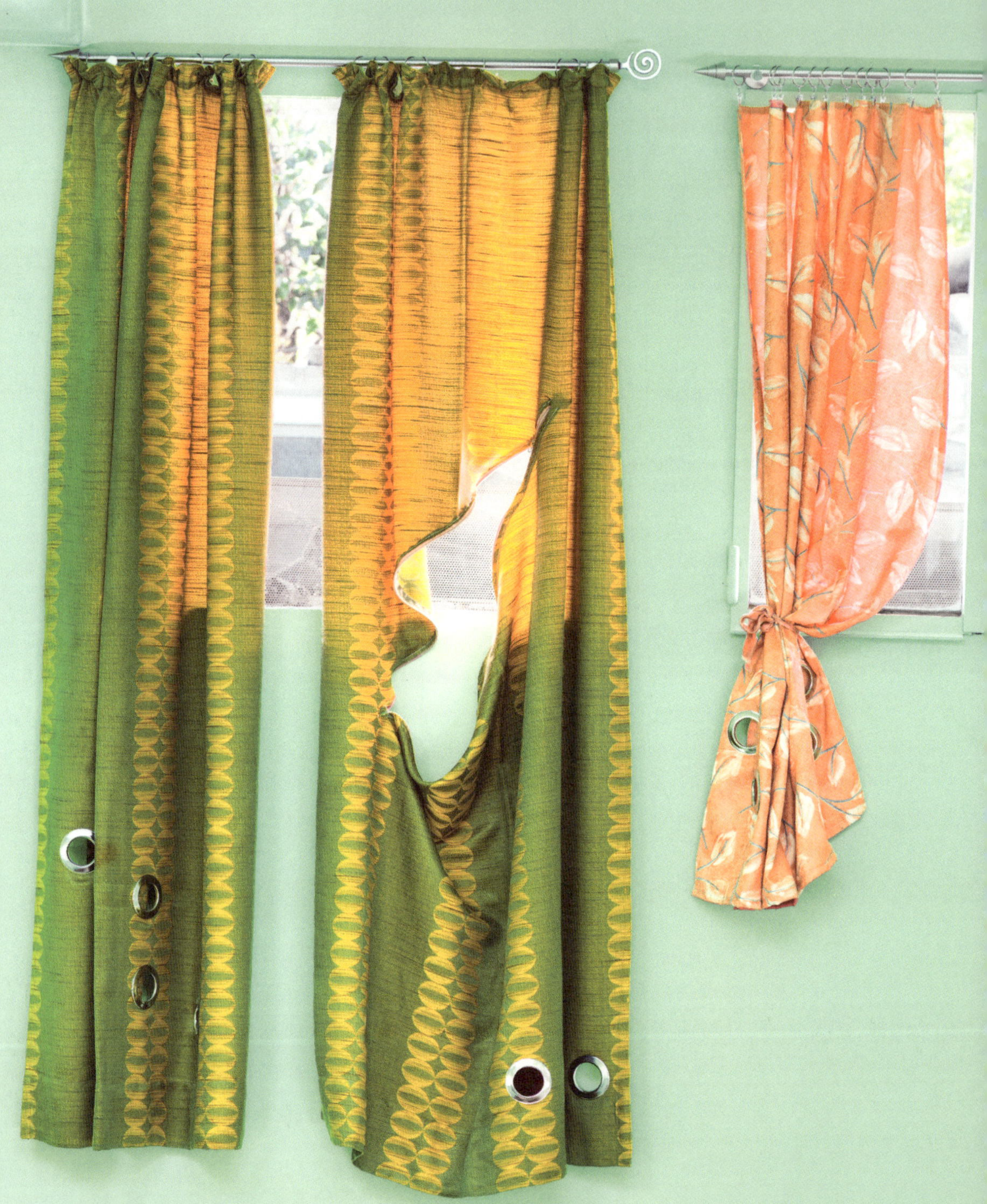

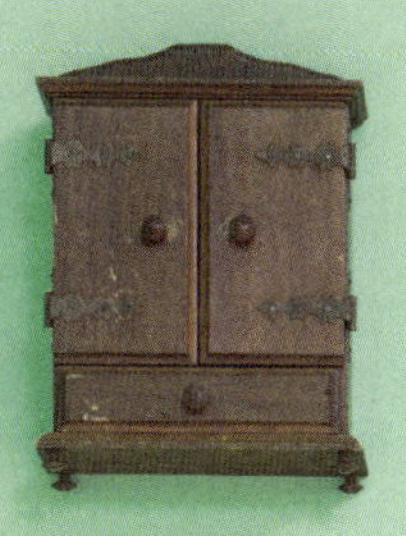

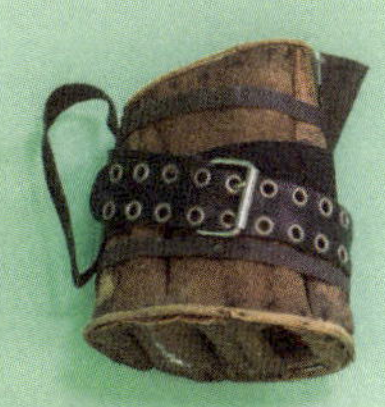

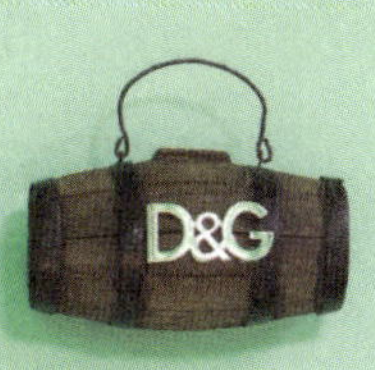
D&G

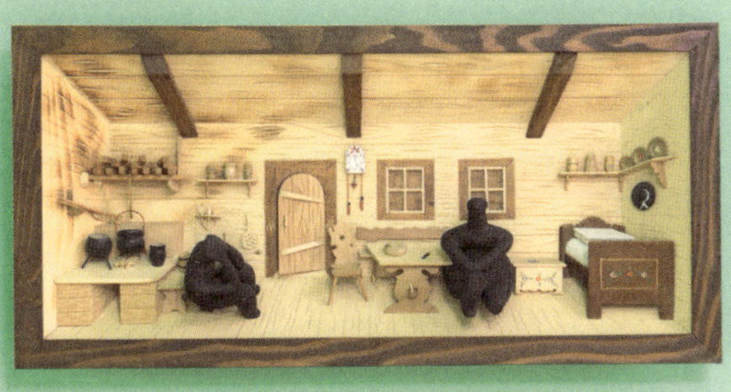

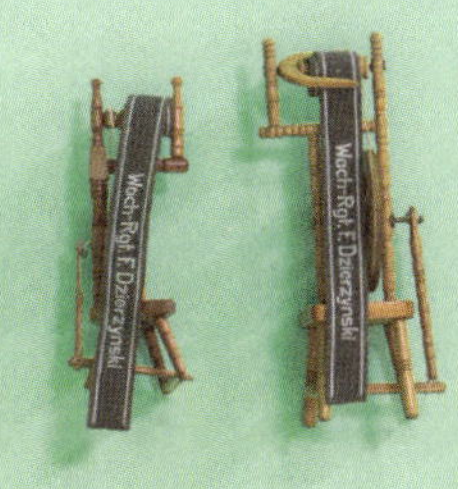
Wach-Rgt. F. Dzierzynski
Wach-Rgt. F. Dzierzynski

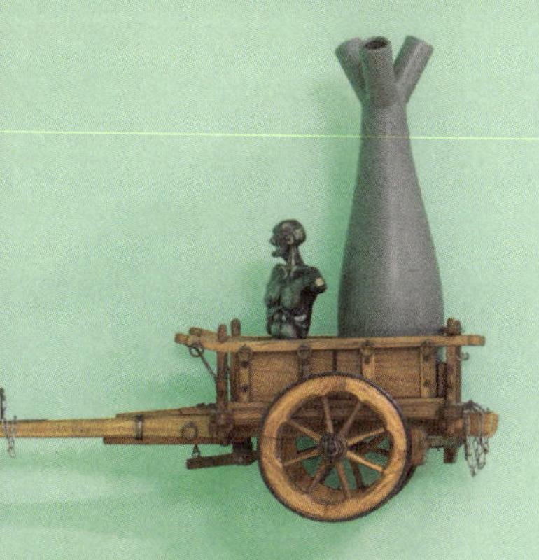

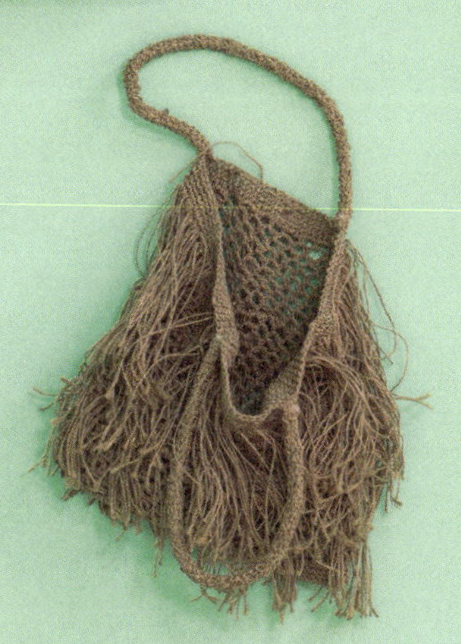

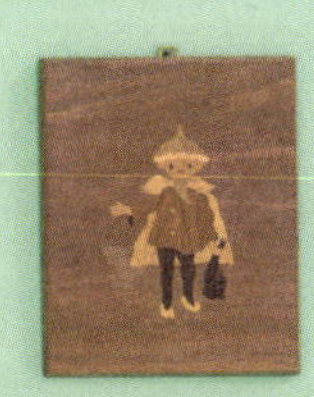

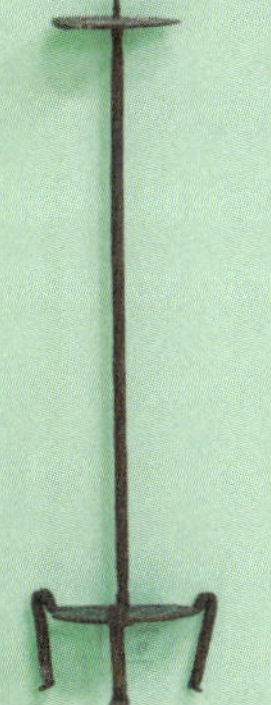

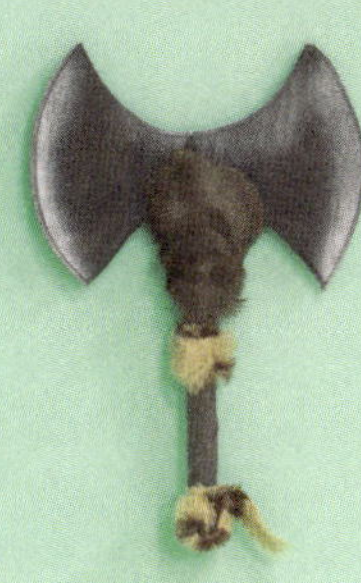

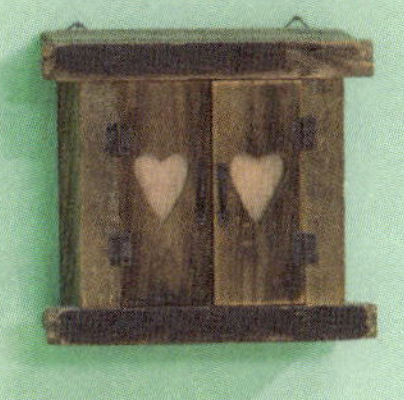

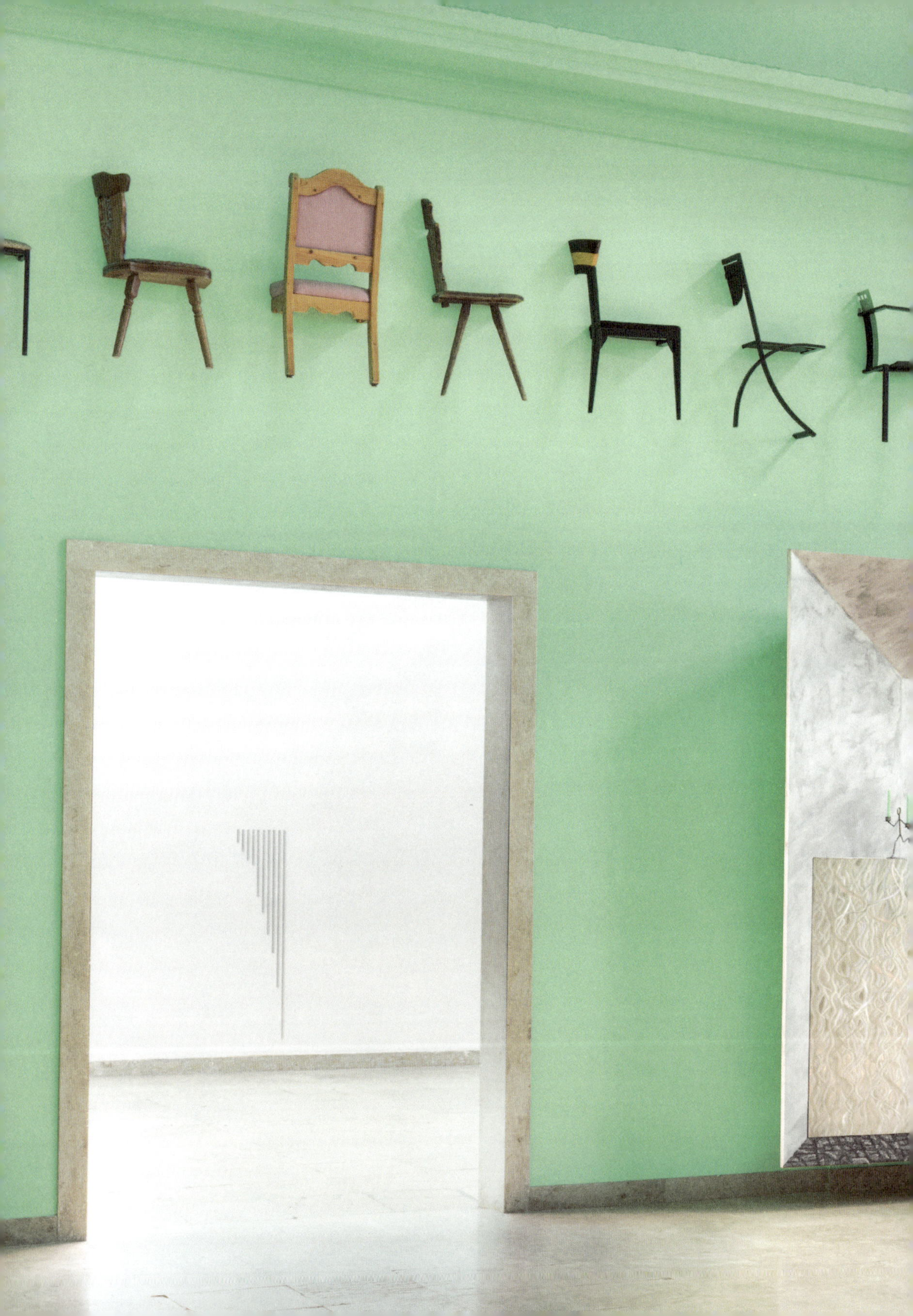

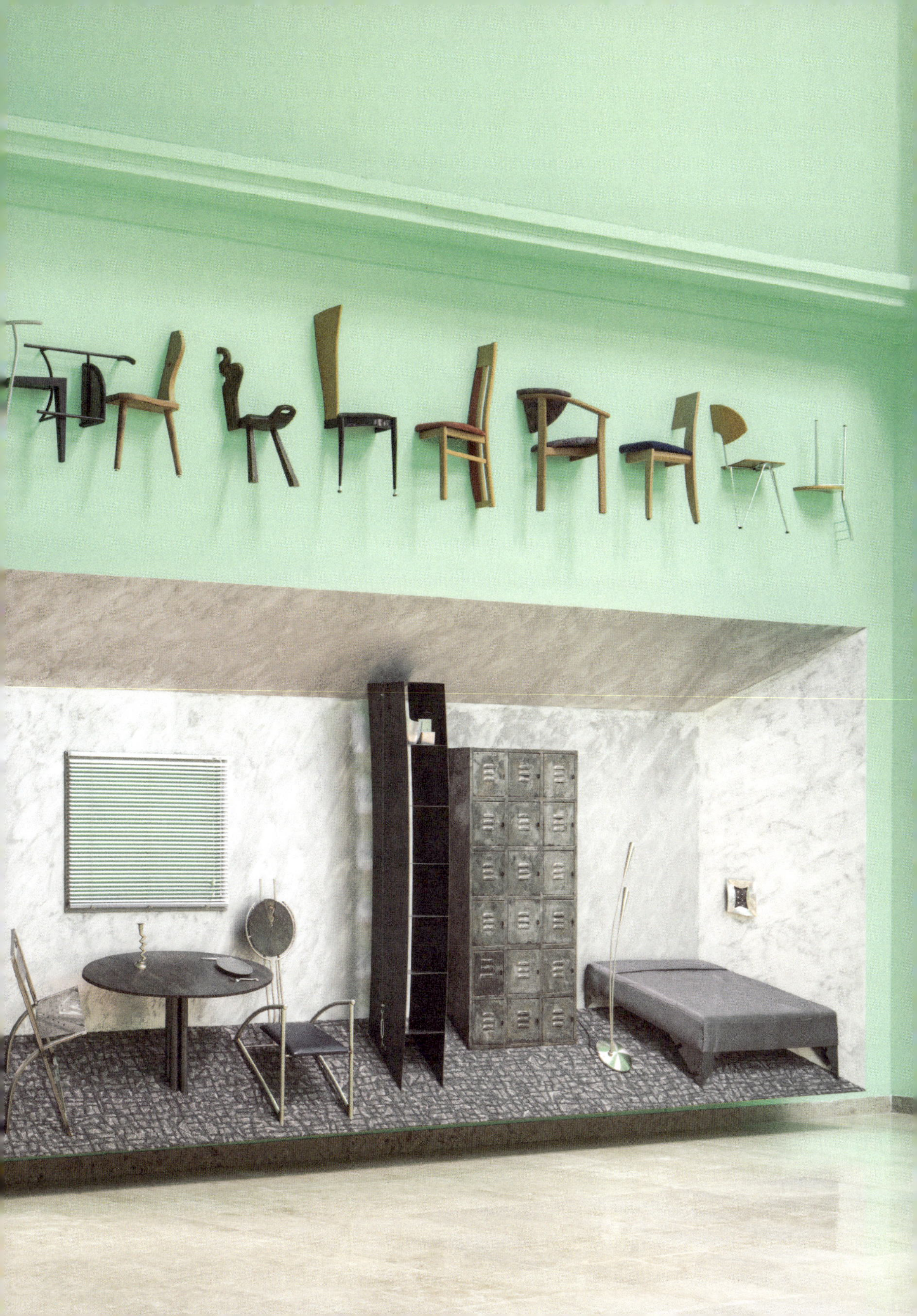

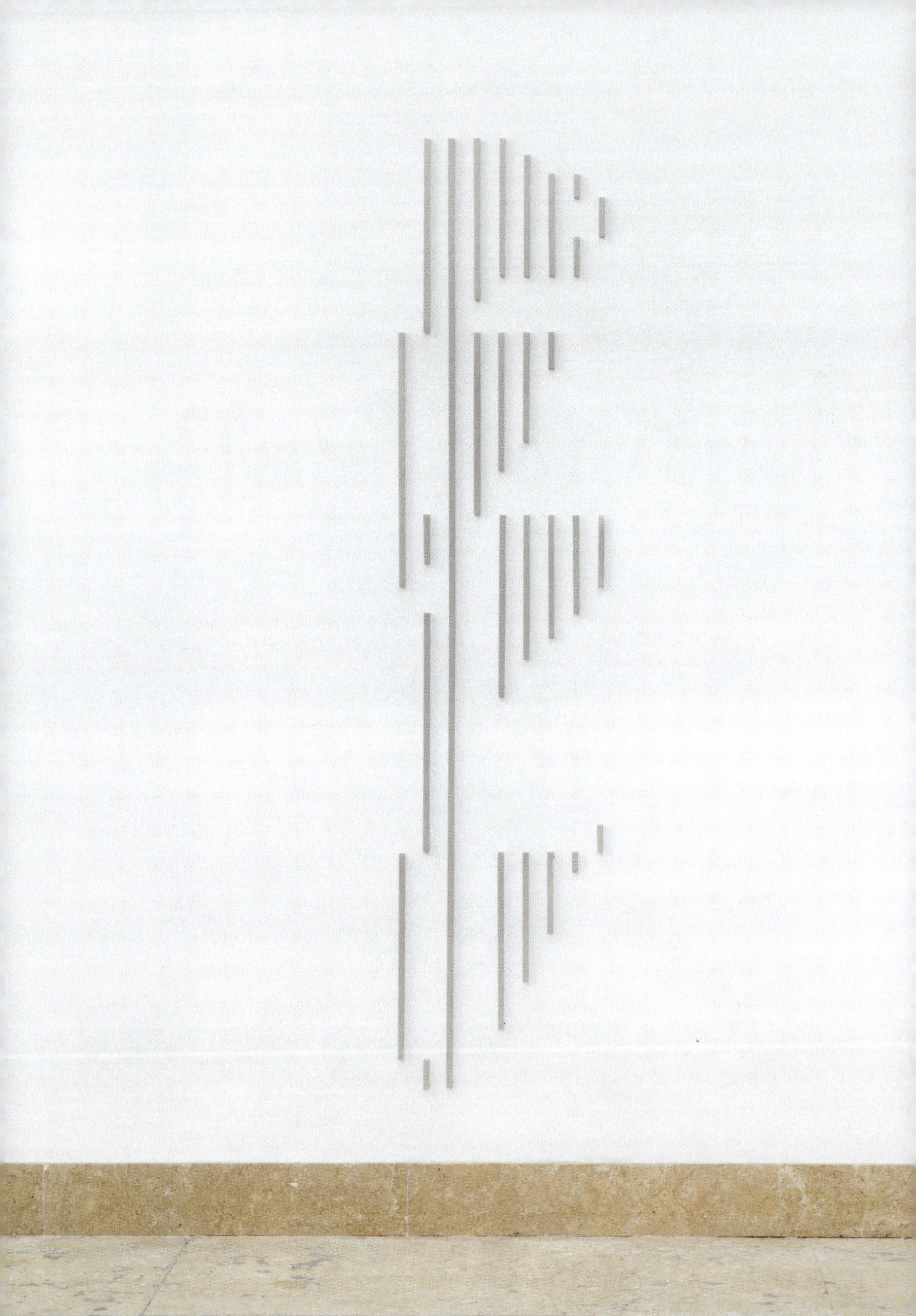

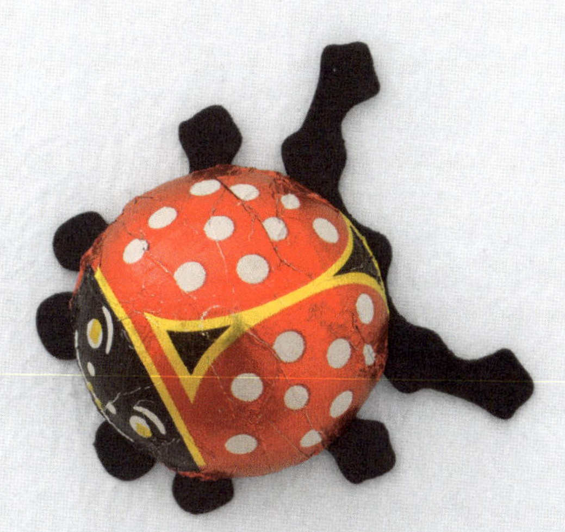

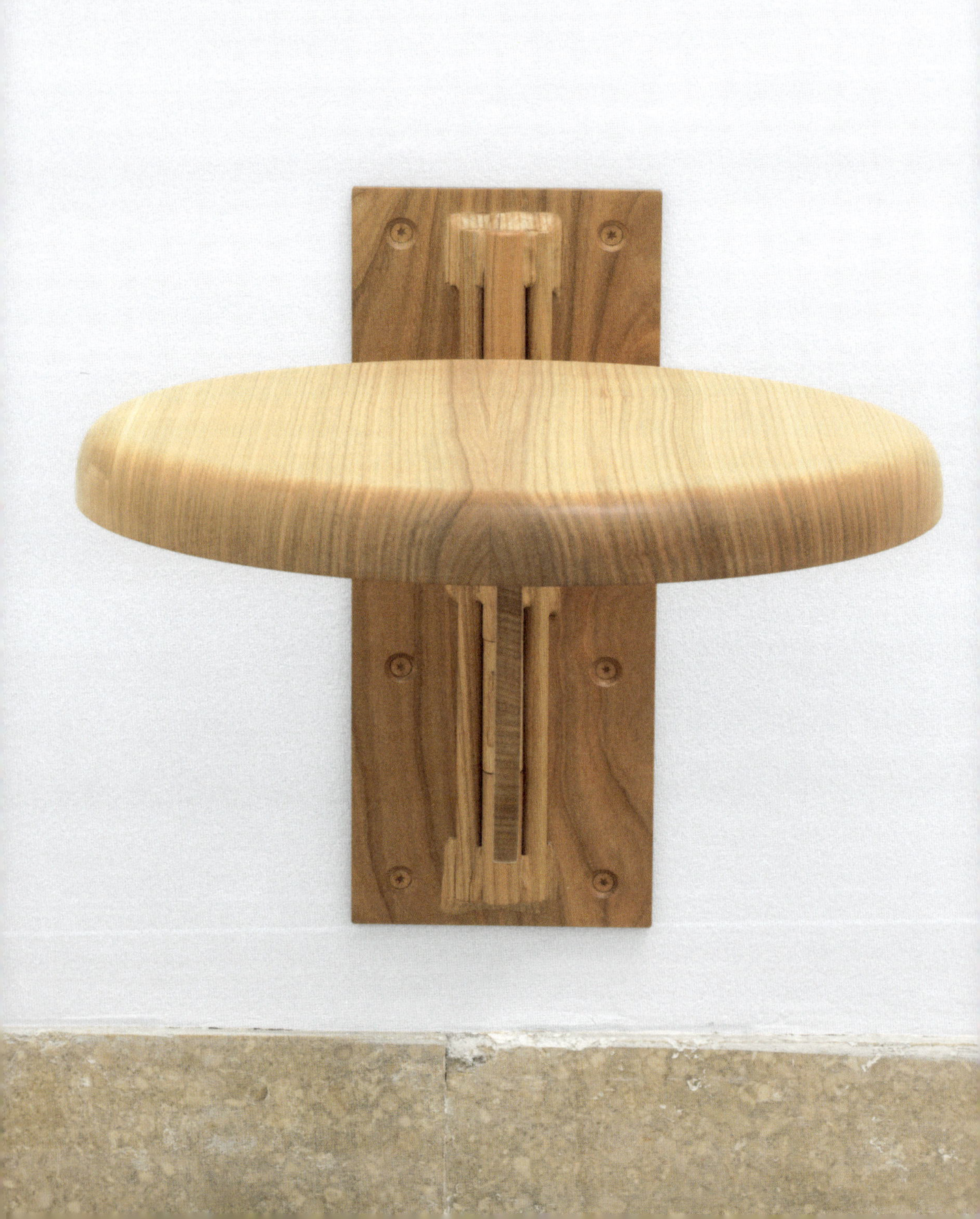

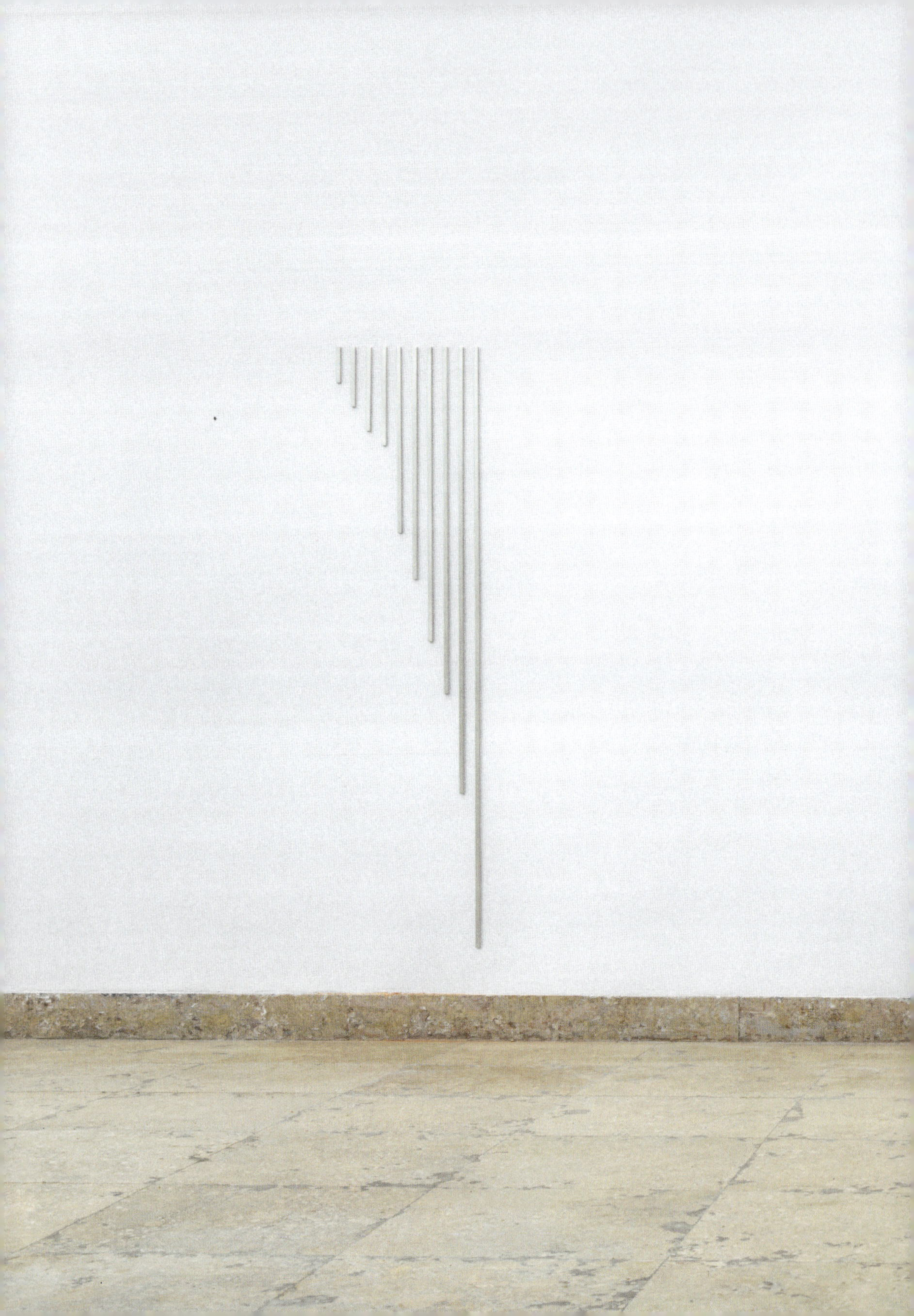

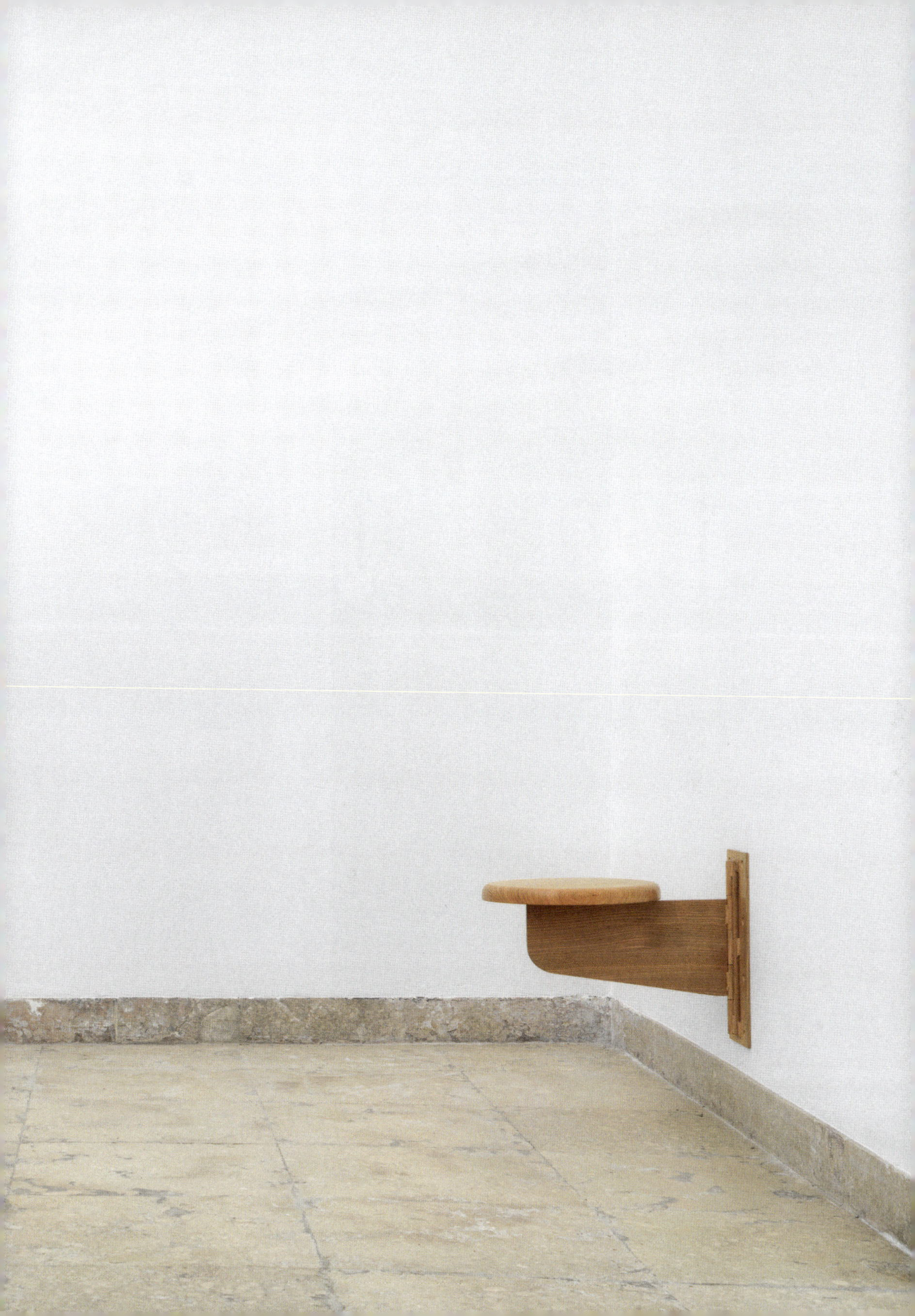

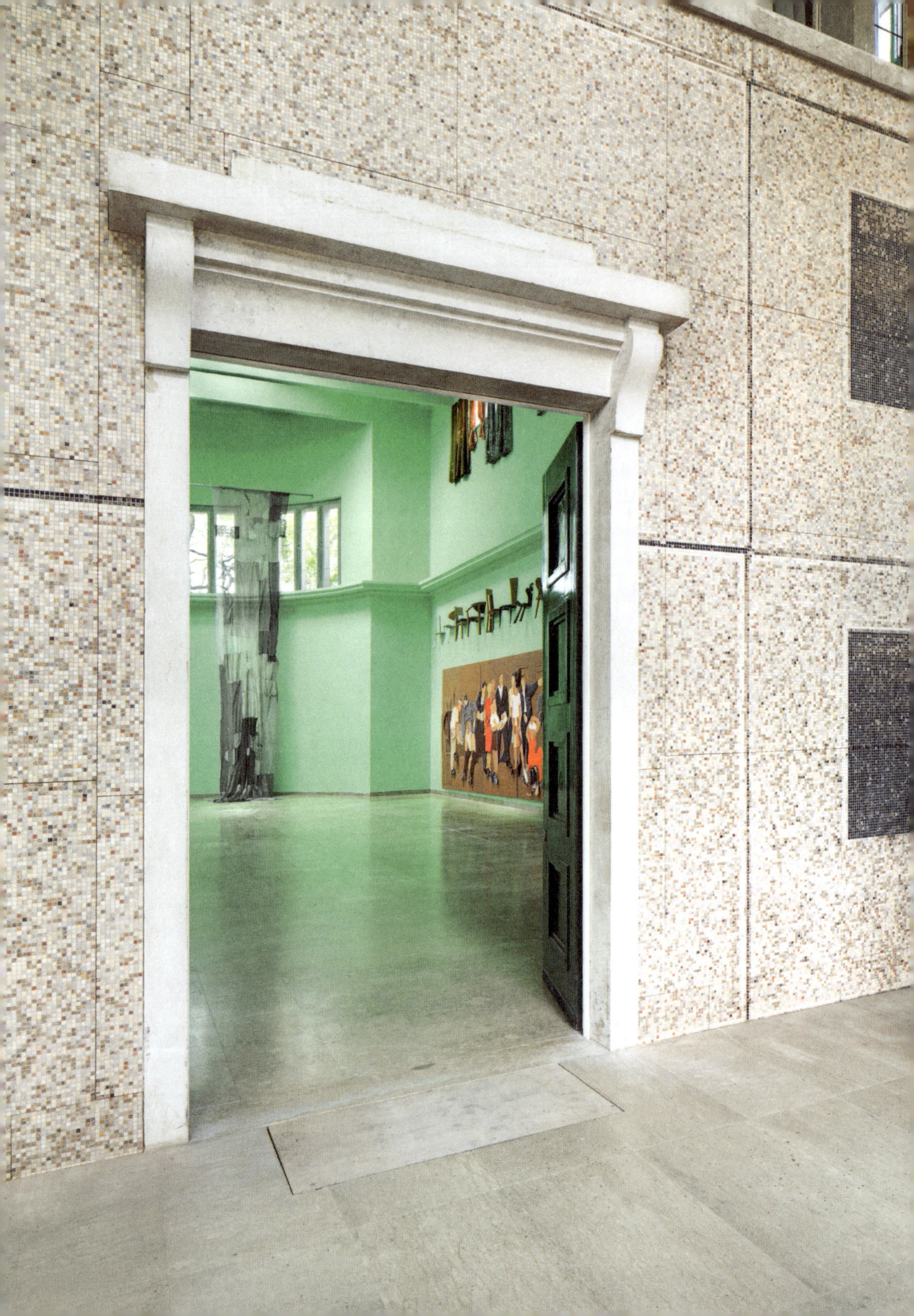

HENRIKE NAUMANN'S REALISM: THE INNER FRONT

Kerstin Stakemeier

Henrike Naumann creates provincial spaces. She does not conceal the national romantic origins of late-eighteenth-century modern aesthetics and its arts, but reconstructs and exhibits them. Naumann brings the omnipresence of what Bertolt Brecht called "suspiciousities" (*verdächtige Tümlichkeiten)*[1] into the space. Their romanticism is embedded in the color of the walls and imbues the curtains; it's in the shape of the chairs and has settled into every surface. The "freedomity" of the arts survived largely as a nostalgia of form, as a romantically nationalized educational ideal. Naumann incorporates into her installations the very things that had to be successively excluded from this ideal in order to present its arts as free: their provincial origins, trickery, and decorum; the artisanal intricacies of economically obsolete handicraft; the regional artistic creations and skills that in Nazi Germany were transformed into industrially reproduced emblems of a nationalized folkic.[2] Yet "the concept of the folkic itself," as Brecht wrote in the late 1930s, "is not particularly folkic. It is not realistic to believe that it is."[3] On the contrary, for Brecht it lay at the heart of the politics of the Popular Front,[4] at the heart of an anti-fascist Realism. And in the underground journal *Die Innere Front* (The Inner Front), which from 1941 was published twice a week in five languages by a Neukölln-based branch of the German Communist Party, the folkic again appears not as an extension of the national, but as its breaking point, as an anational communion against national violence.

In Henrike Naumann's spaces, these conflicting historical traces of the folkic—its anti-fascist realism and its romantic nationalism—coalesce into a horizon within which all modern art has to reveal itself as glorified minor art. In Naumann's installations, the decorative, applied, and fine arts are inextricably linked through questions of form, all of which lead back to a shared, beleaguered sense of the folkic. Within a national framework, all art is always also minor art. And with Bertolt Brecht and Henrike Naumann, it is precisely this connection that leads to its anti-fascist horizon. Yet this fact remains uncomfortable, particularly in the non-applied arts, which to this day are relentlessly plagued by a looming loss of educational status, a looming erosion of legitimacy. Like Henrike Naumann, Bertolt Brecht privileged the dubiously folkic that was looming amidst the educated cultural freedom, since the latter is usually merely struggling

1) Bertolt Brecht, "Popularity and Realism," *Aesthetics and Politics*. London: New Left Books, 1977, pp. 79–85. See note 5.

2) Cf. *Formen der Anpassung: Kunsthandwerk und Design im Nationalsozialismus*, ed. Frank Werner, GRASSI Museum für Angewandte Kunst Leipzig, Munich: Hirmer Verlag, 2025.

3) Brecht 1977, pp. 79–85. The original translation uses "popularity" for *Volkstümlichkeit*, a translation that has effectively made an understanding of Brecht's argument in English impossible. The German word *Volkstümlichkeit* was at the time a direct translation from the Russian, as *Volktsümlichkeit* had been officiated as one of the pillars of Realism in the debates around the politics of the Popular Front from 1934. I decided to translate it as *folkic*, using a neologism by the writer Fumi Okiji, because it qualifies a form of conscious provinciality that is characterized by its communal, ahierarchical and decommodified sense of culture. See Fumi Okiji, Billie's Bent Elbow: *Exorbitance, Intimacy and a Nonsensuous Standard*, Stanford: Stanford University Press, 2025.

4) Cf. Wilhelm Pieck, *Die Offensive des Faschismus und die Aufgaben der Kommunisten im Kampf für die Volksfront gegen Krieg und Faschismus. Referate auf d. 7. Kongress d. Kommunist. Internationale* (1935), Berlin: Dietz Verlag, 1957; Werner Herden, *Wege zur Volksfront: Schriftsteller im antifaschistischen Bündnis*, Berlin: Akademie-Verlag 1978; Hans J. Schmitt, *Die Expressionismus-Debatte: Materialien zu einer marxistischen Realismuskonzeption*, Frankfurt am Main: Suhrkamp, 1974.

to prevent itself from slipping out of the realm of educational culture into being an accessory, out of modern art's origin myth of the Romantic eighteenth century into the origin myth of the German state. State art is always minor art. And in this regard, as Brecht phrased it, "there is a whole series of abstract nouns ending on 'ity' which must be viewed with caution. Think of *utility, sovereignty, sanctity*; and we know that the concept of *folkdom* has a quite particular, sacramental, pompous and suspicious connotation, which we dare not overlook. We must not ignore this connotation, just because we so urgently need the concept of the folkic."[5] To this day, the national ends of modern art find solace in these and other suspicious "-ities": in the national romantic origin of modern aesthetics as a cultural good and in the industrial standard as the emblem of an imagined "national culture." Both canons are composed of educated cultural nostalgias built on the colonial plunder at the core of European nation-building.

The Berlin publicist and feminist Marxist Lu Märten coined a fitting term for this in 1920s Berlin: "material-seizure" (*Stoffergreifung*).[6] She used the term to describe art's freedom as a lamentable right of access to any content, which, according to Märten, it "prekills" (*ertötet)*[7] where the art does not refigure itself from it. Art as appropriation. Culture as appropriation. Henrike Naumann does not reproduce Romanticism; she does not prekill new content for art. Rather, she strings together its folkicness as a series of remnants, fissures, and patchwork pieces that emerge wherever the material-seizure is integrated into cultural education, wherever Romanticism becomes embedded into the furniture. The lack of refiguration in the material-seizures that amount to artistic culture is no less persistent than that of nationally industrialized Romanticism. Henrike Naumann combines these two elements to create a folkic panorama of the *Inner Front*: the panorama of a Realism made of fissures, remnants, and patchwork; an interior space assembled from domesticated hieroglyphs, homey parlors, wartime curtains, and a realistic relief—a panorama of the realistically folkic.

Henrike Naumann too calls upon art's fabled freedom—but in her case, it lies in the refiguration and reworking of former material-seizures along their fissures. This is not about advancing cultural education, but about deconstructing and dismantling it. Henrike Naumann creates patchworks from that which is no longer realistic. The socialist group portrait, which she mounted on the wall of the German Pavilion can now only be vaguely discerned beneath its upholstering. It turned into a relief because its painterly form could no longer withstand the nostalgia it inspired. Former attempts at

5) Brecht 1977, pp. 79–85.

6) Lu Märten, *Wesen und Veränderung der Formen (und Künste)*, Frankfurt/Main: Taifun Verlag, 1924, p. 272.

7) Lu Märten, "Historisch-Materialistisches über Wesen und Veränderung der Künste. Eine pragmatische Einleitung" [1921], in: *Lu Märten, Formen für den Alltag. Schriften, Aufsätze, Vorträge*, ed. Rainhard May, Dresden: Verlag der Kunst, 1982, p. 58.

realistic state art as a socialist minor art were undone by the increasing illegibility that resulted from their transformation into kitsch, by the rise of "Ostalgie" as a diminutive national aesthetic, and consequently by the descent of generations of realists into the status of hieroglyphs. GDR art. Henrike Naumann's buildup seeks art's freedom in the material ends of its national romanticism, in the patchwork and cracks. In hieroglyphs that become the legends for Henrike Naumann's Realism. All of which stands in stark contrast to the form of freedom that manifests in the aesthetics of material-seizure and their romantic origins, which, purged of their fault lines, inevitably solidify the arts into a never-ending ironclad form of propaganda, a cultural education consisting of serially produced colonial minor arts—with the artist figure as a national romanticist freedom fighter. FRG art. Henrike Naumann dissects heroism into its constituent parts and makes her art from its colonial, warmongering fissures, arranging them life-sized and, in the process, inevitably posing unpleasant origin questions to herself, and to us—not in terms of her legitimation, not in terms of our legitimation, but to pry open the interstices that every origin reveals in order to collect what has remained of it and within it. In the German Pavilion at the Venice Biennale, Henrike Naumann constructs a space of origin legends, an endless relief of decayed forms of legitimation. We read the hieroglyphs of a controlled deconstruction.

The question of origin is particularly crucial where an attempt is made to anchor the present in it. Willi Baumeister posed this question in West Germany in 1947; his answer, entirely in keeping with the times, was to rebuild from nothing. In his seminal pamphlet on artistic creation, *Das Unbekannte in der Kunst* (The Unknown in Art), he writes that it is "[s]imilar to how the artist draws new values from the unknown through his works."[8] The discovery of cave paintings becomes the discovery of the artist, the origin of a creator in caves that will always resemble ruins. Baumeister wrote his book in 1943, formulating what he perceived as his escape from national socialist Germany into his interiority, his "center"—the "neutral, purified, natural condition of the artist."[9] His reorigination became epochal, style-defining in postwar Germany. In the context of Henrike Naumann's work, Baumeister's painterly postwar abstractions become West German cave paintings made of upholstered, painted, and sculpted cracks that merge seamlessly into the decorations of the living spaces of their time and become indistinguishable from them. Both in Baumeister's book and in the subsequent discussion with Johannes Itten and Hans Sedlmayr over *Das Menschenbild*

8) Willi Baumeister, *The Unknown in Art* [1947], Stuttgart: Willi Baumeister Stiftung, 2013, p. 143.

9) Ibid, p. 200.

in unserer Zeit (The Image of Humanity in Our Time) at the Darmstadt Mathildenhöhe in 1950,[10] the German choice of National Socialism retrospectively emerges as something unspeakable: the romantic origin of a nonsentient abstraction, a formalism of the wounded, failed German colonial subject. In Henrike Naumann's work, the unending material-seizures of this subject descends into the upholstery of the chairs that she makes impossible to sit on in the German Pavilion. But they do remain in the space and become its cornice, a relief of an accommodation within the unlivable.

And yet, it's not the question of origin itself through which Brecht's "suspiciousities" (*verdächtige Tümlichkeiten)* are nationally reproduced, but rather its being answered as a hieroglyph of nationalizing romanticism. The question of origin also arises where the denationalization of the present is concerned. Bertolt Brecht posed it, too. Henrike Naumann poses it, too. But to her mind, its answer lies in dismantling, in transforming the fissures of colonial powers into cartographies, into legends of decolonization. *The Inner Front.* Wil B. Mirimanov's standard work *Kunst der Urgesellschaft* (The Art of the Primitive Society), translated from the Russian in the GDR, begins with the sentence: "Labor created man."[11] A few pages later, he enthusiastically quotes the Soviet psychologist L. S. Vygotsky: "Art is the social within us."[12] In Mirimanov's work, instead of appearing as a product of intellectual education, art emerges in the process of physical formation. In Henrike Naumann's pavilion, the Western and Eastern variants of national form-building appear as unequal, inverted creation narratives, each of which leads to the ultimately never free arts, as the *Inner Front* of German national culture. At their transitions from and within the hieroglyphs of social groundlessness, what arises in the German Pavilion is a prehistory of our present, which also finds its model in a sketch by Waldemar Grzimek, a relief sketch he made in the 1950s as part of a proposal by the artists' group *Die Fähre* for a Thälmann monument in Berlin. It depicts modern history as a series of pre-modern hieroglyphs, a panorama of working people that extends across spinning chairs and war machines, across private and public forms of communal life. A prehistory of modern forms of work with an uncertain outcome. If Western art exhausts itself in a groundless spirit, Eastern art is built from limitless work.

Lu Märten began her major work, *Wesen und Veränderung der Formen (und Künste)* (The Essence and Transformation of Forms [and Arts]), first published in 1924, with a lengthy quotation from Friedrich Engels' *Anti-Dühring,* in which Engels writes of "humanity's leap from the realm of necessity

10) *Das Menschenbild in unserer Zeit. Darmstädter Gespräch 1*, ed. Hanns Gerhard Evers, Darmstadt: Neue Darmstädter Verlagsanstalt, 1951.

11) Wil B. Mirimanov, *Kunst der Urgesellschaft und traditionelle Kunst Afrikas und Ozeaniens*, Dresden: Verlag der Kunst, 1973, p. 12.

12) Ibid., p. 15.

into the realm of freedom."[13] Engels goes on to say that this "world-emancipating act" is the mission of the proletariat. It is definitely not the task of the artist, whose artistic freedom is projected as real only within the "kingdom of reason" (Engels' term for "the idealized kingdom of the bourgeoisie").[14] It is this condition, the existence of the artist as a colonial decal of the realm of freedom, that Henrike Naumann meticulously articulates for us as a fissure—a fissure cracking open between Realism and the folkic. Henrike Naumann produces big minor art, masterpieces of a desocialized craft, that of art, forced into national self-aggrandizement due to the proletariat's unfindability. Henrike Naumann is perfectly positioned in the German Pavilion. She has always worked towards its purpose. From the national histories of its arts and their industrial, artisanal, and dilettante fringes and outposts, she rearranges it into a cave painting of our folkicness. Not least, Henrike Naumann also always produces us as provincial recipients.

Where Henrike Naumann's works fill the German Pavilion, origin myths and the folkic meet postmodernism and Realism. In Naumann's view, colonization is never merely an externalized movement, neither spatially nor temporally. As a form of continuous warlike consumption, it extends to the *Inner Front*. Clemens Villinger's work traces its historicization. Recently, he addressed a question the historiography of Germany seeks to clarify: who survived in the German Reich of Reason?[15] Villinger's starting point is a distinction, which already began to emerge in the late 1940s in research on Nazi perpetrators, namely the distinction "between normal and abnormal personalities."[16] The attempt to identify the political subject of a postwar West led to the dilemma of distinguishing between the National Socialist state subject, the *perpetrator*, and the National Socialist private subject, the *normal citizen*: if the National Socialist man—and these studies, according to Villinger, always concern men—was a normal *citizen*, his normality did not preclude practicing genocide; if the National Socialist man was a *perpetrator*, then his continued existence in the new German state is that of a genocidal subject. In both cases, the *Inner Front* of state normality forms the stage for a continuing genocidal capability—a connection whose origin can also be traced back to German colonial policy and its national socialist continuation. Origins. Prehistories. Panoramas in which, as Villinger demonstrates, the concept of normality becomes a kind of fissure that shifts, a yardstick of state-supported violence that is deployed wherever a still-extant state subject must, but cannot be, distinguished from it.

13) Friedrich Engels, *Herr Eugen Dühring's Revolution in Science (Anti-Dühring)* [1877], New York: International Publishers, 1939, p. 310.

14) Ibid., p. 24.

15) Clemens Villinger, "Endlich normale Nazis? Normalität als Begriff in der Alltags- und Täterforschung zur NS-Zeit," *Vierteljahrshefte für Zeitgeschichte*, 74, no. 1, 2026, pp. 117–51.

16) Ibid., p. 125.

In Henrike Naumann's buildup, these fissures are drifting through the space as markers of the folkic. The GDR, in which Naumann was born in 1984, inevitably drifts within the forms of the Federal Republic it was transferred into. Remnants of the GDR drift within the present-day German state. Remnants of National Socialist Germany drift within the present-day German state. Normalities and fissures. Fissures also in the pavilion itself, whose Nazi-era reconstruction in 1938 by Ernst Haiger was repeatedly referenced by the West German artists who exhibited there. With Naumann, its interior is painted in the same green that once adorned the interiors of Soviet barracks in the GDR. The artists of the GDR, their Realism under the mint-green Soviet protectorate, have no past in this architecture. Henrike Naumann searched the Federal Archives to trace the GDR's attempts to change this, to bring its art into the National Pavilion. As early as 1956, the socialist Academy of Arts attempted to invite its imperialist counterpart, the West German Foreign Office, to negotiate East German participation in the German Pavilion at the 1958 Venice Biennale. However, the West insisted on its property as the successor state to Nazi Germany, and turned down the invitation. Eberhard Hanfstaengl had been responsible for the selection of West German artists since 1948. He had already taken on this task in 1935 and 1936. Figures of origin. Competencies of normalcy. The Federal Archives also document, in the form of letters and reports, an attempt of the then newly instated Venice Biennale management launched toward the end of 1978 to grant socialist countries visibility in Venice. However, their invitations to Czechoslovakia, Cuba, Poland, East Germany, the People's Republic of China, Romania, Hungary, and the Soviet Union to take part in talks, initially went unanswered. Hungary was the only country to respond. Negotiations with the Soviet Union and the GDR didn't begin until a year later. From 1982 onward, visual artists from the GDR exhibited their work in the former Pavilion of Decorative Arts in Venice. But they never moved into the German Pavilion. The documents in the Federal Archives contain neither installation views nor the catalogues whose production Hermann Raum, the GDR's long-serving commissioner to the Venice Biennale, described at length in government reports. His dispatches merely record the impossibility of viewing even the contributions of the socialist brother states in Venice within the short installation period—which was repeatedly disrupted by the GDR's own lack of experience and by the Biennale changing its plans. They describe an infrastructural failure to reconstruct the phalanx of socialist art, the monumental works of late Socialist Realism, in Venice. Henrike Naumann makes up for this. In miniature. She brings a mural of commissioned socialist art to the German Pavilion: a 3×8 meter painterly variation on the mural *Die Mechanisierung der Landwirtschaft* (The Mechanization of Agriculture), produced in the late 1950s by her grandfather, the painter and graphic artist Karl Heinz Jakob. A large-scale piece of minor art that still adorns the former wall of the former chamber hall of the former Chamber of Industry and Commerce in former Karl-Marx-Stadt. Today, Jakob's mural in Chemnitz is covered over by drywall. And Henrike Naumann's reworked quotation of its monumental Realism takes the socialist form and manifests it as a cave painting of the present day. Reconfigured into a relief in the German Pavilion, she salvages it as a postmodern hieroglyph, as it had already been perceived at the time of its unveiling. The social realization of Jakob's mural never materialized. Workers writing in the daily press accused him of material-seizure. The working clothes were deemed inaccurate, as were the tools. Jakob had not taken them to transform his form. Already during the painting process, the commissioning state institutions had already judged the machines that framed the group of people in Jakob's paintings to be nonfigurative. Jakob transformed them, made them more socialist. But Karl Heinz Jakob's Realism was still too painterly, not utilitarian enough for the chamber hall in Karl-Marx-Stadt. His large-scale painting of postwar reconstruction in the East incorporated motifs from late nineteenth-century naturalism, early 1910s Expressionism, and 1920s Constructivism, gathering images of humanity from *these* periods into a mural of his *own* socialist present: a painterly present of work, constructed from the transformed pasts of its themes. A prehistory that tied Karl Heinz Jakob's Realism to modern art history. Henrike Naumann reworks the Realism demanded from her grandfather in the form of a relief, thereby anchoring his group of workers even more distinctly in the realm of necessity. Naumann's intervention renders Jakob's mural, that, as an example of social realist painting, had become a hieroglyph of bygone state socialism, legible as a fissure between Realism and the folkic, between the image of a community and its working reality. Naumann incorporates precisely the kind of everyday life into Jakob's scene that, contrary to the hopes of the critical workers at the time, has thus far failed to achieve the leap into the realm of freedom. Between relief and inlay, between oversized decoration and small-scale realism, Naumann's reworking demonstrates what, in the sense of the East German publicist Heinz Hirdina, could be called Jakob's postmodernism: the positioning of working people in a postwar scenario the humanization of which must seem questionable.[17] In a series of lectures on "Functionalism—Postmodernism" that Hirdina gave in Berlin in the mid-1980s, he argued that only functionality allows "aesthetic enjoyment to shift from form in itself to form in use."[18] This is one reason why Hirdina considered the 1950s the beginning of postmodernism. The transition was fissured, and this is precisely what Jakob's painting was accused of. His Realism remained an attempt to humanize the present through historical recourse. Postwar painting East. Henrike Naumann has always worked postmodernly, has always proceeded from the fissures. Into a Realism of the fissure. Postmodernity, which in Henrike Naumann's work often organizes the space as a furniture-shaped driftwood collection, giving rise to places of worship, adolescent rooms, and memorials, climbs the walls here in the German Pavilion, grows into life-size, and incorporates Jakob into the legends of our present-day prehistories. For Henrike Naumann,

17) Heinz Hirdina, "Postmodernismus: Experiment oder Produktleitbild?," in: Bruno Flierl, Heinz Hirdina, *Postmoderne und Funktionalismus. Sechs Vorträge*, Berlin: Verband der Bildenden Künstler, 1985, p. 21.

18) Heinz Hirdina 1985, p. 10.

everything becomes a mural, everything becomes a hieroglyph, everything becomes postmodern Realism, everything becomes folkic. The furnishing loses its depth and scale; the proportions are skewed. Yet within their social context, the proportions are absolutely true to scale. In the German Pavilion, Henrike Naumann constructs *The Inner Front*, in a ratio of 1:1. Fissure by fissure.

In 1978, the East Berlin theater director Heiner Müller gave a lecture on postmodernism in New York, stating what Henrike Naumann would demonstrate in 2026: "In the *realm of necessity*, Realism and the folkic are two separate things. The split goes through the author."[19] It runs through Henrike Naumann. Müller hoped to bridge this rift with the GDR, in the GDR. And so he added: "Periodization is the politics of colonialism as long as history ... does not become universal history."[20] It was meant to become universal history. The colonial politics of the GDR. The colonial politics of the FRG. Their deconstruction into universal history failed to materialize. In the German Pavilion, Henrike Naumann's art is itself positioned firmly outside this universal history. Yet Henrike Naumann produces in it and for it a postmodern Realism of the colonially folkic. Like Brecht, Müller insisted on the anational origins of the folkic and deliberately revived it from the late-1930s Realism debates of the Popular Front against fascism, and from Bertolt Brecht's later comments on these debates, his appeal to "Realism and the Folkic" as art's only viable socialization. Henrike Naumann lays out for us how the socialization of art in the origin myths of East and West Germany drifted from the Realism of the Popular Front into the folkic of colonial history. Yet she keeps Realism and the folkic in play. Because the folkic remains attached to Realism and "the increasing pressure of authentic experience develops the ability to look history into the white of the eye."[21] Müller's words speak directly to Naumann's *Inner Front*.

At *Ambiente Berlin*, a 1990 exhibition dedicated to the newly coalesced city of Berlin that had grown out of the Venice Biennale of 1988, Hermann Raum presented "Still Berlin," a retrospective evaluation of his former protectorate, the visual arts of the GDR: "The artistic achievements do not require any special recognition in this context."[22] This, too, is a distinctively realist statement—realist in the sense that the question of origin in the GDR had been answered with the Peasants' War of the early seventeenth century.[23] The workers' and peasants' state intended to fulfill its legacy—including through the arts it produced. Within the horizon of integrating artistic labor into the diverse crafts employed in the struggle against class rule, Raum's statement could also

19) Heiner Müller, "Reflections on Post-Modernism," in: *New German Critique*, Milwaukee: Duke University Press, 1979, p. 55. As in the case of the earlier Brecht quotes I changed the English translation to accommodate the meaning of *Volkstümlichkeit.*

20) Ibid., p. 56.

21) Heiner Müller, *"Für Alle reicht es nicht." Texte zum Kapitalismus*, Frankfurt/Main: Suhrkamp Verlag, 2017, p. 48.

22) Hermann Raum, "Immer noch Berlin," in: *Ambiente Berlin*, ed. Marie-George Gervasoni, Venice: Edizioni Biennale Realizzazione Fabbri Editori, 1990, p. 175.

23) Cf. the authors' collective Adolf Laube, Max Steinmetz, Günter Vogler (director), *Illustrierte Geschichte der deutschen frühbürgerlichen Revolution*, Berlin: Dietz Verlag, 1974.

point to the simple fact that the question of realistic potential arises less from individual artistic achievements than from the sum of their social mediation. Henrike Naumann didn't bring her grandfather to the German Pavilion to showcase his masterful craftsmanship or to honor his artistic achievements, but to explore the fissures in his Realism with him. Yet, for Raum, it was precisely realist art's social potential—which his colleague, art historian Peter H. Feist, had identified in the 1960s in the materialist principle of art's "relative autonomy as the 'autonomy of the material'"[24]—that, in looking back, he decided the artists of the GDR had lost. In 1990, Raum declared the visual arts of the GDR to be a hieroglyph.

Feist had also been one of the editors of Mirimanov's prehistory. The two were united in the search for the "intrinsic laws of the material" within art, which led Mirimanov to recognize the courtly arts of Europe as "significantly poorer"[25] in terms of artistic expression compared to those of West and Central Africa at the time. A poorer civility that would soon resort to colonial plunder in order to become richer. Mirimanov's contemporary visual example of this plundering poverty is Pablo Picasso's *Les Desmoiselles d'Avignon* (1907).[26] Uncommented. Here, the history of artistic freedom has always been a history of material-seizure, of an artistically desocialized loss of form, as it is in Henrike Naumann's German Pavilion. A rich collection of colonial fissures, on both the inner and outer fronts. In the catalogue for the 10th Art Exhibition in Dresden in 1988, Raum wrote that, due to its "steep over-artification," GDR art had become nothing more than "a minor special case in the overall experience of powerlessness."[27] He had already given up on it prior to 1989. And Feist's earlier basic principles for a materialist understanding of art, the second point of which was "the conviction of the primacy of *content*," can still be traced back to the powerlessness Raum described. Its content ended. But if, as Feist further explains, "the content of the artwork... is of course not synonymous with its theme or subject," but rather "the meaning that the artist gives to their theme through the form, ... the statement that the artist wants to make and that reaches the viewer only in the guise of a form that can be perceived with the senses,"[28] then once again it's easy to identify Henrike Naumann as a realist in the German Pavilion. Henrike Naumann is an antagonist of material-seizure. And yet she inevitably finds the origins of her art within it, in the national framework of minor art, whose *Inner Front* she builds up for us. In Brecht's words, it still holds true that "there is not only such a thing as *being folkic*, there is also the process of *becoming folkic*."[29]

24) Peter H. Feist, *Prinzipien und Methoden marxistischer Kunstwissenschaft. Versuch eines Abrisses*, Leipzig: Seemann Verlag, 1966, p. 12.

25) Ibid., p. 277.

26) Cf. ibid., p. 278.

27) Martin Damus, *Malerei der DDR: Funktionen der bildenden Kunst im Realen Sozialismus*, Reinbek bei Hamburg: Rowohlt, 1991, p. 345.

28) Feist 1966, p. 24f.

29) Brecht 1977, p. 85.

HENRIKE NAUMANNS REALISMUS. DIE INNERE FRONT

Kerstin Stakemeier

Henrike Naumann produziert provinzielle Orte. Der nationalromantische Ursprung moderner Ästhetik und ihrer Künste im ausgehenden 18. Jahrhundert wird von ihr nicht verdeckt, sondern aufgebaut und ausgestellt. Henrike Naumann bringt die Allgegenwart dessen, was Bertolt Brecht die „verdächtigen Tümlichkeiten"[1] nannte, in den Raum. Ihre Romantik steckt in der Wandfarbe und sie hängt in den Gardinen, sie formt die Stühle und sie legt sich auf alle Oberflächen. Auch die Freiheitstümlichkeit der Künste überlebte maßgeblich als ebensolche nostalgische Form, als romantisch nationalisiertes Bildungsideal. Henrike Naumann führt in ihre Aufbauten das ein, was aus dem Ideal dieser Künste sukzessive ausgeschlossen werden musste, um sie als frei vorstellen zu können: Die provinziellen Ursprünge, Kunststücke und Dekore, die kunsthandwerklichen Feinheiten ökonomisch ausgedienter Handwerksformen und die regionalen Kunststücke und Fertigkeiten, die im nationalsozialistischen Deutschland in industriell wiederholte Embleme nationalisierter Volkstümlichkeiten verwandelt wurden.[2] Doch „der Begriff *volkstümlich* selber ist", wie Brecht Ende der 1930er-Jahre schrieb, „nicht allzu volkstümlich. Es ist nicht realistisch, dies zu glauben".[3] Für Brecht steht er ganz im Gegenteil im Zentrum einer Politik der Volksfront,[4] im Zentrum eines antifaschistischen Realismus. Und auch in der Zeitschrift *Die Innere Front,* die von einer Neuköllner Ortsgruppe der Kommunistischen Partei Deutschlands ab 1941 im Untergrund zweimal die Woche in fünf Sprachen produziert wurde, taucht das Volkstümliche nicht als Fortsetzung des Nationalen, sondern als dessen Bruchstelle, als anationale Gemeinschaft gegen die nationale Gewalt auf.

Die widerstrebenden historischen Spuren der Volkstümlichkeit, ihr antifaschistischer Realismus und ihre nationalistische Romantisierung, fügen sich in Henrike Naumanns Räumen in einen Horizont, innerhalb dessen jede moderne Kunst sich als glorifizierte Kleinkunst offenbaren muss. Denn die dekorativen, die angewandten und die unangewandten Künste treten in Henrike Naumanns Werkkomplexen als untrennbar miteinander verbundene Formfragen einer gebeutelten Volkstümlichkeit auf. Im nationalen Rahmen ist jede Kunst immer auch Kleinkunst. Und mit Bertolt Brecht und mit Henrike Naumann eröffnet gerade diese Verbindung ihren antifaschistischen Horizont. Doch vor allem (in) der unangewandten Kunst ist dies immer noch unangenehm.

1) Bertolt Brecht, „Volkstümlichkeit und Realismus", *Sinn und Form*, Jahr 10, Heft 4, 1958, S. 496.

2) Vgl. etwa *Formen der Anpassung: Kunsthandwerk und Design im Nationalsozialismus*, hrsg. Frank Werner, Ausst.-Kat., GRASSI Museum für Angewandte Kunst Leipzig, München: Hirmer Verlag, 2025.

3) Brecht 1958, S. 496.

4) Vgl. hierzu etwa Wilhelm Pieck, *Die Offensive des Faschismus und die Aufgaben der Kommunisten im Kampf für die Volksfront gegen Krieg und Faschismus. Referate auf d. 7. Kongress d. Kommunist. Internationale (1935)*, Berlin: Dietz Verlag, 1957; Werner Herden, *Wege zur Volksfront: Schriftsteller im antifaschistischen Bündnis*, Berlin: Akademie-Verlag, 1978; Hans J Schmitt, *Die Expressionismus-Debatte: Materialien zu einer marxistischen Realismuskonzeption*, Frankfurt am Main: Suhrkamp, 1974.

Es ist vor allem sie, die bis heute stetig vom drohenden Statusverfall, vom drohenden Bildungsverfall ihres Legitimationshorizonts geplagt ist. Bertolt Brecht zog wie Henrike Naumann ihre fragwürdige Volkstümlichkeit inmitten ihrer gebildeten Freiheit hervor, da letztere doch meist nur darum kämpft, nicht aus der Bildung ins Beiwerk abzurutschen, aus dem Ursprungsmythos der modernen Kunst im romantischen 18. Jahrhundert in den Ursprungsmythos des deutschen Staats. Staatskunst ist immer Kleinkunst. Und hier müssen „eine ganze Reihe von ‚Tümlichkeiten'", so Brecht, „mit Vorsicht betrachtet werden. Man denke nur an *Brauchtum*, *Königstum*, *Heiligtum*, und man weiß, daß auch *Volkstum* einen ganz besonderen, sakralen, feierlichen und verdächtigen Klang an sich hat, den wir keineswegs überhören dürfen. Wir dürfen diesen verdächtigen Klang nicht überhören, weil wir den Begriff *Volkstümlichkeit* unbedingt brauchen."[5] In diesen und anderen verdächtigen Tümlichkeiten beruhigen sich bis heute die nationalen Enden der modernen Künste: im nationalromantischen Ursprung moderner Ästhetik als Bildungsgut und im industriellen Standard als Emblem ausgedachter „Nationalkultur". Beider Kanon setzt sich zusammen aus den gebildeten Nostalgien der kolonialen Plünderungen europäischer Nationenbildung.

Die Berliner Publizistin und feministische Marxistin Lu Märten erfand hierfür in den 1920er-Jahren in Berlin ein treffendes Wort: die „Stoffergreifung"[6]. Mit ihr beschrieb sie die Freiheit der Künste als beklagenswertes Zugriffsrecht auf ihren Inhalt, den sie mit Märten „ertötet"[7], wo sie sich nicht aus ihm umbildet. Die Kunst der Aneignung. Die Kultur als Aneignung. Henrike Naumann reproduziert nicht die Romantik, sie ertötet der Kunst keine neuen Inhalte, sondern sie reiht ihre Volkstümlichkeiten als eine Serie von Resten, Rissen und Flickwerken auf, die überall dort entstehen, wo die Stoffergreifung ins Bildungsgut übergeht, wo die Romantik ins Mobiliar eingepflegt wird. Der Mangel an Umbildungen in den Stoffergreifungen des künstlerischen Bildungsguts ist nicht weniger nachhaltig als der der national industrialisierten Romantik. Henrike Naumann bildet aus ihnen beiden ein volkstümliches Panorama der *Inneren Front:* das Panorama eines Realismus aus Rissen, Resten und Flickwerk. Henrike Naumann setzt einen Innenraum aus domestizierten Hieroglyphen, häuslichen Stuben, kriegerischen Gardinen und einem realistischen Relief zusammen, ein Panorama realistischer Volkstümlichkeiten.

Es gibt sie auch bei Henrike Naumann, die sagenumwobene Freiheit der Kunst, doch bei ihr liegt sie in der Umbildung und Ausbildung der vergangenen Stoffergreifun-

5) Brecht 1958, S. 496.

6) Lu Märten, *Wesen und Veränderung der Formen (und Künste)*, Frankfurt/Main: Taifun Verlag, 1924, S. 272.

7) Lu Märten, „Historisch-Materialistisches über Wesen und Veränderung der Künste. Eine pragmatische Einleitung" [1921], in: Lu Märten, *Formen für den Alltag. Schriften, Aufsätze, Vorträge*, hrsg. Rainhard May, Dresden: Verlag der Kunst, 1982, S. 58.

gen anhand ihrer Risse. Hier geht es nicht um Fortbildung, sondern um Rückbau und Abbau. Henrike Naumann baut Flickwerke des nicht länger Realistischen auf. Das sozialistische Gruppenporträt, das sich unter Henrike Naumanns Aufpolsterungen an der Wand des deutschen Pavillons nur mehr erahnen lässt, wurde zum Relief, weil es sich malerisch nicht mehr aus der Nostalgie retten konnte. Auf die Versuche realistischer Staatskunst als sozialistischer Kleinkunst folgte deren zunehmende Unlesbarkeit durch Verkitschung, folgte der Aufstieg der Ostalgie als deminuitiver Nationalästhetik, folgte das Absinken von Generationen von Realist*innen in den Status von Hieroglyphen. Henrike Naumanns Aufbau sucht die Freiheiten der Künste in den materiellen Enden ihrer Nationalromantik, in Flickwerken und in Rissen. In Hieroglyphen, die zu Legenden von Naumanns Realismus werden. Ganz entgegen der Freiheit des von Rissen gereinigten romantischen Ursprungs ästhetischer Stoffergreifungen, der die Künste unweigerlich als eine nicht endende, eherne Propaganda, ein Bildungsgut aus seriell kolonialen Kleinkünsten verfestigt; mit der Künstler*in als nationalromantischer Freiheitsheldin. Henrike Naumann zerlegt den Heroismus in seine Einzelteile und macht dessen koloniale, kriegerische Risse selbst zu ihrer Kunst, richtet sie in Lebensgröße ein und stellt ihnen, sich und uns, dabei unweigerlich unschöne Ursprungsfragen: nicht zu ihrer Legitimation, nicht zu unserer Legitimation, sondern um die Zwischenräume aufzureißen, die jeder Ursprung eröffnet, um einzusammeln, was von ihm und in ihm hängenblieb. Henrike Naumann errichtet im Deutschen Pavillon der Venedig Biennale einen Raum aus Ursprungslegenden, ein endloses Relief aus verfallenen Legitimationsformen. Wir lesen die Hieroglyphen eines kontrollierten Rückbaus.

Die Ursprungsfrage hat vor allem dort Konjunktur, wo die Gegenwart aus ihr heraus befestigt werden soll. Willi Baumeister hatte sie 1947 in Westdeutschland gestellt und ganz zeitgemäß als Aufbaufrage aus dem Nichts beantwortet. Sein epochemachendes Pamphlet künstlerischer Schöpfung, *Das Unbekannte in der Kunst,* sieht den „künstlerischen Mensch[en] ... dem Unbekannten durch seine Werke neue Werte“[8] entreißen. Die Entdeckung der Höhlenmalerei wird zu der des Künstlers, zum Ursprung eines Schöpfers aus Höhlen, die immer aussehen wie Ruinen. Baumeisters 1943 verfasste Flucht vor dem nationalsozialistischen Deutschland ins verursprünglichte eigene Innere, in das „grundsätzliche Kraftfeld ... des Künstlers, ...(als) neutraler, gereinigter, naturhafter Zustand“[9], sie war stilbildend. Baumeisters malerische Nachkriegsabstraktionen gehen in Henrike Naumanns

8) Willi Baumeister, *Das Unbekannte in der Kunst [1947]*, Stuttgart: Deutscher Bücherbund, 1962, S. 160.

9) Ebd., S. 200.

Horizont als westdeutsche Höhlenmalereien aus verkleideten, ausgemalten und durchgeformten Rissen fließend in die Dekorationen der Wohnräume ihrer Zeit über und werden von diesen ununterscheidbar. Nicht nur bei Baumeister, sondern ebenso bei Johannes Itten und Hans Sedlmayr, seinen Mitstreitern in der auf sein Buch folgenden Diskussion um *Das Menschenbild in unserer Zeit* auf der Darmstädter Mathildenhöhe 1951,[10] wird die deutsche Wahl des Nationalsozialismus rückblickend als Unaussprechliches zum romantischen Ursprung einer bewusstlosen Abstraktion, eines Formalismus des gekränkten, gescheiterten deutschen Kolonialsubjekts. Bei Henrike Naumann lässt sich dessen nicht abreißende Stoffergreifung in der Polsterung der Stühle nieder, auf denen zu sitzen sie im Deutschen Pavillon verunmöglicht. Aber sie bleiben im Raum, werden sein Fries, ein Relief der Einrichtung in der Unlebbarkeit.

Und doch ist es nicht die Ursprungsfrage selbst, durch die sich Brechts Tümlichkeiten national reproduzieren, sondern ihre Beantwortung als Hieroglyphe nationalisierender Romantik. Die Frage nach dem Ursprung stellt sich auch dort, wo es um die Denationalisierung der Gegenwart geht. Sie stellte sich auch Bertolt Brecht. Sie stellt sich auch Henrike Naumann. Doch für sie liegt ihre Beantwortung im Rückbau, in der Verwandlung der Risse kolonialisierender Gewalten in Kartografien, in Legenden einer Dekolonialisierung. *Die Innere Front.* Wil B. Mirimanows aus dem Russischen übersetztes DDR-Standardwerk zur *Kunst der Urgesellschaft* beginnt seinen Haupttext mit dem Satz: „Die Arbeit schuf den Menschen."[11] Wenige Seiten später zitiert er enthusiastisch den sowjetischen Psychologen L. S. Wygotski: „Die Kunst ist das Soziale in uns."[12] Statt als Produkt geistiger Bildung tritt die Kunst bei Mirimanow als Prozess körperlichen Bildens auf. Die West- und die Ostvarianten nationaler Formwerdung, sie treten in Henrike Naumanns Pavillon als ungleich invertierte Schöpfungsgeschichten auf, die beide in die letztlich nie so freien Künste als *Die Innere Front* deutscher Nationalkultur führen. An ihren Übergängen aus der und in Hieroglyphen sozialen Haltlosigkeit entsteht im Deutschen Pavillon die Einrichtung einer Urgeschichte unserer Gegenwart, die ihr Vorbild auch in einer Studie Waldemar Grzimeks hat, die dieser in den 1950ern als Teil eines Vorschlags der Künstlergruppe *Die Fähre* für ein Berliner Thälmann-Denkmal produziert hatte, einer Reliefstudie. Sie zeigt die moderne Geschichte als vormoderne Serie aus Hieroglyphen, ein Panorama arbeitender Menschen, das zwischen Spinnstühlen und Kriegsmaschinerien aufgespannt ist, zwischen privaten und öffentlichen Formen eines gemeinschaftlichen Lebens.

10) *Das Menschenbild in unserer Zeit. Darmstädter Gespräch 1*, hrsg. von Hanns Gerhard Evers, Darmstadt: Neue Darmstädter Verlagsanstalt, 1951.

11) Wil B. Mirimanow, *Kunst der Urgesellschaft und traditionelle Kunst Afrikas und Ozeaniens*, Dresden: Verlag der Kunst, 1973, S. 12.

12) Ebd., S. 15.

Eine Urgeschichte moderner Arbeitsformen mit ungewissem Ausgang. Erschöpft sich die Westkunst aus einem haltlosen Geist, wird die Ostkunst aus grenzenloser Arbeit erbaut.

Lu Märten begann ihr 1924 erstmals erschienenes Hauptwerk *Wesen und Veränderung der Formen (und Künste)* mit einem langen Zitat aus Friedrich Engels *Anti-Dühring*. Engels schreibt hier vom „Sprung der Menschheit aus dem Reich der Notwendigkeit in das Reich der Freiheit“[13]. Engels schreibt weiter, dass diese „weltbefreiende Tat“ die Aufgabe des Proletariats sei. Es ist definitiv nicht diejenige der Künstler*in, deren künstlerische Freiheit nur im „Reich der Vernunft“ (Engels Name für „das idealisierte Reich der Bourgeoisie“[14]) als real projiziert wird. Es ist dieser Zustand, die Existenz der Künstlerin als kolonialem Abziehbildchen des Reichs der Freiheit, den Henrike Naumann uns minutiös als Riss auslegt, als Riss zwischen Realismus und Volkstümlichkeit. Henrike Naumann produziert große Kleinkunst, Meisterwerke eines in der Unauffindbarkeit des Proletariats in die nationale Selbstüberschätzung gezwungenen, desozialisierten Handwerks, dem der Kunst. Im Deutschen Pavillon ist Henrike Naumann perfekt positioniert. Sie arbeitet von jeher an seiner Bestimmung. Aus den Nationalhistorien seiner Künste und deren industriellen, handwerklichen und dilettantischen Rändern und Außenposten richtet sie ihn neu ein, in eine Höhlenmalerei unserer Volkstümlichkeit. Henrike Naumann produziert nicht zuletzt immer auch uns als provinzielle Rezipient*innen.

Dort wo Henrike Naumanns Arbeiten den Deutschen Pavillon füllen, treffen Volkstümlichkeit und Ursprungsmythos auf Postmoderne und Realismus. Kolonialisierungen sind in Naumanns Horizont niemals nur externalisierte Bewegungen, weder räumlich noch zeitlich. Sie verlängern sich als Formen fortgesetzter kriegerischer Konsumption an *Die Innere Front*. Clemens Villinger verfolgt in seiner Arbeit deren Historisierung. Kürzlich anhand einer Frage, die in den auf Deutschland bezogenen Geschichtswissenschaften klären will, wer im deutschen Reich der Vernunft überlebte:[15] Ausgangspunkt ist für Villinger die bereits in den 1940er-Jahren in der NS-Täterforschung aufkommende Unterscheidung „zwischen normalen und abnormalen Persönlichkeiten“[16]. Der Versuch, das politische Subjekt des Nachkriegswestens zu identifizieren, führte in das Dilemma der Unterscheidung zwischen dem nationalsozialistischen Staatssubjekt *Täter* und dem nationalsozialistischen Privatsubjekt *Normaler*: War der nationalsozialistische Mann, und es geht in diesen Studie, so Villinger, stets um Männer, ein *Normaler,* schließt seine Normalität eine genozidale Praxis nicht aus, war der nationalsozialistische Mann ein *Täter*, dann ist sein Fortleben im

13) Friedrich Engels, Herrn *Eugen Dührings Umwälzung der Wissenschaft. ‚Anti-Dühring‘* [1877], Berlin: Karl Dietz Verlag, 2020, S. 264.

14) Ebd., S. 17.

15) Clemens Villinger, „Endlich normale Nazis? Normalität als Begriff in der Alltags- und Täterforschung zur NS-Zeit“, *Vierteljahrshefte für Zeitgeschichte*, 74, Nr. 1, 2026, S. 117–151.

16) Ebd., S. 125.

neuen deutschen Staat das eines genozidalen Subjekts. Im einen wie im anderen Fall ist *Die Innere Front* der staatlichen Normalität der Schauplatz eines fortgesetzt genozidalen Vermögens. Eine Verbindung, deren Ursprung in der deutschen Kolonialpolitik ebenso aufgesucht werden kann wie in deren nationalsozialistischer Fortsetzung. Ursprünge. Urgeschichten. Panoramen, in denen, wie Villinger demonstriert, der Begriff der Normalität zu einer Art verschiebbarem Riss wird, ein Gradmesser staatstragender Gewalt, der überall dort zum Einsatz kommt, wo ein weiterhin bestehendes Staatssubjekt von ihr unterschieden werden muss, aber nicht kann.

In Henrike Naumanns Aufbauten treiben diese Risse als Volkstümlichkeiten durch den Raum. Hier treibt die DDR, in der Henrike Naumann 1984 noch geboren wurde, unweigerlich in den Formen der BRD, an die sie übertragen wurde. Reste der DDR treiben im gegenwärtigen deutschen Staat. Reste des nationalsozialistischen Deutschlands treiben im gegenwärtigen deutschen Staat. Normalitäten und Risse. Risse auch im Pavillon selbst, dessen nationalsozialistische Wiedererbauung 1938 durch Ernst Haiger von den Westkünstler*innen, die in ihm hiernach ausstellten, immer wieder aufgegriffen wurde. Unter Naumann ist sein Innenraum in demjenigen Grün gestrichen, das alle Innenräume der Sowjetkasernen in der DDR zierte. Die Künstler*innen der DDR, ihr Realismus unter mintgrünem sowjetischem Protektorat, sie haben keine Vergangenheit in dieser Architektur. Henrike Naumann verfolgte die vergangenen Versuche der DDR, dies zu ändern, ihre Künste in den Nationalpavillon zu bewegen, im Bundesarchiv. Bereits 1956 versuchte die sozialistische Akademie der Künste ihr imperialistisches Gegenüber, das Auswärtige Amt der BRD, zu Verhandlungen über die Beteiligung von DDR-Künstlern am Deutschen Pavillon in Venedig 1958 einzuladen. Doch der Westen bestand auf sein Eigentum als Nachfolgestaat des nationalsozialistischen Deutschlands und schlug die Einladung aus. Zuständig für die westdeutsche Künstlerauswahl war seit 1948 Eberhard Hanfstaengl, der diese Aufgabe bereits 1935 und 1936 übernommen hatte. Ursprungsfiguren. Normalitätskompetenzen. Im Bundesarchiv wird auch in Brief- und Berichtform der Ende 1978 startende Versuch der damals neuen Leitung der Venedig Biennalen dokumentiert, den sozialistischen Ländern in Venedig Sichtbarkeit einzuräumen. Doch ihre Einladungen zum Gespräch an die CSSR, Kuba, Polen, DDR, VR China, Rumänien, Ungarn und die Sowjetunion blieben zunächst unerwidert. Nur Ungarn antwortete. Die Verhandlungen wurden erst ein Jahr später aufgenommen. Nicht nur von der Sowjetunion, auch von der DDR. Ab 1982 zeigen bildende Künstler der DDR in Venedig Arbeiten im ehemaligen Pavillon der dekorativen Künste. Doch zum Einzug in den Deutschen Pavillon kommt es nie. Die Dokumente im Bundesarchiv enthalten weder Installationsansichten noch die Kataloge, über deren Produktion die Regierungsberichte des langjährigen Kommissars der Venedig Biennale für die DDR, Hermann Raum, über Seiten berichten. Sie protokollieren nur die Unmöglichkeit, innerhalb der kurzen und immer wieder von Umentscheidungen der Biennale und der eigenen Unbedarftheit durchbrochenen Aufbauzeit auch nur die Beiträge der sozialistischen Bruderstaaten in Venedig zu sichten. Sie beschreiben das infrastrukturelle Scheitern daran, die Phalanx der eigenen Künste, die Monumentalwerke des späten sozialistischen Realismus in Venedig zu rekonstruieren. Henrike Naumann holt dies nach. In Miniatur. Sie bringt ein Wandgemälde der sozialistischen Auftragskunst mit in den Deutschen Pavillon: eine 3×8 Meter große malerische Variation des Ende der 1950er-Jahre von ihrem Großvater, dem Maler und Grafiker Karl Heinz Jakob, produzierten Murals *Die Mechanisierung* *der Landwirtschaft*. Eine große Kleinkunst. Sie schmückt immer noch die ehemalige Wand des ehemaligen Kammersaals der ehemaligen Industrie- und Handelskammer der ehemaligen Karl-Marx-Stadt. Durch eine Trockenwand ist Jakobs Wandgemälde in Chemnitz heute verdeckt. Und Henrike Naumanns überarbeitetes Zitat realistischer Monumentalität manifestiert dessen sozialistische Form als Höhlenmalerei unserer Gegenwart. Im Deutschen Pavillon als Relief überarbeitet birgt sie es als postmoderne Hieroglyphe, als die es bereits zum Zeitpunkt seiner vollendeten Enthüllung wahrgenommen wurde. Die soziale Realisierung von Jakobs Mural blieb immer aus. Seine Wandmalerei wurde von in der Tagespresse schreibenden Arbeiter*innen der Stoffergreifung bezichtigt. Die Arbeitskleidung sei ebenso unzutreffend wie die Werkzeuge. Jakob habe sich nicht an ihnen umgebildet. Die Maschinen, die bei Jakob die Menschengruppe rahmten, waren schon im Prozess der Bildproduktion von den auftraggebenden staatlichen Institutionen als ungegenständlich identifiziert worden. Jakob bildete sie um, machte sie sozialistischer. Doch Karl Heinz Jakobs Realismus blieb zu sehr malerisch, zu wenig funktionalistisch für den Kammersaal in Karl-Marx-Stadt. Seine großformatige Malerei des Nachkriegsaufbaus Ost nahm Motive aus dem Naturalismus des ausgehenden 19. Jahrhunderts, dem frühen Expressionismus der 1910er-Jahre und dem Konstruktivismus der 1920er-Jahre auf, und setzte die Menschenbilder *dieser* Zeiten zu einem Wandbild *seiner* eigenen sozialistischen Gegenwart zusammen: eine malerische Gegenwart der Arbeit, aufgebaut aus umgebildeten Vergangenheiten ihres Sujets. Eine Urgeschichte, mit der Karl Heinz Jakobs Realismus in der modernen Kunstgeschichte blieb. Henrike Naumann arbeitet den Realismus, der von ihrem Großvater gefordert wurde, als Relief nach und verankert seine Arbeiter*innengruppe damit noch weitaus deutlicher im Reich der Notwendigkeit. Als Malerei des sozialistischen Realismus zur Hieroglyphe vergangenen Staatssozialismus abgesunken, wird Jakobs Mural durch Henrike Naumanns Eingriff als Riss lesbar, zwischen Realismus und Volkstümlichkeit, zwischen dem Bild einer Gemeinschaft und deren arbeitender Realität. Henrike Naumann baut genau den Alltag in Jakobs Szenerie ein, der, entgegen der damaligen Hoffnung der kritischen Arbeiter*innen, den Sprung ins Reich der Freiheit bis hierhin nicht schaffte. Zwischen Relief und Intarsie, zwischen überdimensioniertem Dekorum und unterdimensioniertem Realismus demonstriert Naumanns Umarbeitung das, was man im Sinne des ostdeutschen Publizisten Heinz Hirdina Jakobs Postmodernismus nennen könnte: die Platzierung der arbeitenden Menschen in einem Nachkriegsszenario, dessen Humanisierung fraglich erscheinen muss.[17]

17) Heinz Hirdina, „Postmodernismus: Experiment oder Produktleitbild?", in: Bruno Flierl, Heinz Hirdina (Hg.), *Postmoderne und Funktionalismus. Sechs Vorträge*, Berlin: Verband der Bildenden Künstler, 1985, S. 21.

In einer Serie von Vorträgen, die Hirdina Mitte der 1980er-Jahre in Berlin zu „Funktionalismus – Postmodernismus" hielt, argumentierte er, dass nur die Funktionalität es zulasse, dass der „ästhetische Genuss von der Form an sich auf die Form im Gebrauch"[18] übergehe. Auch daher sind die 1950er-Jahre für Hirdina der Anfang der Postmoderne. Der Übergang war gerissen, und ebendies wurde Jakobs Bild vorgeworfen. Sein Realismus blieb ein Versuch, die Gegenwart aus dem historischen Rückgriff zu humanisieren. Nachkriegsmalerei Ost. Henrike Naumann arbeitet von jeher postmodern, von jeher vom Riss ausgehend. In einen Realismus des Risses. Die Postmoderne, die in Henrike Naumanns Arbeiten oft als möbelförmige Treibholzsammlung den Raum strukturiert, in ihm Anbetungsstätten, Jugendzimmer und Gedenkstätten aufbaut, sie wandert hier im Deutschen Pavillon die Wände hoch, wächst in die Lebensgröße, und sie reiht Jakob in die Legende unserer gegenwärtigen Urgeschichten ein. Alles wird hier für Henrike Naumann Wandbild, alles wird Hieroglyphe, alles wird postmoderner Realismus, alles wird unrealisierte Volkstümlichkeit. Die Einrichtung verliert ihre Tiefe, ihre Größe, die Maßstäbe verziehen sich. Doch die Größenverhältnisse sind in ihren sozialen Verhältnissen absolut maßstabsgetreu. Henrike Naumann baut im Deutschen Pavillon *Die Innere Front*, maßstabsgetreu. Riss für Riss.

1978 hielt der Ost-Berliner Theatermacher Heiner Müller einen Vortrag über die Postmoderne in New York. In ihm stellte er das fest, was Henrike Naumann 2026 demonstriert: „Im *Reich der Notwendigkeit* sind Realismus und Volkstümlichkeit zwei Dinge. Der Riß geht durch den Autor."[19] Er geht durch Henrike Naumann. Müller hoffte in der DDR, mit der DDR darauf, seinen Riss rückzubauen. Und so fügte er hinzu: „Periodisierung ist Kolonialpolitik, solange die Geschichte nicht Universalgeschichte"[20] ist. Sie sollte es werden. Die Kolonialpolitik der DDR. Die Kolonialpolitik der BRD. Ihr Rückbau in die Universalgeschichte blieb aus. Henrike Naumanns Kunst ist selbst deutlich jenseits dieser Universalgeschichte positioniert, im Deutschen Pavillon. Doch Henrike Naumann produziert in ihm und für ihn einen postmodernen Realismus kolonialer Volkstümlichkeit. Müller hatte, wie Brecht, auf den anationalen Ursprung der Volkstümlichkeiten bestanden und sie bewusst aus den Realismusstreits der Volksfront gegen den Faschismus in den späten 1930ern wieder aufgenommen, und aus Bertolt Brechts Nachworten zu diesem Realismusstreit, seinem Appell an „Volkstümlichkeit und Realismus" als alternativloser Sozialisierung der Kunst. Henrike Naumann legt für uns aus, wie die Sozialisierung der Kunst in den Ursprungsmythen der BRD und der DDR aus dem Realismus

18) Heinz Hirdina 1985, S. 10.

19) Heiner Müller, „Postmoderne", in: Wolfgang Storch (Hg.), *Geländewagen 1*, Berlin: Verlag Ästhetik und Kommunikation, 1979, unpaginiert.

20) Ebd.

der Volksfront in die Volkstümlichkeit der Kolonialgeschichte abdriftete. Doch sie hält Realismus und Volkstümlichkeit im Spiel. Denn die Volkstümlichkeit haftet am Realismus und „der zunehmende Druck authentischer Erfahrung entwickelt die Fähigkeit, der Geschichte ins Weiße im Auge zu sehen“[21]. Müller beschreibt Naumanns *Innere Front*.

1990, in *Ambiente Berlin*, einer seit 1988 aus der Venedig Biennale herausgewachsenen Ausstellung zur frisch verschmolzenen Mauerstadt, schreibt Hermann Raum unter der Überschrift „Immer noch Berlin“ rückblickend über sein Protektorat, die bildende Kunst der DDR: „Die künstlerischen Leistungen bedürfen in diesen Zusammenhängen keiner besonderen Würdigung.“[22] Auch dies ist eine überaus realistische Aussage. Realistisch in dem Sinne, dass die Ursprungsfrage in der DDR mit den Bauernkriegen des frühen 17. Jahrhunderts beantwortet worden war.[23] Ihre Erbschaft gedachte der Arbeiter- und Bauernstaat zu erfüllen, auch durch die in ihm produzierten Künste. Im Horizont einer Eingliederung der künstlerischen Arbeit in die vielfältigen Handwerke, die im Kampf gegen die Klassenherrschaft zum Einsatz kamen, konnte Raums Aussage auch auf die schlichte Tatsache verweisen, dass die Frage des realistischen Vermögens weniger in künstlerischen Einzelleistungen hervortritt als vielmehr in der Gesamtheit ihrer gemeinschaftlichen Vermittlung. Henrike Naumann brachte ihren Großvater nicht in den Deutschen Pavillon, um sein baumeisterliches Schöpfertum zu bergen oder seine künstlerischen Leistungen zu würdigen, sondern um die Risse seines Realismus mit ihm auszubauen. Doch bei Raum war es ebendieses soziale Vermögen der realistischen Künste, das, was Raums Kollege, der Kunsthistoriker Peter H. Feist, in den 1960er-Jahren in dem materialistischen Prinzip der „relativen Eigengesetzlichkeit der Kunst als ‚Eigengesetzlichkeit des Stoffes‘“[24] identifiziert hatte, dass er rückblickend in den Künstler*innen der DDR verloren gab. Raum erklärt die bildende Kunst der DDR 1990 zur Hieroglyphe.

Feist war auch einer der Herausgeber von Mirimanows Urgeschichte gewesen. Beide einte die Suche nach der „Eigengesetzlichkeit des Stoffes“ in der Kunst, was letzteren dahin führte, schon die höfischen Künste Europas gegenüber denjenigen West- und Zentralafrikas als bildnerisch „bedeutend ärmer“[25] zu erkennen. Eine ärmere Sozialität, die bald darauf zur kolonialen Plünderung ansetzen würde, um reicher zu werden. Mirimanows visuelles Gegenwartsbeispiel für diese plündernde Armut sind Pablo Picasssos *Les Desmoiselles d'Avignon* (1907).[26] Unkommentiert. Die Geschichte der künstlerischen Freiheit ist hier, wie in Henrike

21) Heiner Müller, *‚Für Alle reicht es nicht.‘ Texte zum Kapitalismus*, Frankfurt/Main: Suhrkamp Verlag, 2017, S. 48.

22) Hermann Raum, „Immer noch Berlin“, in: *Ambiente Berlin*, hrsg. von Marie-George Gervasoni, Venedig: Ed. Biennale Realizzazione Fabbri Ed., 1990, S. 175.

23) Vgl. hierzu etwa Autorenkollektiv Adolf Laube, Max Steinmetz, Günter Vogler (Leiter), *Illustrierte Geschichte der deutschen frühbürgerlichen Revolution*, Berlin: Dietz Verlag, 1974.

24) Peter H. Feist, *Prinzipien und Methoden marxistischer Kunstwissenschaft. Versuch eines Abrisses*, Leipzig: Seemann Verlag, 1966, S. 12.

25) Ebd., S. 277.

26) Vgl. ebd., S. 278.

Naumanns Deutschem Pavillon, von jeher eine Bildungsgeschichte der Stoffergreifung, des künstlerisch entsozialisierten Formverlusts. Eine reiche Sammlung kolonialer Risse, an der inneren wie der äußeren Front. Im Katalog zur 10. Kunstausstellung in Dresden 1988 hatte Raum geschrieben, dass durch „steile Verkunstung" die Kunst der DDR nurmehr „ein kleiner Spezialfall der Gesamterfahrung von Ohnmacht" sei.[27] Er hatte sie bereits vor 1989 aufgegeben. Und Feists frühere Grundlegungen eines materialistischen Kunstverständnisses, dessen zweiter Punkt „die Überzeugung vom Primat des *Inhalts*" war, lässt sich noch bis in die von Raum charakterisierte Ohnmacht weiterverfolgen. Ihr Inhalt endete. Doch wenn, wie Feist weiter ausführt „der Inhalt des Kunstwerkes ... selbstverständlich nicht gleichbedeutend mit seinem Thema oder Sujet" ist, sondern „der Inhalt ... vielmehr der Sinn, den der Künstler seinem Thema vermittels der Gestaltung gibt, ... die Aussage, die der Künstler zur Sache machen will und die beim Betrachter nur in Gestalt der sinnlich wahrnehmbaren Form ankommen"[28], dann wird Henrike Naumann ein weiteres Mal unschwer als Realistin im Deutschen Pavillon erkennbar. Henrike Naumann ist eine Gegnerin der Stoffergreifung. Und doch findet sie den Ursprung ihrer Kunst unweigerlich in ihr, im nationalen Rahmen der Kleinkunst, deren *Innere Front* Henrike Naumann für uns aufbaut. In Brechts Worten gilt weiterhin, „es gibt nicht nur das *Volkstümlichsein*, sondern auch das *Volkstümlichwerden*"[29].

27) Martin Damus, *Malerei der DDR: Funktionen der bildenden Kunst im Realen Sozialismus*, Reinbek bei Hamburg: Rowohlt, 1991, S. 345.

28) Feist 1966, S. 24f.

29) Brecht 1958, S. 502.

OBJECTS IN MULTIPOLAR (INFRA)STRUCTURES

Sabeth Buchmann

A visitor approaching the façade of the German Pavilion, which comprises over three million mosaic tiles, might wonder whether it's a work of art in architecture, a monument, or a panoramic painting. As if the antique-style building had been made to resemble the colorful mosaics of Ravenna, the arrangement of the colored marble tesserae, each of which measures 1.5 centimeters square, produces a trompe-l'œil effect that dates back to an ancient technique of optical illusion revived in the Renaissance and practiced to this day in scenic painting and murals. Yet the gray stripes and yellowish forms of the pavilion's façade are more than virtuosic ornamentation. The work is a realistic depiction of a three-dimensional building of which only the empty, battered, window- and doorless, graffiti-covered walls remain—a prefabricated housing complex evidently slated for demolition. As though she were inverting the architectural model's function of facilitating a real estate sale—or the early-nineties reconstruction of historical buildings like the Berlin Palace, which was torn down in 1950—Sung Tieu draws on a stage-set aesthetic that's deeply ingrained in the public consciousness, one that found its ultimate manifestation when the demolished Palace of the Republic, formerly the seat of the East German parliament, was replaced with a neo-historicist imitation façade. By overlaying this aesthetic register with memories of East Berlin's building ruins, Tieu's mosaic echoes the "building-specific art" prevalent in (late-) modernist East German[1] and Soviet bloc urban planning and the concrete monuments that dominated it. These projects served to aesthetically embellish factories, public buildings, and prefabricated housing blocks constructed according to standardized industrial norms—the SED leadership's response to the post-World War II housing shortage in East Berlin, then the capital of the German Democratic Republic. In *Stadtraumbezogene Orientierungszeichen,* the VEB Stern-Radio factory façade in Berlin-Marzahn designed in 1985 by artist Gertraude Pohl,[2] I see a possible resonance with Tieu's exhibitions *Song for VEB Stern-Radio Berlin* (2021) and *One Thousand Times* (2023). Pohl's colorful, abstract mural,[3] made up of squares of enameled sheet metal, offered an interplay of dynamic tension between surface and line, two- and three-dimensionality, and organic and geometric forms; DIBAG AG Munich, in its capacity as the new owner, destroyed it for the most part in 1992.[4] In this regard, it's a

1) One might also think of Brasília, the capital of Brazil, which was built from scratch in the 1950s.

2) See https://bildhauerei-in-berlin.de/bildwerk/stadtraumbezogene-orientierungszeichen-9781/#:~:text=Die%20Arbeiten%20für%20das%20Stern,dem%20Titel%20%22Stadtraumbezogene%20Orientierungszeichen%22, (accessed December 1, 2025).

3) See https://bildhauerei-in-berlin.de/bildwerk/stadtraumbezogene-orientierungszeichen-9781.

4) Ibid.

telling example of the artistically ambitious "working environment design"[5] (arbeitsplatzbezogene Gestaltung) practiced by state-owned enterprises that employed Vietnamese contract workers, many of whom lived close to the nine buildings of the Gehrenseestrasse prefabricated housing complex depicted in Tieu's façade, erected in 1980 in Berlin's Alt-Hohenschönhausen district.

In light of the dismantling and destruction of "architecture-specific art" in the former GDR, which a post-reunification court ruling deemed "state-affiliated and therefore not worthy of protection,"[6] Tieu's mosaic façade installation can be interpreted as a documentary and commemorative gesture that memorializes both a dreary prefab building and a defunct design practice. Far removed from idealized nostalgia, the temporary transformation of the German Pavilion leaves no doubt as to its ambivalent representational character. The material also evokes the late-socialist feudalism of the Great Hall in the East German embassy in Moscow, for which Pohl used Siberian marble in her design four years after the Gehrenseestrasse complex was built. This mural tradition wasn't limited to GDR history, however; it continued briefly into the post-reunification decade, when prefabricated building façades were adorned with the geometric patterns[7] that Brazilian and other artists had derived from indigenous cultures—works that have since been removed. In other words, Tieu's imitation façade evinces a formal language appropriated from geometric abstraction that has links to both socialist and non-European infrastructure projects.

Marble's low level of hardness makes it relatively easy to handle; its aesthetic, technical, and economic qualities have been inscribed into (art) history far beyond Western modernism. It can be found in temples and palaces as well as in public squares and private housing complexes, kitchens, and bathrooms—this is the extent to which marble has permeated public and private infrastructure.

Tieu's façade defamiliarizes these connotations, which speak to both everyday and artistic contexts; she presents the pavilion, which was built in 1909[8] and refurbished in 1938 to conform to the Nazi Party's pseudo-classical ideal, in a visibly dislocated prefabricated guise. By transposing a claim to national representation onto the marbled ruin of a building formerly inhabited for the most part by contract workers and, from the 1990s onward, by asylum seekers, the mosaics personalize the form, scale, and function of the German Pavilion and defamiliarize it: an artistic device that allows us to view the abstract in the concrete. In this regard,

5) Ibid.

6) Ibid. And for this reason, after "the privatization of public space socialized in the GDR (...)," they were allowed to be destroyed or removed. See https://www.howoge.de/immobiliensuche/neubauprojekte/quartier-gehrenseestrasse-wollenberger-strasse.html, (accessed October 12, 2025).

7) See https://www.alexander-j-herrmann.de/news/lokal/1382/Entfernung-der-Mosaiksteine-im-Gelben-Viertel.html.

8) Initially known as the "Bavarian Pavilion"; see Maria Eichhorn's exposé on the conversion as part of her work for the German Pavilion at the 2022 Venice Biennale.

the façade projects the standardization, regulation, and control the workers' dormitories implemented in managing their inhabitants in extremely close quarters. In turn, the pavilion's two mirror-image side rooms abstract the lives and experiences of the inhabitants of the approximately 1,000 living spaces, each of which measured just over sixteen square meters. Originally planned for nearly 4,000 people, it's possible they were conceived as barracks;[9] from 1982 onward, the building housed primarily Vietnamese, but also Cuban and Mozambican contract workers, as well as foreign students.[10] As Tieu explains on her architectural tours, she moved into the Gehrenseestrasse complex with her mother in 1994 and lived there for three years. The expeditions to the site combine historical and biographical narratives and constitute an autoethnographic relationship to the remnants of architectural infrastructure being explored. In showcasing the building type, which the GDR once exported to its socialist brother countries, including Vietnam, Tieu's pavilion design treats it as a medium of collectively experienced contemporary history. We learn that Tieu and her mother lived on Gehrenseestrasse at a time when the number of tenants had risen to 6,000 due to canceled employment contracts and the termination of state-owned dormitories elsewhere. The Gehrenseestrasse buildings, some of which were also used as accommodations for asylum seekers, were the only alternative for former contract workers who, due to economic or personal reasons, couldn't or didn't want to return to the so-called "brother countries" of the GDR, which was dissolved in 1990.

As such, the mosaic façade references one example of the infrastructure projects the GDR had been promoting since the early 1970s, a period considered to be a phase of international outreach, evidenced, among other things, by the country's first-ever participation in the Venice Biennale in 1982, just eight years before it ceased to exist. In this vein, Tieu's façade imitation, composed of wafer-thin marble squares, can be read as a literal mosaic of layered experience and meaning that all the more explicitly problematizes the definition of artistic contemporaneity. Insofar as 1989—with the collapse of the so-called Eastern Bloc, the accelerating dynamics of globalization, and the remapping of the world into countries of the Global South and North—is considered a watershed moment between (post-)modernity and the present, Tieu's intervention takes on a site- and time-specific as well as a multipolar and multi-temporal character.[11] This is all the more significant given that the art and architecture of the GDR only began to receive serious attention three decades

9) See Sung Tieu's research in this catalogue.

10) According to research by the artist and her team, the buildings on Gehrenseestrasse may have initially served as barracks.

11) See Mi You, *Art in a Multipolar World*, Berlin: Hatje Cantz Verlag, 2024. The professor of "Art and Economics" at the documenta Institute in Kassel is referring to a multiplication of the bipolar power centers that existed until the end of the Cold War.

after German reunification, after a significant rise in the number of exhibitions and publications. While the history of labor migration, apart from a few exceptions,[12] remains chronically neglected, this chapter is far from closed, as even long-established immigrants find themselves faced with a new wave of nationalist-motivated racism. The façade draws a connection to the modernization Asian, African, and Caribbean migrant workers made possible in pre-reunification Berlin; at the same time, it enters into a material-aesthetic continuum with the (art-)historically charged marble floor of the German Pavilion. Laid in 1938 to replace the original parquet flooring, the metamorphic stone is imbued with the so-called Third Reich's phantasm of eternity. Hans Haacke had it torn out in 1993 in response to the racist arson attacks perpetrated the previous year against Vietnamese residents of the Sunflower House in Rostock-Lichtenhagen, and arranged the fragments into a Caspar David Friedrich-esque sea of stones. For its part, the petrification of the workers' dormitory on the pavilion façade can be read as an ironic gesture, aware of its temporality and immortalization of a repressed migration history. In contrast to Haacke's aesthetics of destruction, the mosaic comes across as a palimpsest-like overwriting of an existing structure. Viewed as an anti-monumental hybrid of ruin and memorial, the fake façade testifies to a partially destroyed GDR modernism and the repression of its social history, marked as it was by political upheaval and the exploitation of migrant workers. In other words, it is the lives of contract workers, outsourced to urban peripheries and segregated from the rest of the population, that make each individual mosaic piece a concrete pars pro toto of an abstract whole.

The current state depicted on the façade leaves no doubt that the building is uninhabitable;[13] as an imitation ruin, it marks the beginning of another chapter in the history of urban infrastructure development, one that also touches upon the current debate over the state of public utilities. In this regard, Tieu's guided tours offer information about future modernization plans, which have been put on hold. And so the redevelopment of the 6.3-hectare property on Gehrenseestrasse, which the Berlin state housing company HOWOGE scheduled for the 2020s in cooperation with the real estate developer Belle Époque, will not be realized for the time being: their plan was, and still is,[14] to create a "courtyard and high-rise complex with more than 1,000 apartments (...)" where foreign students, contract workers, and asylum seekers once lived, half of which are to be "government-subsidized" and offer "barrier-free access and

12) Among other things, through the 2024 exhibition *Echoes of the Brother Countries* at Haus der Kulturen der Welt in Berlin: https://www.hkw.de/programme/echos-der-bruderlaender. Previous projects and exhibitions such as *Revolutionary Romances. Transkulturelle Kunstgeschichten in der DDR* (Albertinum Dresden 2019–14) und *Re:connect. Kunst und Kampf im Bruderland* (MdBK Leipzig 2023) should also be considered.

13) During our joint visit in the summer of 2024, however, we found mattresses and other items there, hints that unhoused people were now living at the site.

14) The insolvency proceedings initiated by Belle Époque were stopped in July 2025.

underfloor heating." According to HOWOGE, plans also include "commercial uses for the services industries; housing for students, senior citizens, and nursing care; social and medical services; culture; and retail."[15]

The public-private partnership rhetoric typical of post-reunification Berlin sounds like a distant echo of a life displaced from the former housing complex as Tieu describes it in her October 13, 1995 letter to the editor of *The New York Times*. Titled "Inside the Blocks," the fictional author, a seven-year-old girl named Ching, recounts her overwhelmingly positive memories of Gehrenseestrasse in response to the clichés trotted out by a *NYT* reporter named Alan Cowell—who, among other things, writes of ghetto-like conditions.[16] These recollections included bartering without money and mutual support in organizing food and childcare. Despite the cramped living conditions, Tieu explains that her childhood was happy because it was socially embedded. She also writes about tenants' fears of police crackdowns—not to mention the brutal and occasionally deadly attacks by right-wing extremists. Hostile propaganda from politicians and the press denouncing the chaotic conditions on Gehrenseestrasse further inflamed racist agitation.[17]

Against this backdrop, if I interpret the marble trompe-l'œil as an aesthetic link between the infrastructures responsible for both the social housing developments on the city's outskirts, which were cut off from one another by highways, and state-organized labor migration—that is, the recruitment, management, and control of low-wage workers in labor-deficient industries—it is because they are connected to the production of goods and commodities, travel and transport, consumerism and service industries, and the water and energy supply, which, according to American art theorist Marina Vishmidt, always constitute a "locus of social abstraction."[18] From this perspective, the pavilion appears less as a petrified monument than a form that can be (re)produced through aesthetic perception.[19] Finally, the fact that the all-over mosaic covers the window bays and the "Germania" inscription chiseled in 1938 above the portal suggests that the German Pavilion is not an empty vessel, but a "hyperobject"[20] charged with biographical experience, state-organized life, and national representation: in the words of the Canadian materials scientist Deb Chachra, it represents a node within multiple systems of unimaginable size, reach, and complexity.[21] As if the imitation façade served to temporarily preserve a dysfunctional infrastructure, the spatial and temporal dimensions that determine its form appear as an abstract third element comprised of technical media and social regulations:

15) See https://www.howoge.de/immobiliensuche/neubauprojekte/quartier-gehrenseestrasse-wollenberger-strasse.html, (accessed January 12, 2026).

16) See "Inside the Blocks" in Rob Grosse, Sung Tieu, Richard Sides, *Ars Viva 2021*, exh. cat., Kulturkreis der deutschen Wirtschaft im BDI e.V., Bielefeld/Berlin: Kerber Verlag, 2021, p. 62.

17) Sung Tieu has meticulously explored these and other aspects of Vietnamese life in exhibitions such as *Oath Against Minimalism* (2020), *One Thousand Times* (2023), and in 1992/2025 at the KW Institute for Contemporary Art Berlin, which she realized as part of the 2025 Schering Prize for Artistic Research.

18) Marina Vishmidt, "Between Not Everything and Not Nothing: Cuts Towards Infrastructural Critique," in Maria Hlavajova und Simon Sheik (eds.), *Former West. Art and the Contemporary after 1989*, London/Cambridge, MA: The MIT Press, 2017, pp. 265–68, here p. 265.

19) See the definition of infrastructures as active forms in Keller Easterling, *Extrastatecraft: The Power of Infrastructure Space*, London/New York: Verso, 2014 and *Medium Design: Knowing How to Work on the World*, London/New York: Verso, 2021

20) The reference here is to Tim Morton's *Hyperobjects: Philosophy and Ecology after the End of the World*, quoted in Deb Chachra, *How Infrastructure Works: Inside the Systems That Shape Our World*, New York: Riverhead Books, 2023, p. 19.

21) Ibid., p. 13.

Collective infrastructures are a good candidate for the most complex systems created by humans. They are planetary in scale, build on their own histories, are entangled with each other, and have impacts that extend far into the future. Their design, construction, and operation require a wide range of technical disciplines—civil engineering, obviously, but also electrical engineering, mechanical engineering, environmental engineering, and the science of systems and of networks. All of these fields incorporate not just technologies but practices, ways of thinking, doing, and building. The decision making and funding around these systems, particularly public systems, is the province of policy, finance, and economics. Finally, as systems that require land and resources, it's impossible to extricate infrastructure from a larger history of conquest, colonialism, and capitalism and, particularly (...) from racism and white supremacy. The theorist Timothy Morton coined the word 'hyperobject' for just these sorts of systems that span multiple time scales, length scales, and social settings.[22]

Because human perception can only grasp the dimensions of hyperobjects to a limited degree, the symbolic mirroring of art institution and residential neighborhood is all the more salient, particularly as it intervenes in the mode of aesthetic reception: what if we consider the German Pavilion not as a solitary and temporary exhibition space, but rather as a multifaceted and permanently networked infrastructure? What if it became a long-term repository for the personal memories Tieu's temporary façade evokes? For it is nothing less than a pars pro toto of an infrastructural whole, whose aesthetic (re)production is inherent in its form of remembrance. Accordingly, the way in which the trompe-l'œil synchronizes the past, present, and future of the prefabricated building and pavilion goes beyond associating the façade with a GDR-specific building type. Similar to Pohl's "work environment designs," façade and interior direct the viewer's attention to the composition of color and form, light and proportion: as if these were the media that, in the tradition of geometric abstraction, negotiate what they depict with and within the bodies, perceptions, and memories of their viewers.

In their foreword to the exhibition catalogue *Oath Against Minimalism*, Andrea Lissoni and Sam Thorne, whose respective venues presented Tieu's exhibitions *Zugzwang* and *In Cold Print*,[23] write that these spaces "recall the interiors of immigration bureaus, registration offices, and modern penal institutions."[24] Accordingly, the synchronization of the German Pavilion with the ruins of an East German prefabricated

22) Ibid., p. 18f.

23) Curated by Damian Lentini (Haus der Kunst) and Cédric Fauq (Nottingham Contemporary).

24) Andrea Lissoni and Sam Thorne, foreword, in *Sung Tieu, Oath Against Minimalism*, exh. cat. Haus der Kunst, Munich, and Nottingham Contemporary. Leipzig: Spector Books, 2020, p. 11.

housing block establishes an infrastructural link between cultural, administrative, and disciplinary institutions.

This form of narrative abstraction is typical for a critique of historical Minimal Art's gender-, class-, race-, and colonialism-blind neutrality credo, a critique that has been growing steadily since the 1970s.[25] In her catalogue essay "Sung Tieu—Scannings," for instance, art theorist Pamela N. Corey references Jaleh Mansoor's interpretation of Mona Hatoum's *Keffieh* series (1993–99) by speaking of a transformation of the minimalist grid into a "chain of dissonant particulars."[26] Thus, my reading of Tieu's fusion of the German Pavilion and the East German prefabricated housing complex into an infrastructural hyperobject leads me to the thesis that the system-generating concatenation of distinct elements is based less on a narrative mode than on a social abstraction of the kind that Vishmidt finds in the bridges, tunnels, and canals that make up the infrastructure.

As Corey goes on to explain, for Tieu, "abstraction has served as a key formal strategy (...). These include elements of modernist and brutalist design such as grids, concrete, and steel, materials associated with what the artist herself (under the pseudonym or birth name Tieu Thi Phuong Dung) refers to as "brutally global," or what Jelena Stojanović describes as the monstrously modernist dimensions of functionalism-as-formalism materialized in Cold War architecture and design."[27] Tieu's transformation of the neoclassical pavilion's façade into a trompe-l'œil of late-modernist concrete architecture evinces essential characteristics of a hyperobject, helping us to think about a national institution as a multipolar (infra)structure.

Addendum:

Since this text was written in December 2025, redevelopment plans for the Gehrenseestrasse site have advanced significantly. The project is now being realized by BE Development—a rebranding of the former Belle Époque—in cooperation with HOWOGE. The plans for a courtyard and high-rise complex comprising more than 1,000 apartments remain in place, including HOWOGE's proposal to offer and manage 274 units, half of which are state-subsidized.

A site once inhabited by foreign students, contract workers, and asylum seekers is thus being transformed into a contemporary real estate development, equipped with underfloor heating and barrier-free access—marking a shift not only in architectural form, but also in its social composition, toward privatized, regulated, and economically stratified modes of dwelling.

25) Dan Rees, *A Minimalist Mourning: The Aesthetics of Administration in the Work of Sung Tieu* (unpublished manuscript).

26) Pamela N. Corey, "Sung Tieu—Scannings," in: *Oath Against Minimalism*, op. cit. pp. 18–21, here p. 19.

27) Ibid., p. 19.

OBJEKTE IN MULTIPOLAREN (INFRA-)STRUKTUREN

Sabeth Buchmann

Wer sich der aus über drei Millionen Mosaiksteinchen bestehenden Fassade des Deutschen Pavillons nähert, wird womöglich rätseln, ob es sich hierbei um Kunst am Bau, ein Monument oder ein Panoramagemälde handelt. Als sei dem antikisierten Gebäude ein den bunten Mosaiken Ravennas angelehntes Erscheinungsbild verpasst worden, lässt die Montage der farbigen, 1,5×1,5 cm messenden Marmorquadrate keinen Zweifel an ihrem Trompe-l'œil-Charakter, der auf der antiken, in der Renaissance wiederbelebten und bis heute in der Theater- und Fassadenmalerei praktizierten Technik der Augentäuschung beruht. Komponiert aus gelblichen Flächen und gräulichen Streifen kann indes von einer virtuosen Verzierung der Pavillonfassade keine Rede sein. Auf ihr ist in illusionistischer Manier ein dreidimensionales Gebäude zu sehen, von dem nur noch nackte und ramponierte sowie mit Graffitis übersäte, fenster- und türlose Wände eines offenbar zum Abbruch stehenden Plattenbaus existiert. Als werde die Funktion von Architekturattrappen verkehrt, mit denen für den Erwerb von Immobilien oder auch in den frühen 1990er-Jahren für den Wiederaufbau von historischen Gebäuden, so das 1950 gesprengte Berliner Stadtschloss, geworben wurde, zitiert Sung Tieu eine ins öffentliche Bewusstsein eingebrannte Kulissenoptik, die sich schließlich auch in der Ersetzung des abgerissenen Palastes der Republik durch eine neo-historistische Fassadenimitation manifestiert. Indem diese Optik von Erinnerungen an Ost-Berliner Gebäuderuinen überlagert wird, können wir in Tieus Mosaikfassade auch ein Echo auf „baubezogene Kunst" erkennen, wie sie im (spät-)modernen, von Betonmonumenten bestimmten Städtebau[1] der DDR und des sowjetischen Blocks verbreitet war. Diese dienten nicht nur der ästhetischen Nobilitierung von Betrieben und öffentlichen Gebäuden, sondern auch jener von standardisierter Industrienorm unterworfenen Plattenbauten, mit der die SED-Führung der nach dem 2. Weltkrieg herrschenden Wohnungsnot in Ost-Berlin als damaliger DDR-Hauptstadt beizukommen suchte. Eine hinsichtlich Tieus Ausstellungen *Song for VEB Stern-Radio Berlin* (2021) und *One Thousand Times* (2023) mögliche Resonanz erkenne ich in der 1985 von der Künstlerin Gertraude Pohl für VEB Stern-Radios in Berlin-Marzahn gestalteten Fassade *Stadtraumbezogene Orientierungszeichen.*[2] Das farbig-abstrakte, von dynamischen Spannungen zwischen Fläche und Linie, Zwei- und

1) Zu denken wäre hier auch an Brasilia, die in den 1950er-Jahren neuerbaute Hauptstadt Brasiliens.

2) Siehe https://bildhauerei-in-berlin.de/bildwerk/stadtraumbezogene-orientierungszeichen-9781/#:~:text=Die%20Arbeiten%20für%20das%20Stern,dem%20Titel%20%22Stadtraumbezogene%20Orientierungszeichen%22, letzter Zugriff am 1.12.2025.

Dreidimensionalität, Organik und Geometrie zeugende und aus emaillierten Stahlblechquadraten gebildete Wandbild[3] wurde 1992 von der DIBAG AG München in ihrer Funktion als neue Eigentümergesellschaft weitgehend zerstört[4]: Als solches ist es ein vielsagendes Beispiel für die künstlerisch anspruchsvolle „Arbeitsumweltgestaltung"[5] von Betrieben, in denen auch jene vietnamesische Vertragsarbeiter*innen beschäftigt waren, die unter anderem in dem 1980 fertiggestellten Plattenbauareal in der im Stadtteil Alt-Hohenschönhausen gelegenen Gehrenseestraße mithin in einem jener neun Gebäude wohnten, das sich in Tieus Fassade spiegelt.

Angesichts der Beseitigungen und Zerstörungen „architekturbezogener Kunst" in der ehemaligen DDR, da sie laut Gerichtsbeschluss als „staatsnah und somit nicht als schutzwürdig galt"[6], kann Tieus Anbringung einer Mosaikfassade als zugleich dokumentarische und kommemorative Geste gelesen werden, setzt sie doch nicht nur einem schmucklosen Plattenbau, sondern auch einer verdrängten Gestaltungspraxis ein Denkmal.

Weit entfernt von idealisierender Nostalgie lässt die temporäre Umgestaltung des Deutschen Pavillons keinen Zweifel an ihrem ambivalenten Repräsentationscharakter. So schwingt in dem verwendeten Material auch jener spätsozialistische Feudalismus mit, der den vier Jahre nach Errichtung des Gehrenseestraße-Komplexes von Pohl aus sibirischem Marmor gestalteten Großen Saal der Moskauer DDR-Botschaft kennzeichnet. Zugleich lässt sich die Wandbildtradition nicht auf die DDR-Geschichte beschränken, setzte sie sich doch im Nachwendejahrzehnt für kurze Zeit fort, als Plattenbaufassaden unter anderem von brasilianischen Künstler*innen mit inzwischen wieder abgeschlagenen, auf indigene Kulturen zurückgehenden geometrischen Muster versehen wurden.[7] Mit anderen Worten zeigt sich in Tieus Fassadenimitation eine ebenso für sozialistische Infrastrukturprojekte wie für außereuropäische, von der geometrischen Abstraktion angeeignete Formsprache auf.

Aufgrund seines geringen Härtegrades verhältnismäßig flexibel zu handhaben, verbinden sich im Marmor ästhetische, technische und ökonomische Eigenschaften und Qualitäten, welche sich weit über die westliche Moderne hinaus in die (Kunst-)Geschichte eingeschrieben haben: Marmor findet sich in Tempeln und Palästen genauso wie auf öffentlichen Plätzen und in privaten Wohnanlagen, in Küchen und Bädern – ein Umstand, der zeigt, dass und in welchem Maß Marmor das Bild öffentlicher und privater Infrastrukturen prägt.

3) Siehe https://bildhauerei-in-berlin.de/bildwerk/stadtraumbezogene-orientierungszeichen-9781.

4) Ebd.

5) Ebd.

6) Ebd. So durften sie nach „der Privatisierung des in der DDR vergesellschafteten öffentlichen Raumes (...)" zerstört bzw. entfernt werden. Siehe https://www.howoge.de/immobiliensuche/neubauprojekte/quartier-gehrenseestrasse-wollenberger-strasse.html, letzter Zugriff am 12.10.25.

7) Siehe https://www.alexander-j-herrmann.de/news/lokal/1382/Entfernung-der-Mosaiksteine-im-Gelben-Viertel.html.

Solche der Alltags- und Kunstwahrnehmung gleichermaßen zugänglichen Konnotationen erfahren durch Tieus Fassade insofern eine Verfremdung, als sich der 1909 erbaute[8] und 1938 dem pseudoklassizistischen Ideal der NSDAP angepasste Pavillon im sichtbar dislozierten Plattenbaustil präsentiert. Indem die Wandbilder nationale Repräsentationsansprüche auf die marmorierte Ruine eines ehemals vornehmlich von Vertragsarbeiter*innen und ab den 1990er-Jahren von Asylbewerber*innen bewohnten Gebäudes übertragen, personalisieren und verfremden sie Form, Maßstab und Funktion des Deutschen Pavillons: Ein Kunstgriff, der es erlaubt, das Abstrakte im Konkreten zu betrachten. So reflektiert die Fassade Standardisierung, Regulierung und Kontrolle in Bezug auf die Rolle der Arbeiter*innenwohnheime, ihre Bewohner*innen auf kleinstem Raum zu verwalten. In Entsprechung hierzu abstrahieren die beiden wechselseitig gespiegelten Seitenräume des Pavillons das Leben und die Erfahrungen der in den rund 1000, je 16 qm großen, ursprünglich für knapp 4000 Menschen geplanten Wohnräumen. Möglicherweise zunächst als Kaserne [9] geplant, wohnten hier ab 1982 neben ausländischen Studierenden vor allem vietnamesische, aber auch kubanische und mosambikanische Vertragsarbeiter*innen.[10] Wie aus ihren regelmäßigen Architekturführungen hervorgeht, zog Tieu 1994 mit ihrer Mutter für drei Jahre in das *Objekt Gehrenseestraße* ein. Da die kollektiven Ortsbegehungen historische und biografische Erzählungen verknüpfen, stellen sie eine autoethnologische Beziehung zu den besichtigten Resten architektonischer Infrastrukturen dar. Der ehemals in sozialistische Bruderländer, unter anderem nach Vietnam exportierte und durch Tieus Pavillongestaltung adressierte Bautypus wird so zu einem Medium kollektiv erlebter Zeitgeschichte. Wir erfahren, dass Tieu und ihre Mutter zu einem Zeitpunkt in der Gehrenseestraße lebten, als aufgrund annullierter Arbeitsverträge und andernorts gekündigter Werkswohnungen die Anzahl der Mieter*innen auf 6000 angestiegen war. Denn jenen Vertragsarbeiter*innen, die aus wirtschaftlichen und sozialen Gründen nicht in die sogenannten Bruderländer der 1990 aufgelösten DDR zurückkehren konnten oder wollten, blieb demnach keine Alternative zu den teilweise als Asylbewerbeheime betriebenen Wohnkomplexen.

Als solche verweist die Mosaikfassade auf ein Beispiel jener von der DDR seit den frühen 1970er-Jahren forcierten Infrastrukturmaßnahmen, die als eine Phase der internationalen Öffnung gilt, welche sich unter anderem an der erstmaligen Vertretung der DDR auf der Venedig Biennale im Jahr 1982, also nur acht Jahre vor ihrer Auflösung, ablesen

8) Zunächst als ‚Bayrischer Pavillon'; siehe Maria Eichhorns Freilegung des Umbaus im Rahmen ihres Beitrag zum Deutschen Pavillon der Venedig Biennale 2022.

9) Siehe Sung Tieus diesbezügliche Recherche im vorliegenden Katalog.

10) Laut Recherche der Künstlerin und ihres Teams könnte es sein, dass die Gebäude in der Gehrenseestraße zunächst als Kasernen dienen sollten.

lässt. Tieus aus hauchdünnen Marmorquadraten bestehende Fassadenimitation lässt sich daher als buchstäbliches Mosaik aus Erfahrungs- und Bedeutungsschichten lesen, welche die Bestimmung künstlerischer Zeitgenossenschaft umso expliziter problematisiert: Insofern 1989, mithin der Zusammenbruch des sogenannten Ostblocks, die sich verstärkende Globalisierungsdynamik sowie die Neukartierung der Welt in Länder des globalen Südens und Nordens als Wasserscheide zwischen (Post-)Moderne und Gegenwart gilt, kommt Tieus Intervention neben orts- und zeitspezifischer auch multipolarer[11] und -temporaler Charakter zu. Dies ist umso signifikanter, als die Kunst und die Architektur der DDR erst nach drei Jahrzehnten des Einigungsvertrags durch eine auffällige Zunahme an Ausstellungen und Publikationen verstärkte Aufmerksamkeit erfahren sollte, wobei bis auf wenige Ausnahmen[12] Geschichte der Arbeitsmigration chronisch unterbelichtet bleibt. Dabei handelt es sich um eine alles andere als abgeschlossene Geschichte, sehen sich doch selbst längst eingebürgerte Einwander*innen mit einer neuerlichen Welle von nationalistisch motiviertem Rassismus konfrontiert. Stellt die Fassade einerseits eine Beziehung zu der mithilfe asiatischer, afrikanischer und karibischer Arbeitsmigrant*innen möglichen Modernisierung im Vorwende-Berlin her, bildet sie andererseits ein materialästhetisches Kontinuum zum (kunst-)historisch aufgeladenen Marmorboden des Deutschen Pavillons: 1938 anstelle des ursprünglichen Parkettbodens gelegt, ist dem metamorphen Gestein das Ewigkeitsphantasma des sogenannten Dritten Reichs förmlich eingeschrieben. Von Hans Haacke 1993 in Reaktion auf die im Vorjahr verübten rassistischen Brandanschläge gegen vietnamesische Bewohner*innen des Sonnenblumenhauses in Rostock-Lichtenhagen herausgerissen und zu einem Caspar David Friedrich-haften Steinmeer arrangiert, könnte die Petrifizierung des Arbeiter*innenwohnheims auf der Pavillonfassade ihrerseits als ironische, weil sich ihrer Temporalität bewussten Geste der Verewigung verdrängter Migrationsgeschichte gelesen werden. Im Unterschied zu Haackes Ästhetik der Destruktion stellt sich das Mosaik somit als palimpsesthafte Überschreibung eines bestehenden Baukörpers dar. Als antimonumentaler Hybrid aus Ruine und Denkmal betrachtet bezeugt die Fakefassade nicht eine in Teilen zerstörte DDR-Moderne, sondern auch die Verdrängung ihrer von politischen Umbrüchen und Ausbeutung migrantischer Arbeitskräfte handelnden Sozialgeschichte. Es ist mit anderen Worten das in urbane Peripherien ausgelagerte und von der restlichen Bevölkerung abgetrennte Leben von Vertragsarbeiter*innen, welche jedes einzelne

11) Siehe Mi You, *Art in a Multipolar World*, Berlin: Hatje Cantz Verlag, 2024. Die Professorin für Kunst und Ökonomien am Kasseler documenta Institut meint damit eine Vervielfältigung der bis Ende des Kalten Krieges bipolaren Machtzentren.

12) U. a. durch die Ausstellung *Echos der Bruderländer* 2024 im Berliner Haus der Kulturen der Welt: https://www.hkw.de/programme/echos-der-bruderlaender. Zu denken wäre hier auch an Vorgängerprojekte- und ausstellungen wie z. B. *Revolutionary Romances. Transkulturelle Kunstgeschichten in der DDR* (Albertinum Dresden 2019–2014) und *Re:connect. Kunst und Kampf im Bruderland* (MdBK Leipzig 2023).

Mosaiksteinchen zu einem konkreten Pars pro Toto eines abstrakten Ganzen macht.

Der auf der Fassade reproduzierte Istzustand lässt keinen Zweifel an der Unbewohnbarkeit[13] des Gebäudes und schlägt als Imitation der Bauruine ein weiteres Kapitel jener Geschichte urbaner Infrastrukturentwicklung auf, welche auch die derzeitige Debatte um die Funktionstüchtigkeit öffentlicher Versorgungssysteme berührt. Entsprechend können sich Interessierte im Rahmen von Tieus Führungen über die vorerst gescheiterte Zukunft aktueller Modernisierungspläne informieren. Demzufolge kann die in den 2020er-Jahren geplante Neubebauung der 6,3 Hektar großen Liegenschaft in der Gehrenseestraße durch die HOWOGE, die Wohnungsbaugesellschaft des Landes Berlin, in Kooperation mit dem Immobilienentwickler Belle Époque vorerst nicht realisiert werden: Deren Plan war bzw. ist es,[14] dass dort, wo einst ausländische Studierende, Vertragsarbeiter*innen und Asylbewerber*innen lebten, ein „Hof- und Hochhausquartier mit mehr als 1.000 Wohnungen entstehen (...)", von denen die Hälfte über „sozial gefördert" und „über barrierefreie Zugänge und Fußbodenheizung" verfügen sollte. Geplant waren laut HOWOGE „auch gewerbliche Nutzungen für Dienstleistungen, Student:innen-, Senior:innen- oder Pflegewohnen, soziale und medizinische Versorgung, Kultur und Ladengeschäfte".[15]

Die für das Nachwende-Berlin charakteristische Public-Private-Partnership-Rhetorik klingt dabei wie ein fernes Echo auf das aus dem ehemaligen Wohnkomplex verdrängte Leben, das Tieu in ihrem mit 13. Oktober 1995 datiertem Leser*innenbrief an die *New York Times* beschreibt. „Inside the Blocks" getitelt, geht die fiktive Verfasserin, ein siebenjähriges Mädchen namens Ching, darin auf ihre vorwiegend positiven Erinnerungen an die Gehrenseestraße ein, um sich gegen die von einem *NYT*-Reporter namens Alan Cowell aufgetischten Klischees – so spricht er unter anderem von ghettoähnlichen Zuständen – zu verwahren.[16] Hierzu zählte geldloser Tauschhandel und gegenseitige Fürsorge, etwa bei der Essensversorgung und Kinderbetreuung. Wie Tieu betont, erfuhr sie trotz beengter Wohnverhältnisse eine glückliche, weil sozial eingebettete Kindheit. In ihren Schilderungen tauchen aber auch die Ängste auf, welche die damaligen Mieter*innen angesichts rabiat durchgreifender Polizei durchlitten – ganz abgesehen von den brutalen und zum Teil tödlich endenden Übergriffen rechtsextremer Gewalttäter. Von feindseliger Stimmungsmache seitens Presse und Politik bestärkt, heizten die als chaotisch denunzierten Zustände in der Gehrenseestraße die rassistische Hetze weiter an.[17]

13) Bei unserem gemeinsamen Besuch im Sommer 2024 fanden sich dort allerdings Matratzen und andere Gegenstände, die darauf hindeuteten, dass hier inzwischen Obdachlose leb(t)en.

14) Die zwischenzeitlich von der Belle Époque angemeldete Insolvenz wurde im Juli 2025 wieder aufgehoben.

15) Siehe https://www.howoge.de/immobiliensuche/neubauprojekte/quartier-gehrenseestrasse-wollenberger-strasse.html, letzter Zugriff am 12.1.2026.

16) Siehe „Inside the Blocks", in: Rob Grosse, Sung Tieu, Richard Sides, *Ars Viva 2021*, Ausst.-Kat. des Kulturkreises der deutschen Wirtschaft im BDI e.V., Bielefeld/Berlin: Kerber Verlag, 2021, S. 62.

17) Sung Tieu hat diese und andere Aspekte vietnamesischen Lebens Ausstellungen wie *Oath Against Minimalism* (2020), *One Thousand Times* (2023) und *1992/2025* in den KW Institute for Contemporary Art Berlin, die sie im Rahmen des Schering-Preises für künstlerische Forschung 2025 realisiert hat, minutiös aufgearbeitet.

18) Marina Vishmidt, *Between Not Everything and Not Nothing: Cuts Towards Infrastructural Critique*, in: Maria Hlavajova und Simon Sheik (Hg.), *Former West. Art and the Contemporary after 1989*, London/Cambridge, MA: The MIT Press, 2017, S. 265–268, hier: S. 265.

Wenn ich vor diesem Hintergrund das marmorne Trompe-l'œil als ästhetisches Bindeglied zwischen jenen Infrastrukturen lese, die für Wohnungsbaumaßnahmen an den durch Autobahnen segregierten Stadträndern genauso wie für staatlich organisierte Arbeitsmigration, d. h. für die Anwerbung, Verwaltung und Kontrolle im Niedriglohnsektor beschäftigter Arbeiter*innen in arbeitskraftarmen Industriezweigen stehen, dann weil sie an Güter- und Warenproduktion, Reisen und Transport, Service und Konsum, Wasser- und Energieversorgung angeschlossen sind, die laut der US-amerikanischen Kunsttheoretikerin Marina Vishmidt immer auch „Orte sozialer Abstraktion"[18] darstellen. In diesem Licht betrachtet erscheint der Pavillon weniger als versteinertes Monument, sondern vielmehr als eine wahrnehmungsästhetisch (re-)produzierbare Form.[19] Schließlich trägt die Verdeckung der Fensteröffnungen und des 1938 über das Portal gemeißelten Schriftzugs „Germania" durch das Allover-Mosaik dazu bei, den Deutschen Pavillon nicht als einen leeren Container, sondern als ein von biografisch Erlebtem, staatlich organisiertem Leben und nationaler Repräsentation gefülltes „Hyperobjekt"[20] wahrzunehmen: Mit der kanadischen Materialwissenschaftlerin Deb Chachra gesprochen stellt es einen Knotenpunkt innerhalb multipler Systeme von unvorstellbarer Größe, Ausdehnung und Komplexität dar.[21] Als diene die Fassadenimitation dem vorübergehenden Erhalt einer dysfunktionalen Infrastruktur, erscheinen die Raum- und Zeitmaße, die ihre Form bestimmen, als abstraktes Drittes technischer Medien und sozialer Regeln:

> Kollektive Infrastrukturen zählen zu den komplexesten Systemen, die vom Menschen hervorgebracht wurden. Sie besitzen planetarische Dimensionen, sind historisch gewachsen, vielfach miteinander verschränkt und entfalten Wirkungen, die weit in zukünftige Zeiträume hineinreichen. Ihre Konzeption, Errichtung und ihr Betrieb erfordern die Zusammenarbeit zahlreicher technischer Disziplinen – insbesondere des Bauingenieurwesens, darüber hinaus jedoch auch der Elektrotechnik, des Maschinenbaus, der Umwelttechnik sowie der System- und Netzwerkwissenschaften. Diese Fachgebiete umfassen nicht allein technische Artefakte, sondern ebenso Praktiken, epistemische Zugänge sowie spezifische Formen des Handelns, Produzierens und Bauens. Entscheidungsprozesse und Finanzierungsstrukturen im Zusammenhang mit Infrastruktursystemen, insbesondere im öffentlichen Sektor, sind dem Bereich von Politik, Finanzwesen und Ökonomie zuzuordnen. Da Infrastrukturen als Systeme stets Flächen und Ressourcen in Anspruch nehmen, lassen

19) Siehe die Definition von Infrastrukturen als aktive Formen bei Keller Easterling, *Extrastatecraft: The Power of Infrastructure Space*, London/New York: Verso, 2014 und *Medium Design. Knowing How to Work on the World*, London/New York: Verso, 2021.

20) Gemeint ist hier Tim Mortons *Hyperobjects. Philosophy and Ecology after the End of the World*, zitiert in: Deb Chachra, *How Infrastructure Works. Inside the Systems That Shape Our World*, New York: Riverhead Books, 2023, S. 19.

21) „Collective infrastructures are a good candidate for the most complex systems created by humans. They are planetary in scale, build on their own histories, are entangled with each other, and have impacts that extend far into the future. Their design, construction, and operation require a wide range of technical disciplines—civil engineering, obviously, but also electrical engineering, mechanical engineering, environmental engineering, and the science of systems and of networks. All of these fields incorporate not just technologies but practices, ways of thinking, doing, and building. The decision making and funding around these systems, particularly public systems, is the province of policy, finance, and economics. Finally, as systems that require land and resources, it's impossible to extricate infrastructure from a larger history of conquest, colonialism, and capitalism and, particularly (...) from racism and white supremacy. The theorist Timothy Morton coined the word "hyperobject" for just these sorts of systems that span multiple time scales, length scales, and social settings.", ebd., S. 13.

> sie sich nicht von einer umfassenderen historischen Entwicklung trennen, die durch Eroberung, Kolonialismus und Kapitalismus geprägt ist – und insbesondere (...) durch Rassismus und weiße Vorherrschaft. Der Theoretiker Timothy Morton prägte für derartige Systeme den Begriff des „Hyperobjekts", womit Gebilde bezeichnet werden, die sich über multiple Zeit- und Raumskalen sowie über unterschiedliche soziale Kontexte hinweg erstrecken.[22]

Indem sich die Dimensionen von Hyperobjekten der menschlichen Wahrnehmung nur bedingt und im beschränkten Maß vermitteln, fällt die symbolische Spiegelung von Kunstinstitution und Wohnquartier umso stärker ins Gewicht, zumal sie in den Modus ästhetischer Wahrnehmung eingreift: Was, wenn wir den Deutschen Pavillon nicht als solitären und temporären Ausstellungsort, sondern vielmehr als vielfach und dauerhaft vernetzte Infrastruktur betrachten? Was, wenn er zu einer langfristigen Adresse jener persönlichen Erinnerungen würde, die Tieus temporäre Fassade aufruft? Denn sie ist nichts weniger als ein Pars pro Toto eines infrastrukturellen Ganzen, dessen ästhetische (Re-)Produktion die von ihm repräsentierte Gedenkform innewohnt. Entsprechend geht die Form, in der das Trompe-l'œil Geschichte, Gegenwart und Zukunft von Plattenbau und Pavillon synchronisiert, über die Assoziation der Fassade mit einem DDR-spezifischen Bautypus hinaus. Mit Pohls „Arbeitsumweltgestaltungen" vergleichbar lenken Fassaden- und Innengestaltung den Blick auf die Komposition von Farben und Formen, Licht- und Größenverhältnissen: Als handele es sich hierbei um Medien, die in der Tradition der geometrischen Abstraktion das, was sie zeigen, mit und in den Körpern, Wahrnehmungen und Erinnerungen ihrer Betrachter*innen verhandeln.

In ihrem Vorwort zu dem ausstellungsbegleitenden Katalog *Oath Against Minimalism* schreiben Andrea Lissoni und Sam Thorne, in deren Häusern Tieus Ausstellungen *Zugzwang* und *In Cold Print* [23] gezeigt wurden, dass diese „Assoziationen an die Räumlichkeiten von Einwanderungsbehörden, Meldestellen und modernen Haftanstalten"[24] wecken würden. Entsprechend stellt die Synchronisierung des Deutschen Pavillons mit der Ruine eines DDR-Plattenbaus eine infrastrukturelle Verbindung zwischen kulturellen, administrativen und disziplinären Institutionen her.

Diese Form der narrativen Abstraktion ist für die seit den 1970er-Jahren kontinuierlich weiterentwickelte Kritik am geschlechts-, klassen-, race- und kolonialismusblinden Neutralitätscredo der historischen Minimal Art charakteristisch.[25] So schließt etwa die Kunsttheoretikerin Pamela

22) Ebd., S. 18f.

23) Kuratiert von Damian Lentini (Haus der Kunst) und Cédric Fauq (Nottingham Contemporary).

24) Andrea Lissoni und Sam Thorne, Vorwort, in: *Sung Tieu, Oath Against Minimalism*, Ausst.-Kat. Haus der Kunst, München, und Nottingham Contemporary, Leipzig: Spector Books, 2020, S. 11.

25) Dan Rees, *A Minimalist Mourning: The Aesthetics of Administration in the Work of Sung Tieu* (unveröffentliches Manuskript).

N. Corey in ihrem Katalogessay *Sung Tieu – Scannings* an Jaleh Mansoors Deutung von Mona Hatoums Werkserie *Keffieh* (1993–1999) an, indem sie von einer Umgestaltung des minimalistischen Rasters zu einer „Kette dissonanter partikularer Einheiten"[26] spricht. Meine Lektüre von Tieus Verschmelzung des Deutschen Pavillons und der DDR-Platte zu einem infrastrukturellen Hyperobjekt verleitet mich daher zu der These, dass der systembildenden Verkettung distinkter Elemente weniger ein Modus der narrativen, sondern vielmehr der sozialen Abstraktion jener Art zugrunde liegt, wie sie Vishmidt in infrastrukturbildenden Brücken, Tunneln und Kanälen erkennt.

Wie Corey weiter ausführt, war für Tieu „Abstraktion immer eine zentrale formale Strategie (...). Dazu gehörten Elemente modernistischen und brutalistischen Designs wie das Raster, Beton und Stahl – Materialien, die mit etwas assoziiert werden, das die Künstlerin selbst (unter ihrem Pseudonym bzw. Geburtsnamen Tieu Thi Phuong Dung) als ‚brutally global' bezeichnet hat und das Jelena Stojanović als die monströs modernistischen Dimensionen von Funktionalismus-als-Formalismus beschreibt, wie sie sich in Architektur und Design aus der Zeit des Kalten Krieges materialisiert haben."[27]

Tieus Umgestaltung der neoklassizistischen Pavillonfassade in ein Trompe-l'œil spätmoderner Betonarchitektur macht wesentliche Eigenschaften eines Hyperobjekts sichtbar und hilft dabei, eine nationale Institution als multipolare (Infra-)Struktur zu denken.

Addendum:

Seit der Abfassung dieses Textes im Dezember 2025 sind die Planungen zur Neuentwicklung des Standorts Gehrenseestraße deutlich vorangeschritten. Das Projekt wird nun von BE Development – einer Umbenennung des ehemaligen Unternehmens Belle Époque – in Kooperation mit HOWOGE realisiert. Die Pläne für eine Hof- und Hochhausanlage mit mehr als 1.000 Wohnungen bestehen weiterhin; darunter HOWOGEs Vorhaben, 274 Wohnungen anzubieten und zu verwalten, von denen die Hälfte staatlich gefördert ist.

Ein Ort, der einst von ausländischen Studierenden, Vertragsarbeiter*innen und Asylsuchenden bewohnt wurde, wird somit in ein zeitgenössisches Immobilienprojekt überführt, ausgestattet mit Fußbodenheizung und barrierefreiem Zugang – und markiert damit nicht nur einen Wandel in der architektonischen Form, sondern auch in seiner sozialen Zusammensetzung hin zu privatisierten, regulierten und ökonomisch stratifizierten Formen des Wohnens.

26) Pamela N. Corey, „Sung Tieu – Scannings", in: *Oath Against Minimalism*, a. a. O., S. 18–21, hier: S. 19.

27) Ebd., S. 19.

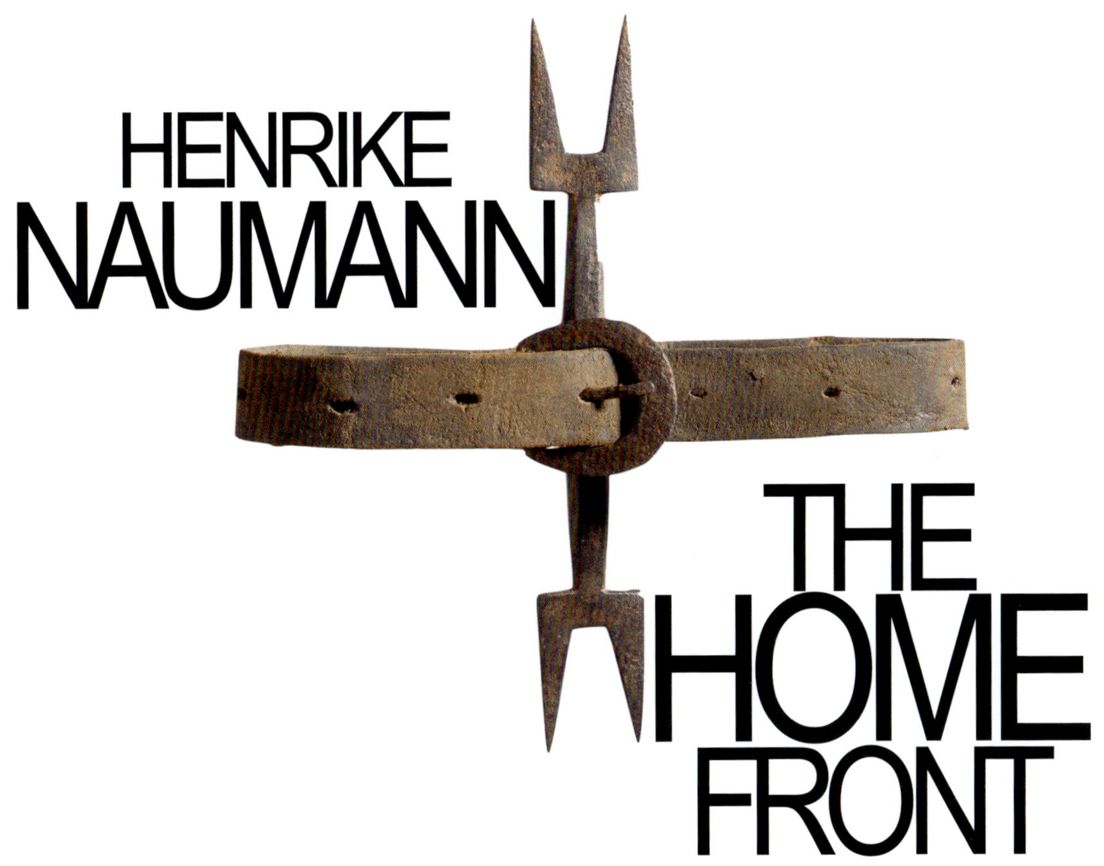
HENRIKE
NAUMANN
THE
HOME
FRONT

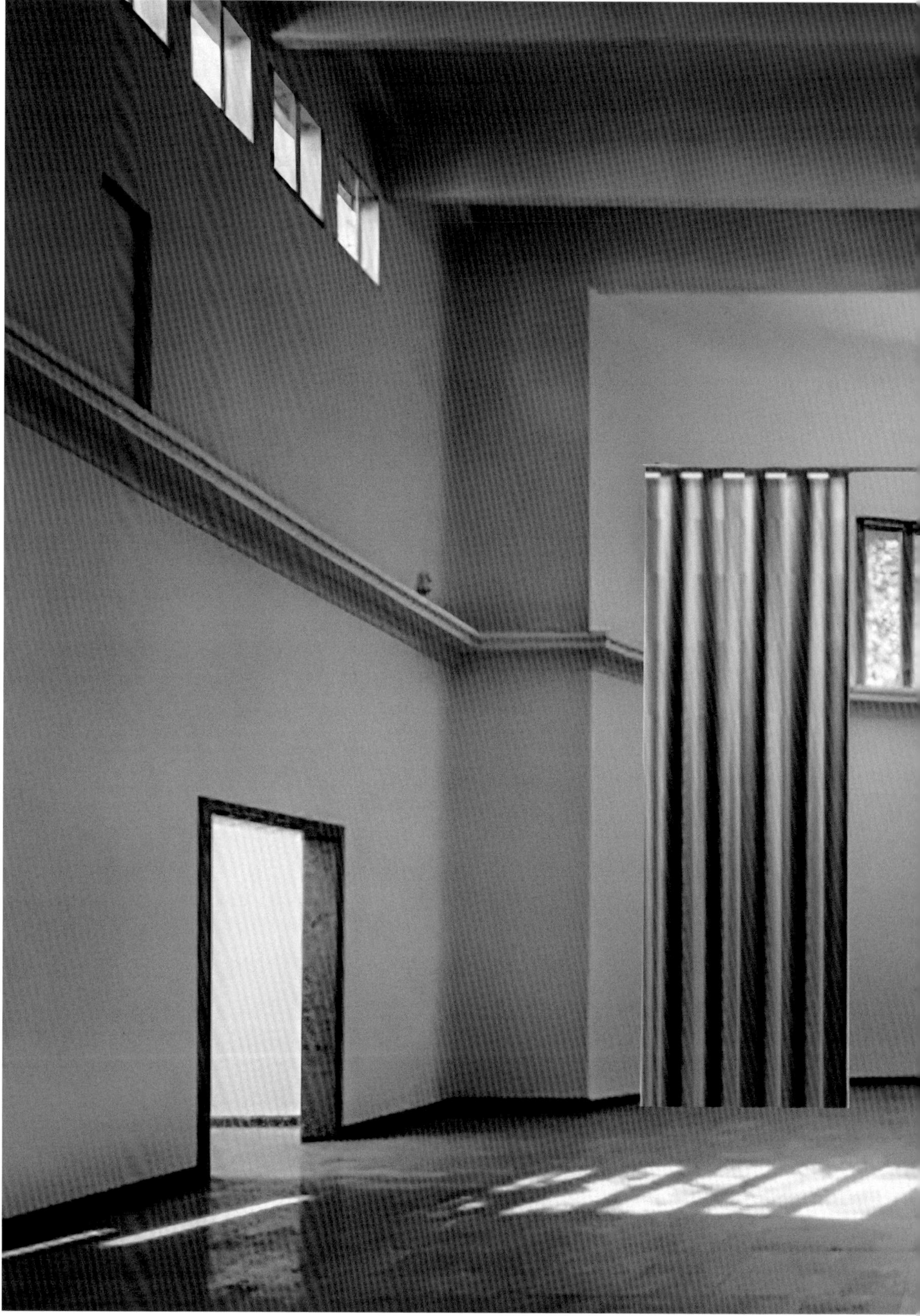

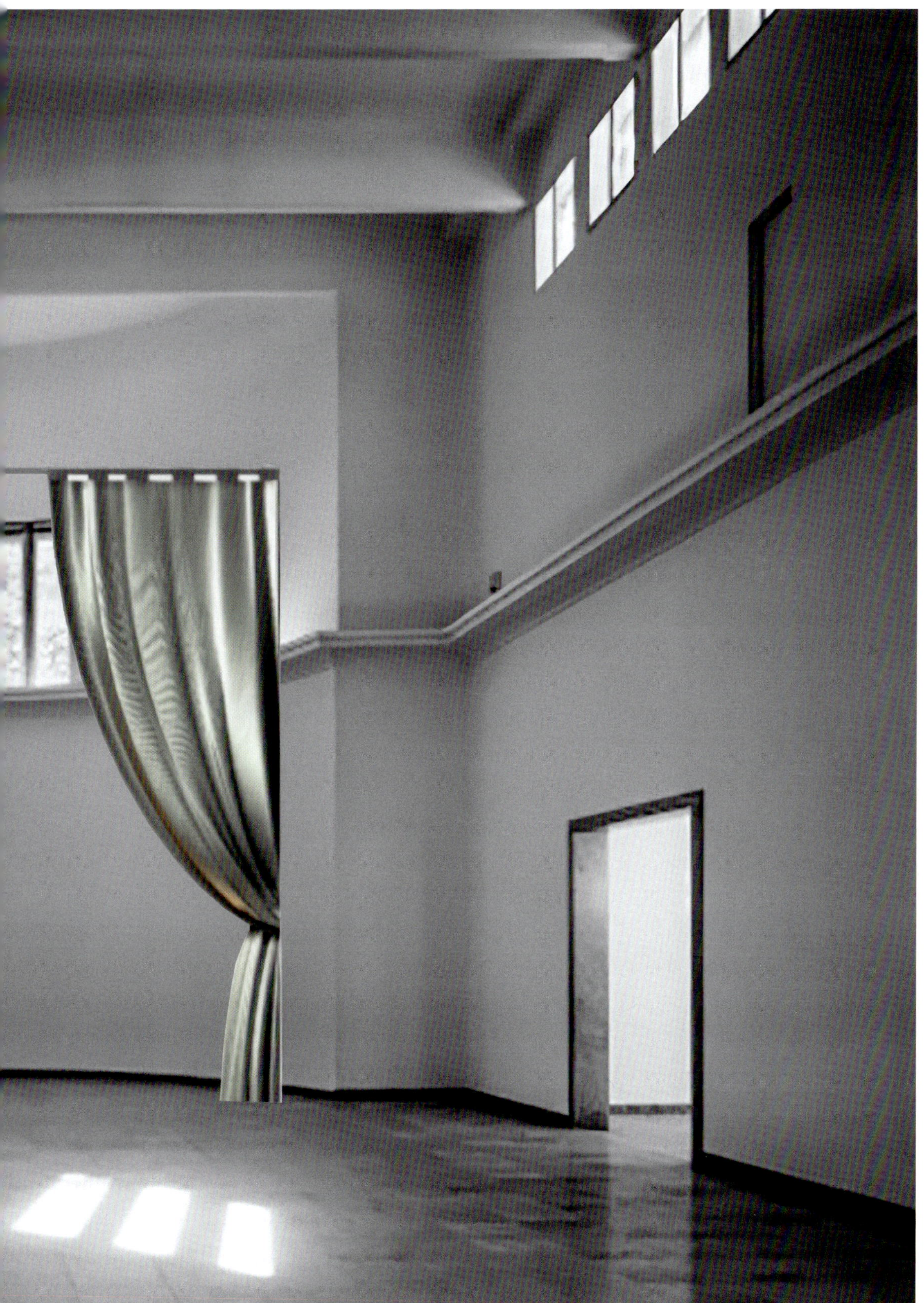

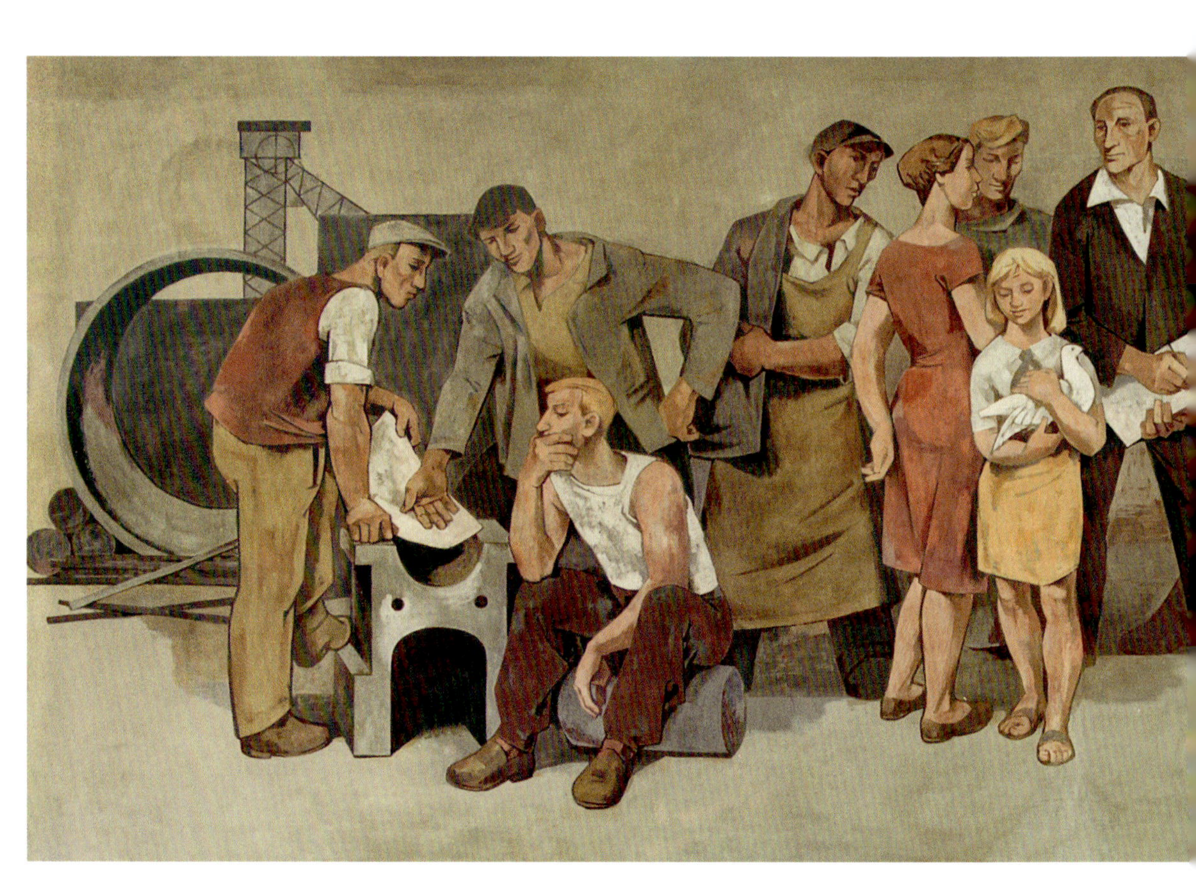

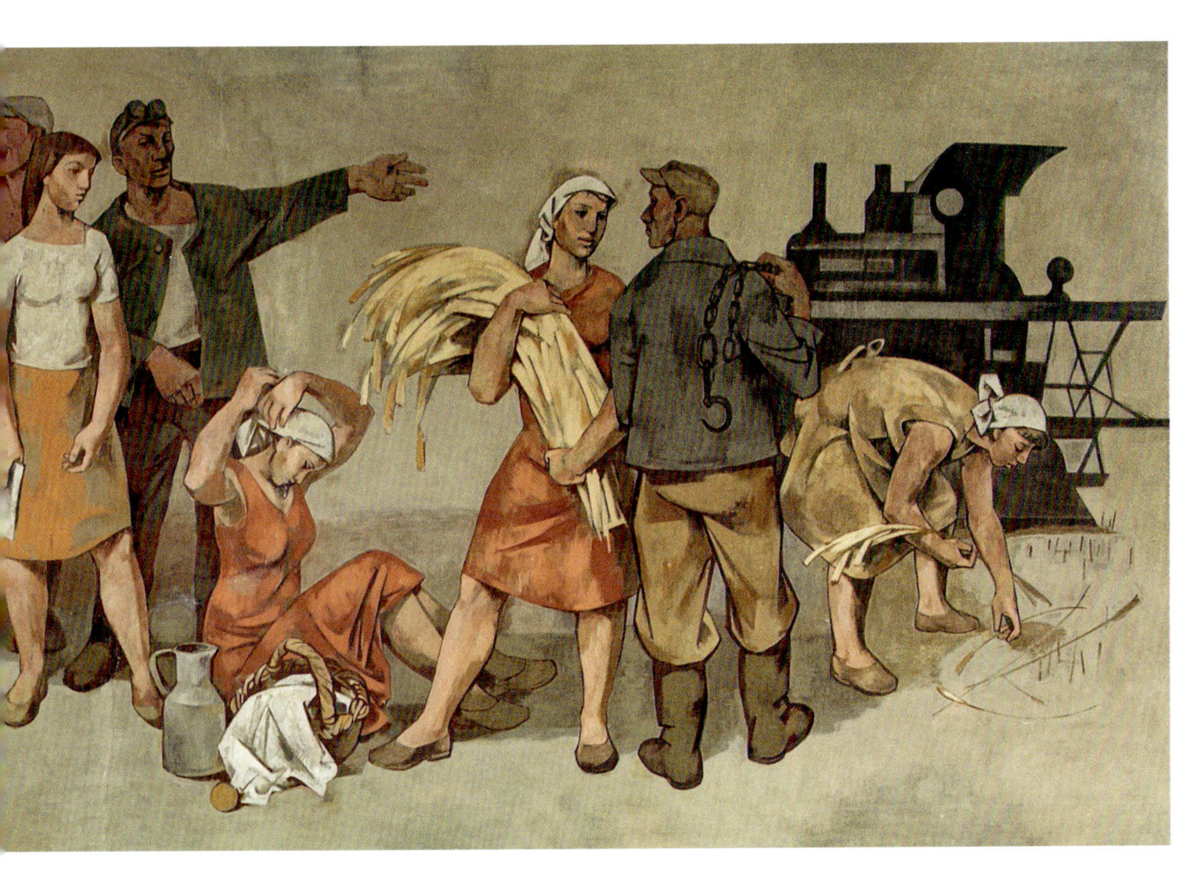

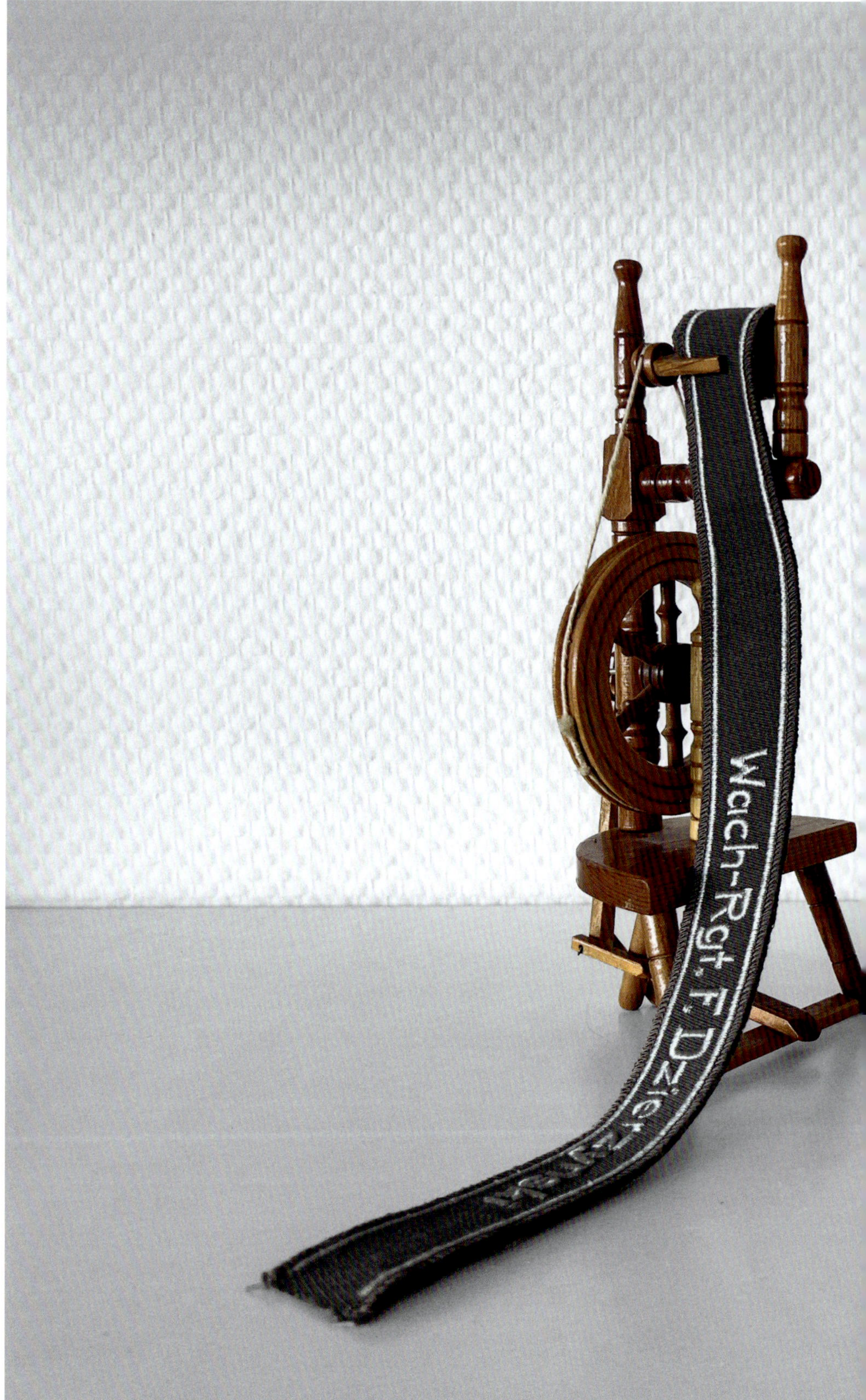
Wach-Rgt. F. Dzier

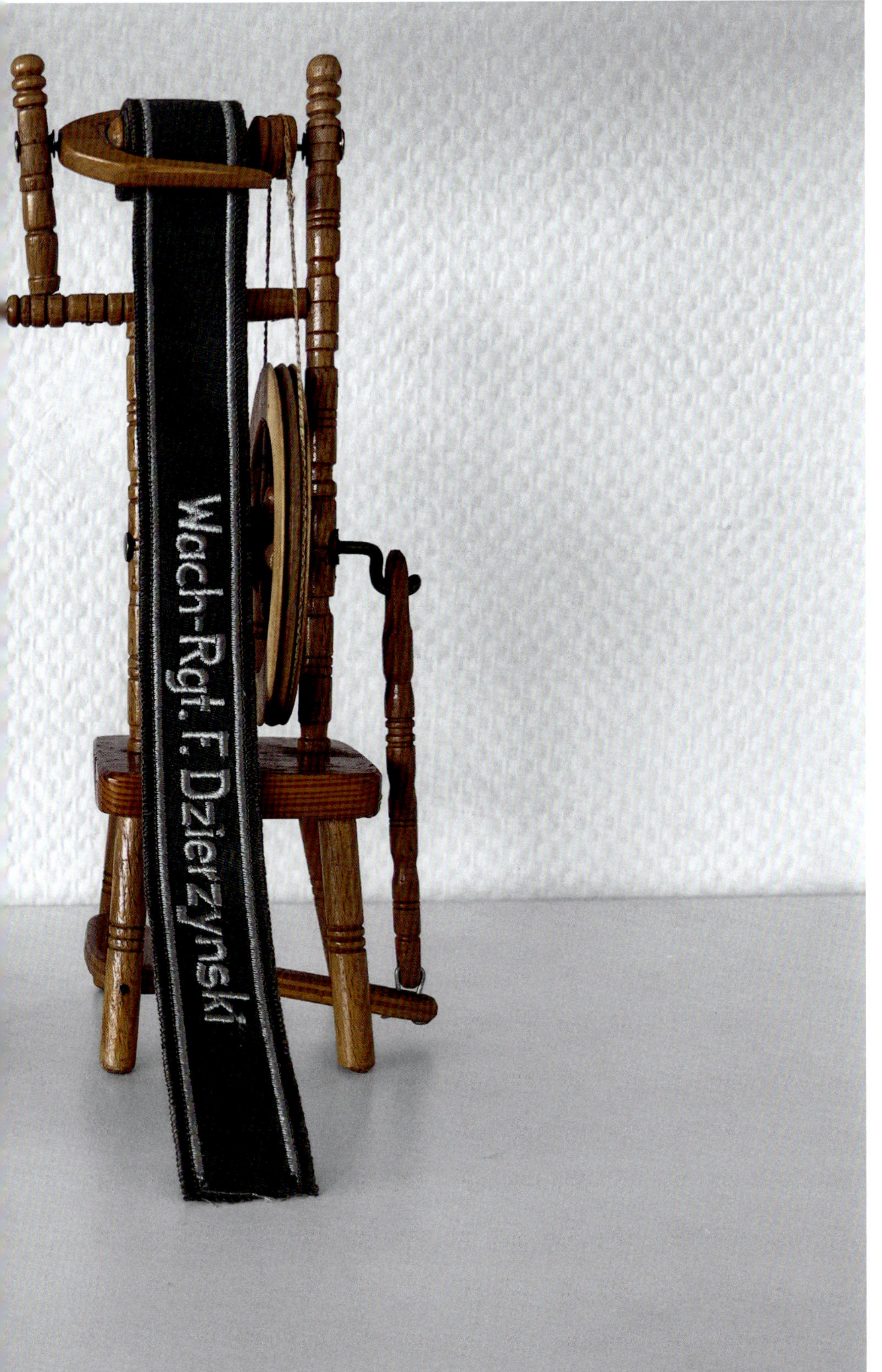
Wach-Rgt. F. Dzierzynski

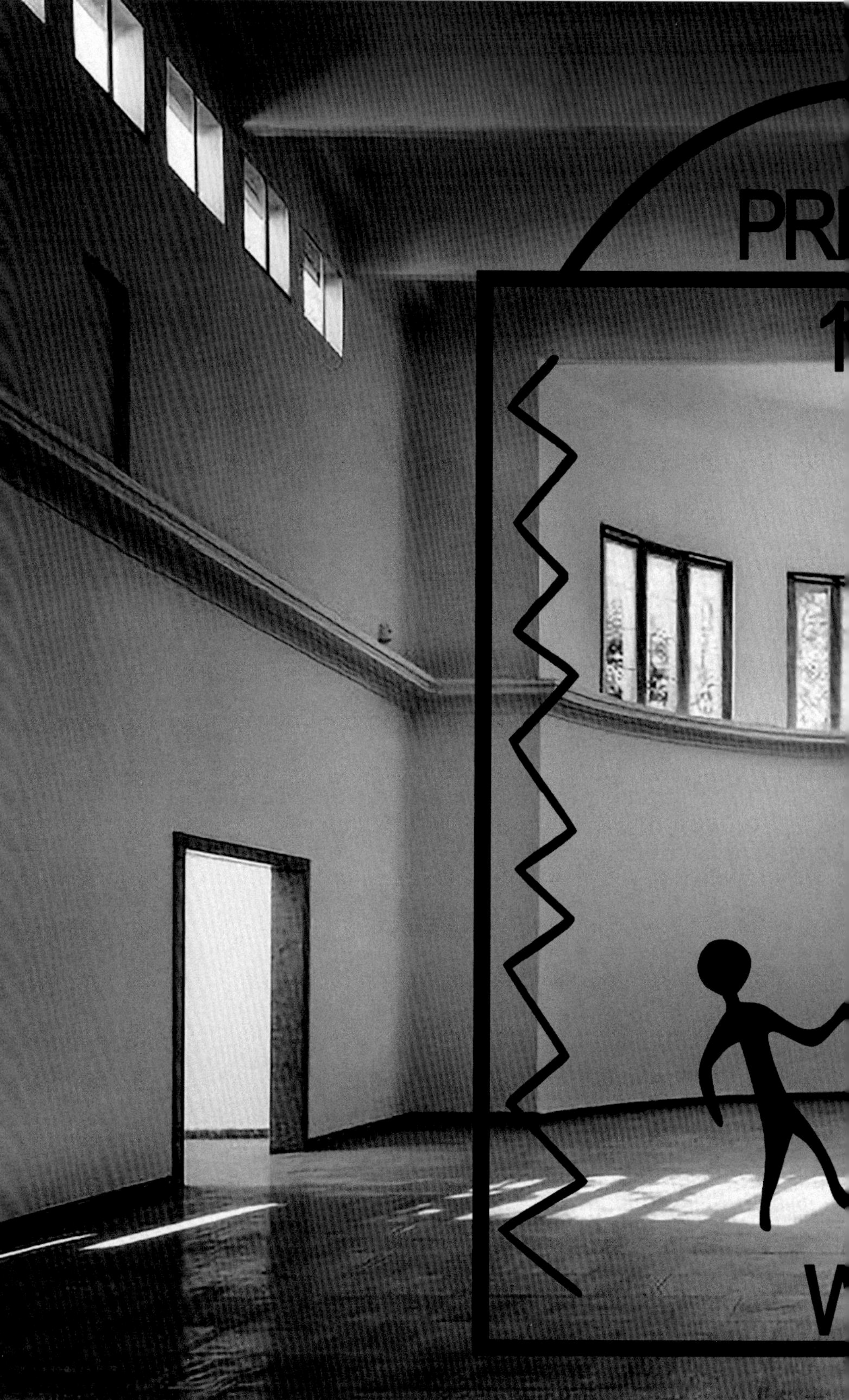

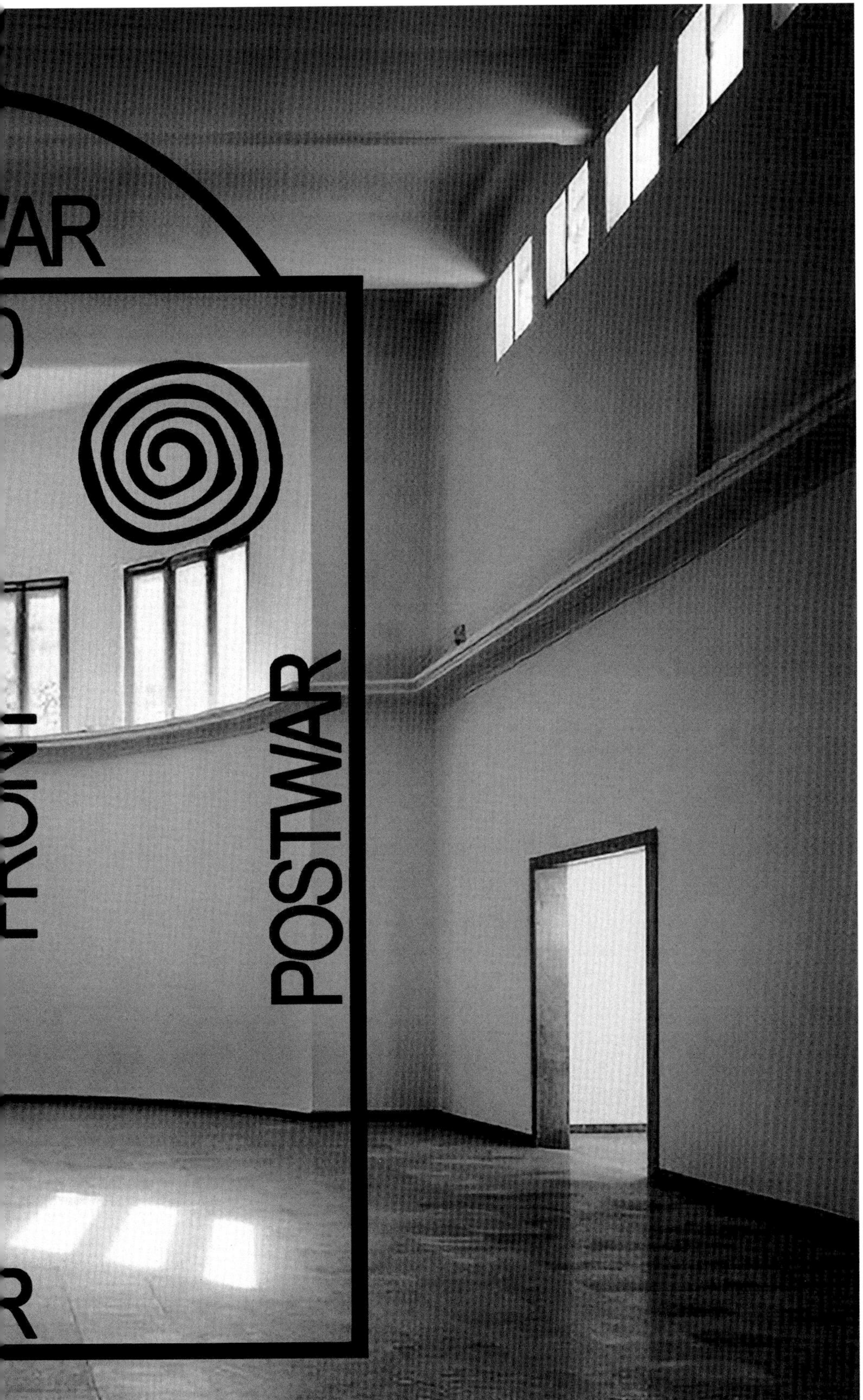
POSTWAR

Deutsche Akademie der Künste
-Der Präsident-

Berlin, den 8. Oktober 1956
Na/Schr.

1

Betrifft: Verhandlungen in Venedig wegen Teilnahme der Künstler der DDR an der nächsten Biennale 1958.

Vorbemerkung: Die Biennale findet seit 1895 regelmässig jedes 2. Jahr in Venedig statt. Auf der letzten Bienn[ale] waren 50 Nationen vertreten (darunter die SU) u[nd] bis auf Ungarn und Volkschina alle Volksdemokra[-] tien. Auf dem Gelände der Biennale befinden sic[h] die Pavillons bzw. Häuser der Nationen, die auf diesen errichtet wurden und ihnen gehören. Das grosse Gebäude "Deutschland" wurde nach 1945 ausschliesslich von der Bundesrepublik in Anspruch genommen, die von der italienischen Regierung ja als Nachfolgerin des ehemaligen Deutschen Reiches betrachtet wird.

Durch Telegrammwechsel war eine Besprechung zwischen mir und

den Verantwortlichen der [...]

Minister vorgelegen 16.10. [illegible]

14

DEUTSCHE AKADEMIE DER KÜNSTE

Berlin N 4, Robert-Koch-Platz 7 · Telefon: Sammelnummer 42 53 11

DER PRÄSIDENT

Berlin, den 8. Oktobe 1956
Na/Schr.

An die
Regierung der Deutschen
Demokratischen Republik
Ministerium für Kultur
Herrn Minister
Dr.h.c. Johannes R. Becher

Berlin C 2
Molkenmarkt 1-3

Abt

Ministerium für Kultur
Sekretariat des Ministers
Eing. 9. OKT. 1956
2200

Lieber Hans!

Hier ein kurzer Bericht über meine Verhandlungen wegen unserer Beteiligung an der Biennale in Venedig. Ich glaube, meine Reise hat sich gelohnt.

Herzliche Grüsse

Otto Nagel

(Professor Otto Nagel)

Anlage:
1 Bericht

(142) B 27846/56 1,5

Wir kamen zu folgender Vereinbarung:
Das Präsidium der Biennale empfiehlt der Vertretung der Bundesrepublik, sich mit uns an den Tisch zu setzen. Ich soll für die Deutsche Akademie der Künste mit einem entsprechenden Vorschlag an die Kommissare der Deutschen Abteilung herantreten.

Von mir wurden folgende Möglichkeiten für eine solche Verhandlung in Betracht gezogen:

1.) Bildung eines gemeinsamen Kommissariats für die Deutsche Abteilung. Gemeinsame Durchführung der Deutschen Ausstellung.

2.) Einen 1. und einen 2. Kommissar (wobei man über die Verteilung reden kann) und Einräumung von Platz im Deutschen Pavillon für die Künstler der Deutschen Demokratischen Republik.
Auswahl der Werke auf beiden Seiten selbstverantwortlich.

3.) Frage von mir: "Ob man uns, wenn es nicht zu einer Verständigung kommt, Platz zur Verfügung stellen würde für die Errichtung eines eigenen Pavillons der Deutschen Demokratischen Republik?"
Demgegenüber ein Vorschlag von italienischer Seite:

Eine Gastausstellung in der Italienischen Abteilung.

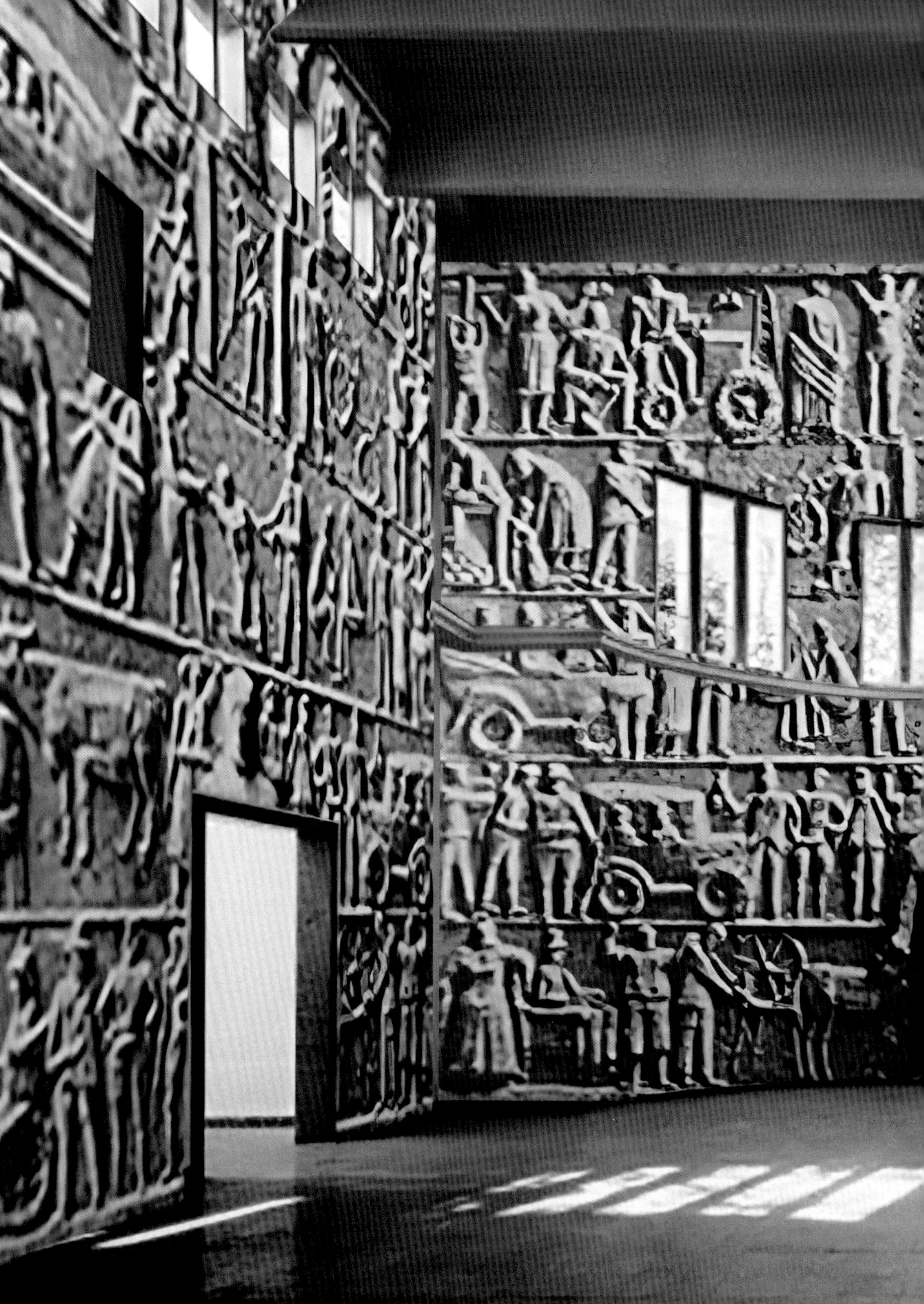

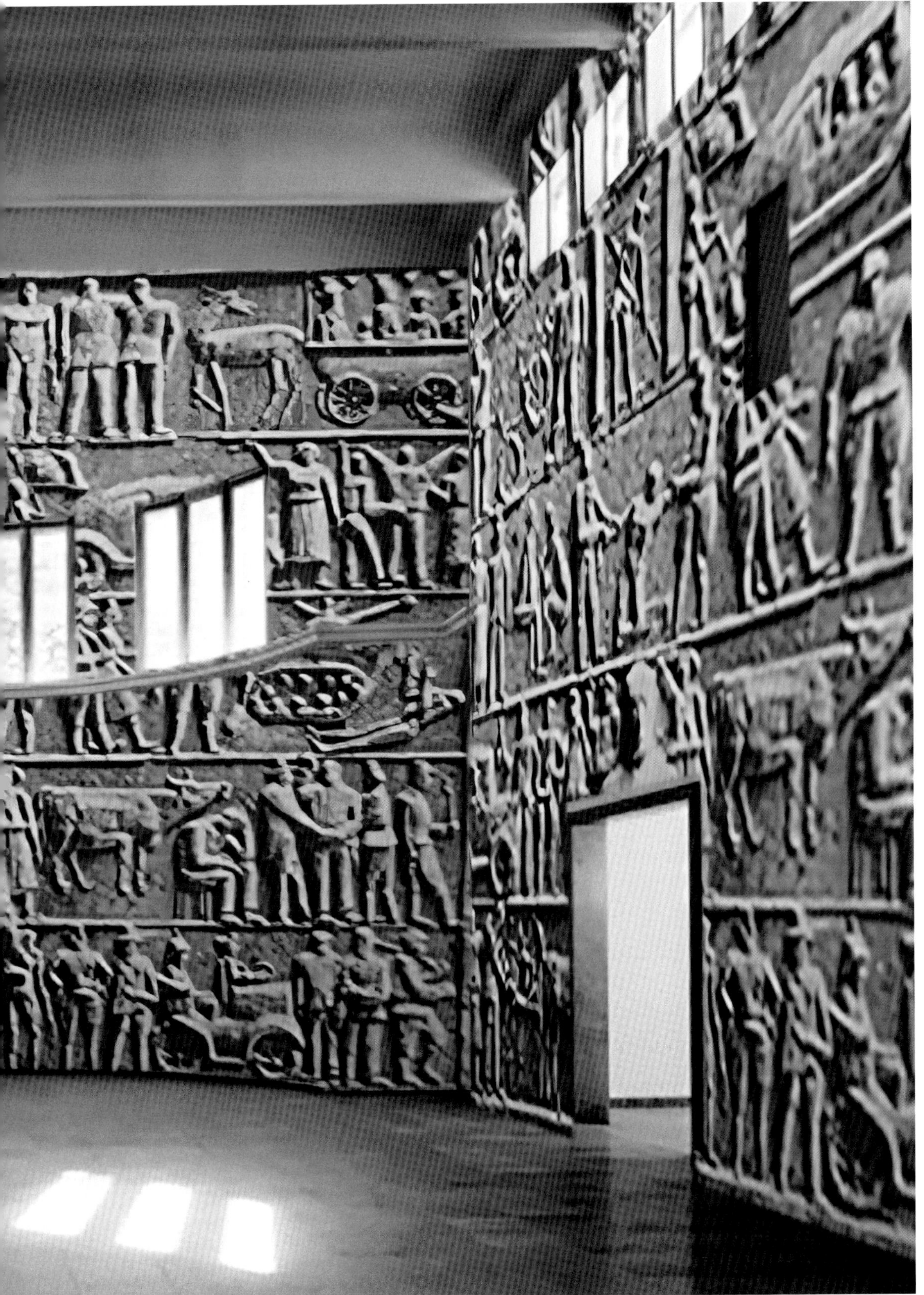

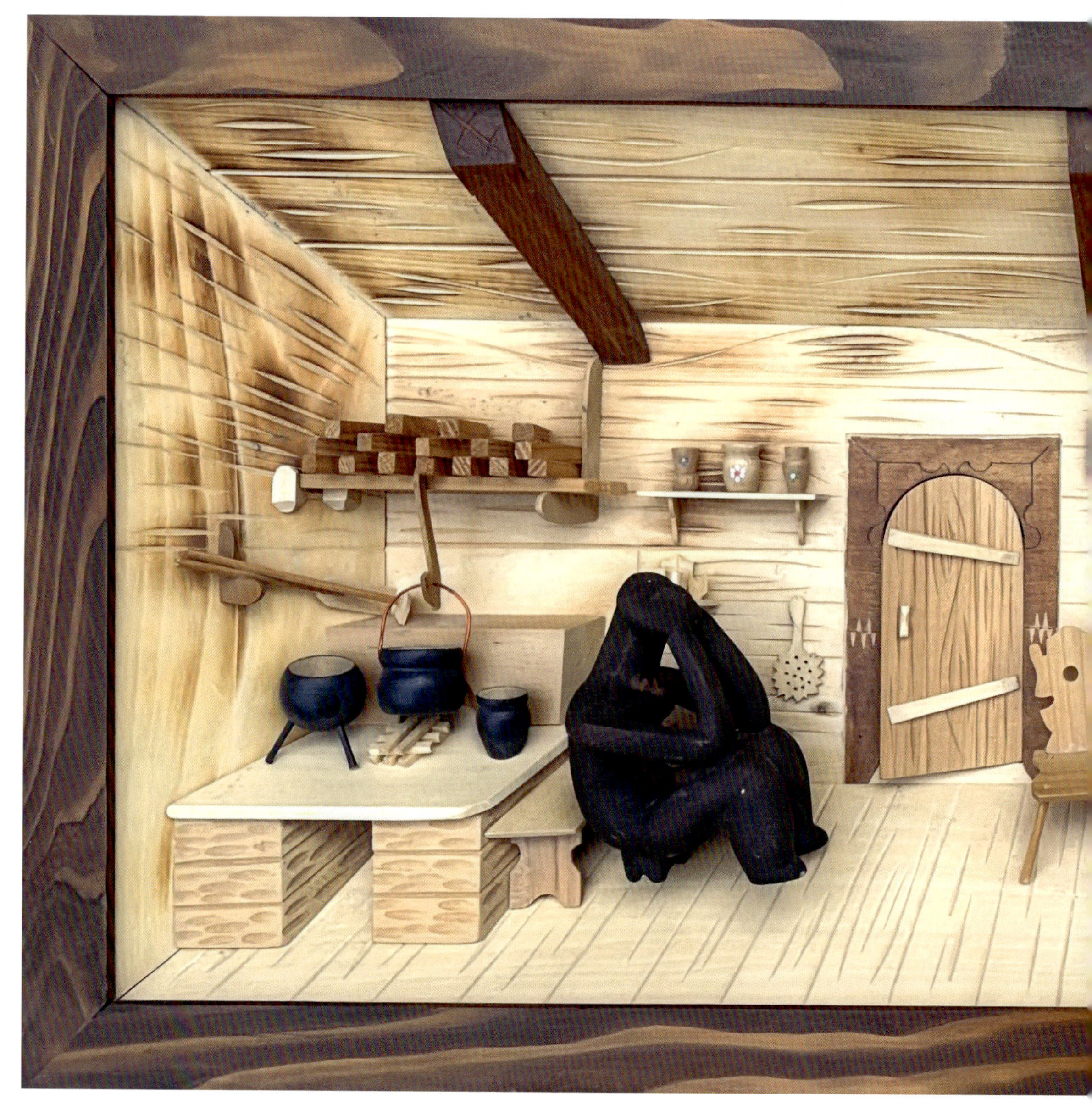

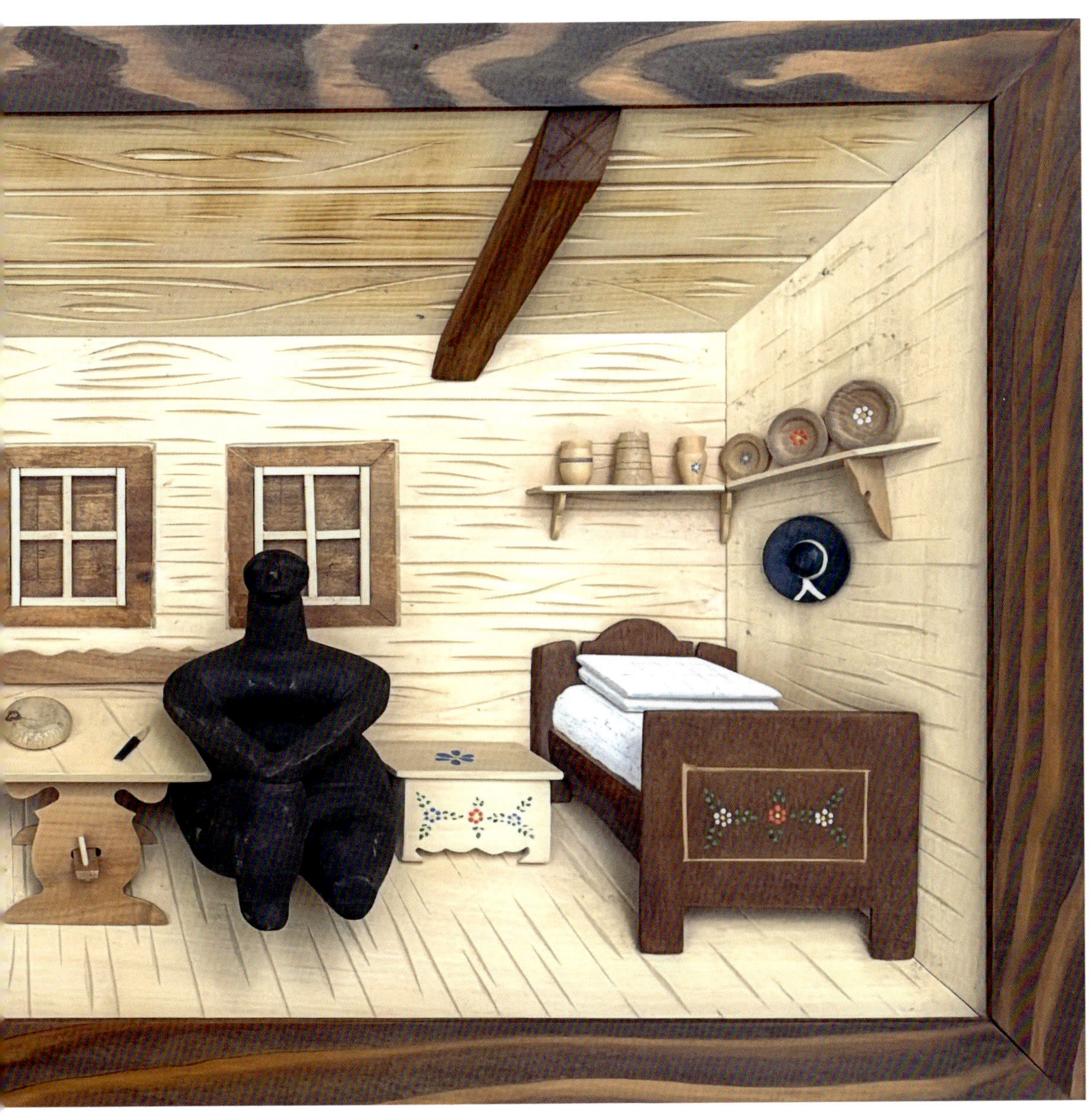

GEHRENSEEESTRASSE, A CHRONICLE/
GEHRENSEEESTRASSE, EINE CHRONIK

Sung Tieu

The housing estate on Gehrenseestrasse in Berlin-Alt-Hohenschönhausen, in ruins today, was once one of the largest residential complexes for foreign contract workers of the German Democratic Republic. From 1994 to 1997, it was also the home of the artist Sung Tieu and her mother. The following chronicle traces the history of the residential complex from 1970 to the present and documents its profound transformation.

1970

Falkenberger Strasse, renamed Gehrenseestrasse in 1980, was located in Hohenschönhausen, a northern district of East Berlin on the outskirts of the capital of the German Democratic Republic (GDR, 1949–1990). On the northern side of the street was a large area used for agriculture.

At the time, the entire GDR was still experiencing a severe housing shortage, caused by the destruction of World War II and reparations payments. The situation was particularly tense in East Berlin: the renovation of old building stock was considered technically complex and nearly impossible to finance.

For the roughly 17 million citizens of the GDR, this meant the housing supply was inadequate in terms of availability, size, location, and amenities. The problem this posed increased the political pressure to initiate new large-scale housing construction projects.

In response to the ongoing housing shortage, the Eighth Congress of the Socialist Unity Party of Germany (SED), under the new Secretary General Erich Honecker, adopted a comprehensive housing construction program in line with the newly proclaimed "unity of economic and social policy," marking a departure from the government's earlier focus on the expansion of East German industry alone. The declared goal was to eliminate the housing shortage by 1990.

To achieve this ambitious target, state housing policy prioritized the rapid and large-scale construction of housing estates using industrialized, prefabricated methods (Plattenbau). These buildings consisted of large prefabricated concrete panels for walls and ceilings, significantly reducing the required materials, construction time, and labor. Although housing estates built in this way had already been constructed since 1958, the program now expanded their production dramatically: by 1990, around 1.5 million units would be completed, most of them in newly built large-scale housing estates on the urban periphery. These new buildings epitomized the promise of socialist modernization.

1973

As part of the housing construction program, the SED decided to develop Berlin's eastern outskirts. The new district of Marzahn was slated to be built by 1985; at the same time, around 30,000 new apartments were planned for Hohenschönhausen. These projects fundamentally transformed the previously rural surroundings of Berlin. The later Gehrenseestrasse estate was also part of these large-scale urban development projects.

1975

For the construction of the new residential areas, workers were mobilized from across the entire GDR. The newly planned blocks along what later became Gehrenseestrasse were initially conceived as residential dorms to accommodate these workers.

The site was planned to consist of nine six-story apartment blocks. Presumably, the dormitory floor plans were based on army barracks designs. The complex was designed to include around 1,000 rooms, with three to four people assigned to each room, which measured a little over sixteen square meters. Kitchens and bathroom facilities were conceived as communal areas on each floor, while the design did not provide dedicated community spaces for recreation and leisure.

1977

The construction phase began under the management of HAG Komplexer Wohnungsbau, commissioned by the "Magistrate of Berlin, Capital of the GDR" (HAG is the acronym for "Hauptauftraggeber" or main contracting authority). The main contractor appointed for the project was the VEB Housing Construction Combine Neubrandenburg (a VEB, or "Volkseigener Betrieb," was a state-run, people-owned enterprise in the GDR). The completed apartment blocks would later come under the management of the Workers' Housing Administration on behalf of the "Magistrate of Berlin."

1978

The first construction workers of the Neubrandenburg Housing Construction Combine moved into the now-completed dormitory rooms, while the necessary utility lines for electricity, sewage, and telephone service were still being installed. From the late 1960s onward, despite a near-100% employment rate, the GDR faced a growing shortage of skilled workers. To combat this, the government concluded agreements with various so-called "socialist brother states" to send foreign workers for training and fixed-term employment to the GDR. The first such contracts were signed with Poland (1963), Hungary (1967), and Algeria (1974). In 1978, a further agreement was signed with Cuba, which formed the basis for what would become an influx of approximately 25,000 Cuban citizens to the GDR by 1989. These workers were typically housed either within or in close vicinity of the factory premises where they worked, which were often separated from the residential areas where East Germans lived. From 1982 onward, Cuban contract workers would also occupy rooms in the housing complex on Gehrenseestrasse.

1979

The construction phase of the residential complex on Gehrenseestrasse was completed.

In February 1979, the GDR government also signed a "Treaty of Friendship and Cooperation" with the People's Republic of Mozambique. As part of this agreement, the first contract workers were sent to the country. By 1989, nearly 20,000 Mozambican citizens had arrived in the GDR, some of whom later moved into the dormitories on Gehrenseestrasse.

1980

In April 1980, the GDR signed the most extensive and politically significant bilateral agreements of its kind to date with the Socialist Republic of Vietnam to regulate "the training and temporary employment of Vietnamese workers in GDR factories." By 1989, around 60,000–70,000 Vietnamese workers had arrived in the GDR, constituting the largest population of foreign workers in the country; a considerable number of them were housed on Gehrenseestrasse from 1982 onward. Similar agreements were later concluded with other socialist "brother countries," including Mongolia (1982), Angola (1985), China, and North Korea (1986).

The bilateral agreement between the countries regulated in detail the type and duration of employment, wages, social benefits, and residency conditions of the workers. Before relocating to the GDR, contract workers would undergo medical examinations in their countries of origin, so-called "fitness examinations," to assess their suitability for work. After arriving in the GDR, they were also required to undergo further health examinations, which often intruded upon their privacy and in some cases were documented by the Stasi (Ministry for State Security). From 1985 onward, these examinations were also expanded to include testing for HIV.

Wage agreements included a basic salary of approximately 600 DDR marks, a daily separation reimbursement of four marks, and a clothing allowance depending on the country of origin. Vietnamese workers were also required to pay twelve percent of their earnings to the Vietnamese state, while personal money transfers and goods shipments home were subject to restrictions from 1989 onward.

Simultaneously, educational and training opportunities were limited, with German language courses usually lasting only a few months and shortened to about one month from 1987 onward. Vietnamese workers were employed in nearly 1,000 factories across the GDR, primarily in light and heavy industry and mechanical engineering, often assigned to jobs that were considered undesirable for GDR citizens.

1982

Most of the construction workers had moved out of the dormitories on Gehrenseestrasse. The buildings were now primarily occupied by contract workers, the majority from Vietnam, and fewer from Cuba, Angola, and Mozambique. The complex would become one of the largest housing complexes for contract workers in the GDR.

Living conditions in the dormitories were regulated by strict rules and surveillance. Contractually, each individual was allocated approximately five square meters of living space. The rooms were sparsely furnished with a bed, bedside table, chair, and basic household items. Men and women were generally housed separately. According to the agreement, the rent for each contract worker should not exceed thirty marks per month. In practice, however, living conditions were often below par, as the rooms offered little to no privacy and were frequently overcrowded, while bathroom and kitchen facilities proved inadequate—in some cases a single cooking area served fifty people, and the required beds, tables, and wardrobes barely fit into many of the rooms.

Guards monitored the housing blocks, and a curfew regulated nighttime hours from 10 p.m. to 7 a.m. Rooms were regularly inspected by staff from the district's Department of the Interior as well as by group leaders, who often came from the respective embassies of the workers' home countries. These leaders acted as intermediaries between the workers and the factory and dormitory managements and kept tabs on the laborers' discipline and work ethic.

Social integration was neither intended nor desired. Contact with the East German population was monitored and often forestalled. Couples were usually assigned to different cities or factories. Marriages to East German citizens were prevented wherever possible. Until 1987, pregnancy usually led to job loss and repatriation or was terminated by forced abortion.

1987

Sung Tieu's father, Tiêu Dũng Tiến, arrived in Freital near Dresden as a 27-year-old Vietnamese contract worker, where he began working at the VEB Freital stainless steel plant (Edelstahlwerk Freital).

His arrival coincided with a period in which the GDR increasingly recruited labor from Vietnam in order to support an anticipated leap in productivity and to address the ongoing labor shortage. In this year alone, around 50,000 additional Vietnamese workers arrived in the GDR—by far the largest influx. As the number of contract workers increased, strict supervision in the dormitories gradually began to loosen. During this period, informal means of generating income emerged to supplement the low wages, such as the production and sale of denim goods, which were highly sought after in the GDR's shortage economy.

1989

In the GDR's final year, another 9,000 Vietnamese contract workers arrived in the country.

The local elections held in May were overshadowed by widespread, proven election fraud, which further fueled public discontent. Only two months earlier, the government had decided that foreigners living in the GDR should have the right to vote and run for office in local elections—a reform that was never realized.

Over the summer, thousands of GDR citizens fled to the West via the West German embassies in Prague and Warsaw, while opposition and civil rights groups formed to demand democratic reform, freedom of expression, and an end to the SED's claim to power. The Peaceful Revolution reached its peak in October with the Monday Demonstrations in Leipzig, where tens of thousands of people took to the streets.

On November 9, the Berlin Wall fell and the inner-German border was opened for GDR citizens. Initially the unintended result of a new travel regulation announced by the SED leadership, the event soon came to signal the end of the GDR. Shortly after, the People's Chamber removed the SED's leading role from the constitution, while the Central Round Table began its work.

The opening of the borders marked a profound turning point for the people of East Germany. While the majority of the population experienced the moment as liberation, the situation for many contract workers was increasingly overshadowed by existential fear, insecurity, and discrimination.

1990

The Treuhand privatization agency was established on March 1 to manage East German state-owned enterprises. Its main task was to liquidate large state-owned conglomerates and transform their successor companies into limited liability corporations.

On March 18, the GDR's last government was elected, led by East CDU (the Christian Democratic Union party), providing democratic legitimacy for the path to German reunification.

The rapid transition to a market economy triggered severe economic disruptions. Many East German factories reduced their workforce, leading to growing competition between local workers and foreign contract workers, who increasingly found themselves in precarious circumstances. Although many employment contracts formally remained valid—some until 1995—contract workers were nevertheless frequently unlawfully dismissed. At the same time, numerous state-run dormitories were closed due to rising operational costs. The Gehrenseestrasse complex, however, remained in operation, initially under the municipal Arbeiterwohnheimverwaltung (AWHV). In August 1990, the organization was privatized and renamed ARWOGE. Following the withdrawal of municipal funding, rents rose sharply: by 1992, single rooms cost around 280 Deutsche marks, while larger rooms ranged from 450 to 1,070 Deutsche marks by 2002.

In response to the precarious situation of foreign contract workers, the first support initiatives and associations were founded in Hohenschönhausen. In the following years, many of these used the premises on Gehrenseestrasse for their activities, promoting intercultural exchange and offering German courses, leisure programs, and legal and psychological support.

During this period, Diedrich Wulfert served as Commissioner for Foreigners in Hohenschönhausen until 1994.

On May 18, East and West Germany signed their first State Treaty, which brought the monetary, economic, and social union into effect on July 1. The Deutsche mark was introduced in the East, triggering profound economic restructuring: prices, wages, and pensions were recalculated, subsidies were reduced, and many East German companies suddenly lost their competitive standing.

On June 13, the East German government changed the contract workers' employment status. This measure retroactively legalized the premature layoffs that had occurred in the preceding months. The new regulations allowed companies to carry out early dismissals for economic reasons, resulting in the majority of contract workers losing their employment. By the end of 1990, for instance, around 81 percent of the Mozambican contract workers had lost their jobs. Of the approximately 4,600 Vietnamese workers in Berlin's eastern districts, around 3,800—more than 80 percent—were unemployed. In addition, the obligation to provide company-run dormitories was abolished.

On June 17, the Treuhand agency was legally restructured. In addition to managing the companies, its specific task was now to prepare them for sale to private investors.

At the same time, an increasing number of asylum seekers from different countries moved into Gehrenseestrasse. During the second half of the year, many former contract workers left the country. To encourage this, an incentive was introduced in the form of a "one-time compensation payment" of 3,000 Deutsche marks, along with a plane ticket to their respective home countries. These payments were formally to be covered by the GDR enterprises themselves, many of which were already being liquidated. In practice, the compensation was often organized by local authorities and paid shortly before departure. Even so, many former contract workers reported that the payments were delayed, incomplete, or never made at all.

Other former contract workers chose to remain in East Germany, often with little legal protection, while some left the still-existing GDR for the Federal Republic of Germany (FRG) to apply for asylum there. At this time, only around 28,000 contract workers remained in the country, the majority of them from Vietnam.

On October 3, the Unification Treaty between East and West Germany came into force, formalizing Germany's reunification. Berlin became the capital of the unified country, although it would take until 1999 for most of the federal government to relocate from Bonn to Berlin.

For many Vietnamese residents, life in Germany during this period was marked by growing fear. Repeated brutal attacks by neo-Nazis created a deep sense of insecurity among many of those affected.

1991

The new Aliens Act (Ausländergesetz, AuslG) came into force on January 1, introducing uniform nationwide regulations for foreign residents. Under Section 5, the former contract workers' previous residence rights were converted into limited permits, offering no clear path to permanent residence once their employment contracts ended. Most received only a temporary suspension of deportation (Duldung), valid solely in the five new federal states (former East Germany).

Unlike migrant workers in the Federal Republic of Germany, former contract workers of the GDR were not given a prospect of permanent residence, as their right to remain became invalid upon the termination of their original employment contracts.

Transitioning to self-employment proved equally difficult, as business licenses were frequently denied. Limited German language skills and unrecognized professional qualifications further restricted access to the labor market, especially since any employment had to be approved by the local employment office.

For this reason, many sought new opportunities in the informal labor market, particularly in retail: they opened snack bars, flower shops, and textile stores, or worked in markets, cleaning companies, and restaurants, often without official authorization.

During this period, a trading center emerged at Rhinstrasse 100 in Berlin-Lichtenberg, where Vietnamese wholesalers distributed goods to street vendors in an attempt to establish greater economic independence.

In the same year, ethnic German repatriates from the countries of the former Eastern Bloc also moved into the Gehrenseestrasse complex. Unlike former contract workers, they were granted German citizenship upon arrival and received access to language courses and government support. At the same time, Jewish quota refugees from the former Soviet Union were accommodated in the complex under a special immigration status that granted residence but not automatic citizenship.

In addition, a significant number of former contract workers and other migrants continued to live in the complex, including around 212 Vietnamese, 160 Mozambicans, 103 Poles, and 165 residents of other nationalities. After earlier access restrictions were lifted, overcrowding increased significantly, with some rooms accommodating up to ten people.

Within far-right circles, the concept of "nationally liberated zones" gained increasing traction and began to influence wider public discourse. In the same period, a Vietnamese resident was attacked in front of his apartment on Gehrenseestrasse, an early manifestation of the escalating racist violence in Berlin.

Of the approximately 90,000 contract workers who had been employed in the GDR, only around 6,670 remained in employment by the end of 1991.

1992

Tieu and her mother, Vũ Thị Hạnh, emigrated from Vietnam to Germany. After short stays in Halle and Leipzig, they moved to Freital near Dresden to join Tieu's father. Tieu attended kindergarten there.

That same year, Vietnamese organizations and civic groups increasingly mobilized to demand residence rights for former contract workers. The Federation of Vietnamese People was founded in Berlin, and public demonstrations called for the right to remain in Germany. In March, the Federal Conference of Commissioners for Foreigners supported permanent residence and integration measures.

At the same time, racist violence escalated. On April 24, former Vietnamese contract worker Nguyễn Văn Tú was murdered by right-wing extremists on Brodowiner Ring in Berlin-Marzahn. He was one of the first known victims of far-right violence in Germany since reunification. His memorial march on May 3 intensified public demands for a right to remain. In June, around 500 people demonstrated at Alexanderplatz in support of residence permits for former contract workers, while the Foreigners' Committee of the Berlin House of Representatives endorsed efforts to grant them residence status.

Between August 22 and 26, far-right extremists carried out a pogrom on the so-called Sunflower House, a residential building for former Vietnamese contract workers in Rostock-Lichtenhagen that also housed the Central Reception Center for Asylum Seekers (ZASt). German residents of the surrounding housing estate and neo-Nazis who had traveled to the area formed a mob that the police allowed to act largely unchecked for several days.

Meanwhile in Berlin, around 500 right-wing extremists intended to attack Gehrenseestrasse in September, but local residents intervened and police were able to prevent it before it could take place.

During this same period, an arson attack was carried out on another housing complex on Zingsterstrasse on the outskirts of Hohenschönhausen, in which the majority of tenants were Vietnamese. A tram track worker noticed black smoke billowing out of the building's entrance and alerted the fire department and police. Soot blackened all six floors of the stairwell, although the spread of a larger fire was successfully contained.

Meanwhile, unknown perpetrators carried out an arson attack on the nearby Wurzel youth club, which was under the influence of right-wing extremism. Antifascist groups justified the attack, as the club served as a meeting place for skinheads.

Starting in September, the SOMAG housing association, a subsidiary of ARWOGE, organized refugee accommodation on Gehrenseestrasse and took over the management of two of the nine apartment blocks.

Not far from Gehrenseestrasse, the relocated Central Reception Center for Asylum Seekers opened in Hohenschönhausen. Shortly afterward, right-wing extremist youths gathered outside the nearby residential buildings, chanting racist slogans.

On December 17, under pressure from numerous civic organizations, the federal and state governments instructed the interior ministers to find a solution for former contract workers. A temporary moratorium on deportations was introduced until April 30, 1993. This offered people a certain degree of protection from being returned to countries considered politically or economically unsafe.

1993

War refugees from Bosnia-Herzegovina also moved into the Gehrenseestrasse blocks, mostly on a temporary basis and under restricted conditions. At the same time, SOMAG hired a security firm to monitor the two apartment blocks under its management around the clock, with patrols later extended to other buildings. Amid rising tensions, Manuel T., a resident of Gehrenseestrasse and former contract worker from Mozambique, was seriously injured in a baseball bat attack by six right-wing extremist youths near the complex. In response to the increasingly precarious situation, several initiatives and community associations moved into the Gehrenseestrasse premises to provide support for residents.

At the same time, Vietnamese residents who relied on the sale of untaxed cigarettes as a means of subsistence came under increasing media scrutiny, leading to frequent police raids on the residential blocks. To combat "illegal" activities, the police established a special investigative unit for Gehrenseestrasse.

More broadly, the early 1990s saw a sharp rise in the number of asylum seekers in Germany, triggering intense public debate and growing calls to restrict the right to asylum. On May 26, 1993, Article 16 of the German Basic Law was amended and supplemented by the new Article 16a. This introduced the so-called "safe third country" rule and stipulated that a legal right to asylum would henceforth apply only to individuals persecuted on political grounds.

Nevertheless, on June 17, the interior ministers of the new federal states, in coordination with the Federal Minister of the Interior, agreed on a right-to-remain regulation for former contract workers from Vietnam and Mozambique.

With simultaneous reforms to asylum law, these residence permits, however, were limited to two years and tied to strict conditions: applicants had to demonstrate financial self-sufficiency and prove that they had not committed any criminal offenses. For many former contract workers, this prolonged their precarious circumstances, as their residency status remained insecure.

In response to this situation, the association Reistrommel e.V. was founded to provide counseling, primarily for Vietnamese residents in the eastern districts of Berlin. During the following years, the organization focused particularly on tenancy rights in the ARWOGE housing complexes and played an important role in the struggle for the rights of former contract workers to remain in the country.

Shortly thereafter, the general moratorium on deportations for former contract workers, introduced a few months earlier in 1993, expired.

1994

After her parents' separation, Tieu and her mother moved to the housing complex on Gehrenseestrasse where she attended a nearby elementary school while her mother worked first as an informal meat and fruit vendor, and later, on a food truck.

During this period, multiple cases of police violence against the Vietnamese population became public, including abuses that occurred at a police station in Bernau between March 1993 and June 1994, where several officers were accused of mistreating and torturing Vietnamese detainees. The officers involved were later suspended from duty, but no legal consequences followed.

Meanwhile, on Gehrenseestrasse, refugee and citizens' initiatives set up a symbolic election for migrants in Berlin. This drew attention to the lack of political participation available to the migrant community who lived, worked, and paid taxes in Germany, but were denied the right to vote. Migrants were called upon to symbolically cast their ballots on Gehrenseestrasse and at other designated locations.

During this period, the municipal housing associations ARWOGE (East Berlin) and ARWOBAU (West Berlin) merged under the name ARWOBAU.

1995

Large-scale police raids were carried out in the housing complexes of Hohenschönhausen with increasing frequency. As a crime prevention measure, the Berlin Senate discussed shutting down the residential buildings on Gehrenseestrasse, prompting concern among tenants.

To represent their interests, around 200 residents elected representatives who sought dialogue with the authorities and were able to ensure that the residential buildings remained open. However, two other housing complexes in Hohenschönhausen were forced to close.

When the temporary residence permits granted in 1993 expired, many former contract workers were once again faced with legal uncertainty. Calls grew louder to end discrimination against them, grant residence permits to long-term residents, and also to allow permits for individuals who have committed minor offenses.

In April, 22-year-old Thái Văn Hương was murdered on Gehrenseestrasse by a fellow Vietnamese, a case that remains unresolved. Homicides of this kind became increasingly frequent in the years that followed, with many cases going unreported due to distrust of the police among those involved.

As a consequence, residents of the Gehrenseestrasse housing complex were required to finance security surveillance themselves, with about one third of their rent going to private security services monitoring the premises. In July, after a year of negotiations, Germany and Vietnam signed a repatriation agreement for Vietnamese nationals living in Germany without legal residence status. The agreement provided for the gradual deportation of at least 40,000 Vietnamese citizens by 2000 and included 25 million Deutsche marks in German financial aid, as well as the release of previously frozen development aid.

Advocacy groups strongly criticized this repatriation agreement, which planned for the deportation of 2,500 Vietnamese nationals in the first year alone.

After the agreement came into effect, around 1,000 Vietnamese residents of Gehrenseestrasse faced the threat of immediate deportation.

Given the large number of Vietnamese residents in the complex, authorities conducted large-scale raids to identify individuals subject to deportation. Many residents began considering remaining in Germany without legal status.

Following the mass deportations, only about 22,500 former contract workers—roughly a quarter of the 90,000 contract workers from Vietnam, Angola, Mozambique, Cuba, and other countries—remained in the new federal states by the end of the year.

1997

On January 31, right-wing extremists brutally attacked Phan Văn Toản, a former contract worker, at the Fredersdorf S-Bahn station in Brandenburg, leaving him severely injured. He died in hospital three months later.

In 2020, civil society groups organized the first memorial rally, resulting in the founding of the Phan Văn Toản Memorial Initiative, which advocates for the creation of a public memorial in Fredersdorf.

Since the signing of the 1995 repatriation agreement, Germany had deported approximately 2,800 Vietnamese nationals without "legal" residence status.

After years of activism and legal struggles, the German Federal Government finally decided in November to grant former contract workers of East Germany the same legal status as migrant workers of West Germany.

Following the legal reform in 1997, earlier periods of residence in the GDR were retroactively credited, allowing former contract workers to obtain permanent residence permits, provided they could support themselves financially and had no criminal record.

A number of associations and initiatives, including Reistrommel e.V., played a significant role in pushing for this change. Now former contract workers were, for the first time, entitled to state welfare benefits and could look forward to a more stable long-term perspective in Germany.

Around the same time, Tieu and her mother moved from Gehrenseestrasse to a private flat in Berlin-Friedrichshain, where her mother began working as a factory worker at Larosé GmbH in Berlin-Grünau, a large-scale industrial laundry.

1998

In February, the war in Kosovo began.

Amid growing tensions surrounding migration and security, police conducted nighttime raids on Bosnian refugees in Gehrenseestrasse, despite their protected status, triggering fear, protests, and political criticism.

1999

In Berlin, as part of the federal distribution key, 220 displaced persons from Kosovo were admitted, around 100 of whom were housed in the SOMAG-managed apartment block on Gehrenseestrasse. Rooms with one to five beds were set up for them. They received medical examinations, meals, and residence permits that were initially valid for three months.

The war in Kosovo ended on June 10. Despite hopes for peace, the displaced persons from Kosovo living on Gehrenseestrasse remained wary, as they were severely traumatized and uncertain whether they would be able to return.

2001

On May 1, the far-right National Democratic Party of Germany (NPD) held a demonstration in Berlin-Hohenschönhausen under the slogan "Work for Germans First." Many of the displaced persons from Kosovo left the accommodations on Gehrenseestrasse and emigrated to other countries while ARWOBAU began the complete evacuation of all residents from the premises.

2003

After the last residents of Gehrenseestrasse received eviction notices, the residential complex stood vacant. Although ARWOBAU received a permit to demolish the site, the property was instead sold to a private buyer. Renovations were planned but never implemented. The complex would be resold several times over the following years.

2006

The school annex on the Gehrenseestrasse grounds was demolished.

2007

The Gehrenseestrasse lot was sold to an investor from Neuss in North Rhine-Westphalia, who planned to renovate the nine prefabricated concrete buildings and create a total of 625 apartments of varying sizes at affordable rents.

2008

The buildings on Gehrenseestrasse were gutted and all pipes, bathroom facilities, windows, and doors were removed. Since the property was privately owned, the Lichtenberg district office had little say in the buildings' reconstruction, removal, or future use. In the years that followed, the buildings increasingly fell into a state of ruin.

2010

The site remained unused, while the property changed owners several times.

2013

Two unhoused persons were found dead in the vacant buildings on Gehrenseestrasse. The cause of death remains unclear.

2015

The Syrian conflict, which began in 2011, escalated into a humanitarian catastrophe, forcing over six million people to flee by 2016. Together with asylum seekers from Iraq and Afghanistan, arrivals in the EU had reached unprecedented levels. The developments—widely referred to as the "refugee crisis"—exposed deep political divisions within the EU over the distribution of refugees. Germany faced major administrative and logistical challenges in accommodating around one million refugees, while the situation also intensified social polarization and racist violence. In 2015 alone, 528 attacks on refugee shelters were recorded, including 126 arson attacks, meaning a shelter went up in flames roughly every three days. On the adjacent grounds of Gehrenseestrasse, which were becoming increasingly dilapidated, an empty gymnasium was temporarily used to house refugees. Several racist attacks occurred on the premises.

During this period, Berlin's housing shortage worsened while real estate prices continued to rise. As a result, renewed interest emerged in the city's eastern outskirts and their prefabricated housing estates, which had long been neglected. The municipal housing company HOWOGE purchased over 1,000 apartments in the vicinity of Gehrenseestrasse, thus marking the beginning of a new phase of urban development.

2016

On the neighboring Gehrenseestrasse lot, next to the gymnasium, container housing was built to accommodate approximately 200 refugees, managed by the operator Albatros. For many refugees, moving from the gymnasium to the containers meant a significant improvement in their living conditions.

The northeastern annex of the former residential complex was demolished.

The Gehrenseestrasse site, covering over six hectares, was acquired by real estate service provider Accentro, which planned the construction of 675 apartments with a total of over 40,000 square meters of living space. The renovation and remarketing of the vacant buildings was scheduled to begin in 2017.

2018

Instead of renovating the buildings on Gehrenseestrasse, Accentro sold the property to the Berlin-based investor group Belle Époque, which still owns the site today.

In April, a new development concept was presented. Belle Époque, in partnership with HOWOGE, planned construction on a new 6.3-hectare urban quarter with around 2,200 apartments. While Belle Époque intended to develop 80% of the site, HOWOGE was to take on the remaining 20%.

Initiated by both partners, the new project marked a shift in approach: rather than renovating the former workers' dormitories, the project now called for demolition and complete urban redevelopment. The plan envisioned a mix of rentals and owner-occupied apartments in multi-story buildings, ranging from one- to five-room units, including about 137 state-subsidized apartments.

Eight planning teams participated in the competition. After several rounds of workshops, two finalists emerged. The architecture office MLA+/Studio M³ won first place and was commissioned to create the basis for the "Gehrensee Courts" master plan.

2019

Belle Époque and HOWOGE requested that the district office discontinue the existing planning procedures (development plan 11-95 VE) and initiate the "Gehrensee-Courts" master plan, which was intended to better address the needs of the local population and current urban planning requirements.

2020

The new planning procedure (11-165) officially began. To mark the occasion, the Belle Époque investment group held a public information event.

2021

A district council resolution stipulated that the development plans could only proceed once healthy living conditions and sufficient open space were ensured. An urban planning report recommended significantly reducing the building volume, ultimately limiting the project to around 1,000 apartments. To meet these requirements, extensive studies on daylight access, mobility, and school capacity were carried out.

For the interim period before demolition, the Gehrenseestrasse complex was opened for a temporary graffiti art project. In collaboration with *Street Art Berlin*, the site was intended to become a tourist attraction, with the possibility of integrating selected artworks into future development.

2023

With the intervention of the Senate Commission, the remaining disagreements between the developers and the district office were resolved and a final agreement was reached regarding the permissible building volume.

From the summer of 2023 through 2025, Sung Tieu would regularly lead informal weekend walking tours of the Gehrenseestrasse site, guiding visitors through the former workers' dormitory complex and recounting its layered history of migration, housing, and political change.

2025

As part of the exhibition *Sung Tieu – 1992, 2025* at Kunst-Werke, KW Institute for Contemporary Art in Berlin-Mitte, Sung Tieu and Tamara Hentschel organized a five-hour bus tour through Berlin-Marzahn and Lichtenberg. The route included the former right-wing youth club Wurzel and Brodowiner Ring, where Nguyễn Văn Tú was murdered in 1992, as well as the Gehrenseestrasse residential complex. By the end of 2025, Sung Tieu had brought over 1,000 visitors to Gehrenseestrasse as part of a broader effort to publicly confront and reflect on the site's history.

The container accommodations next to the ruins on Gehrenseestrasse were closed and remained unused.

The company Bairsoft was granted permission to use the vacant buildings and surrounding outdoor areas as an airsoft field, where participants engaged in simulated combat games using replica firearms that shoot small plastic pellets. In the summer, the Charlottenburg District Court initiated preliminary insolvency proceedings against several companies belonging to the Berlin-based project development group Belle Époque, including Belle Époque Quartier Gehrenseestrasse GmbH. The bankruptcy application, based on an incorrect tax assessment, was withdrawn at the end of July. However, it remains unclear when and in what form the construction project would continue.

After an initial delay, construction of the "Quartier Gehrenseestrasse" was now scheduled to begin in October 2028, with completion planned for September 2032. This marked the end Bairsoft's interim use of the site.

2026

In early March, demolition begins in the eastern section of the Gehrenseestrasse complex. The partial demolition of the nine prefabricated concrete blocks will make way for the construction of a school foreseen in the development plan.

As the concrete slab buildings disappear, Sung Tieu re-erects the housing complex as a large-scale mosaic, reconstructing its present condition at full scale. Depicting the ruinous state of her former home, the housing complex on Berlin's Gehrenseestrasse occupies the façade of the German Pavilion of the 61st Venice Biennale.

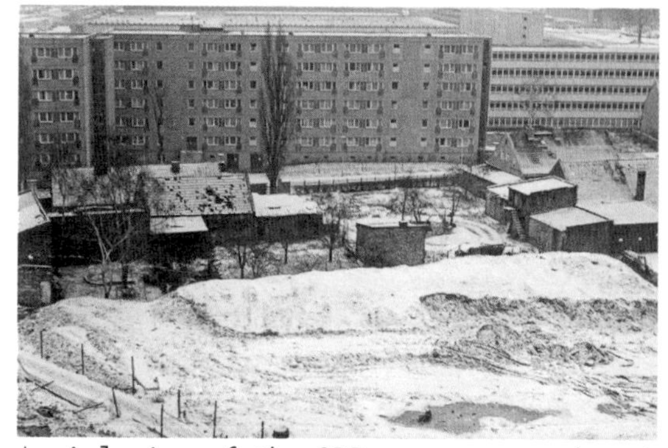

Aerial view of the GDR contract workers' housing complex "Gehrenseestrasse", formerly Falkenberger Strasse, in Berlin-Alt-Hohenschönhausen right after the completion, circa 1979./
Luftansicht auf das DDR-Vertragsarbeiter*innenwohnheim „Objekt Gehrensee-straße", ehemals Falkenberger Straße, in Berlin-Alt-Hohenschönhausen unmittelbar nach der Fertigstellung, circa 1979.

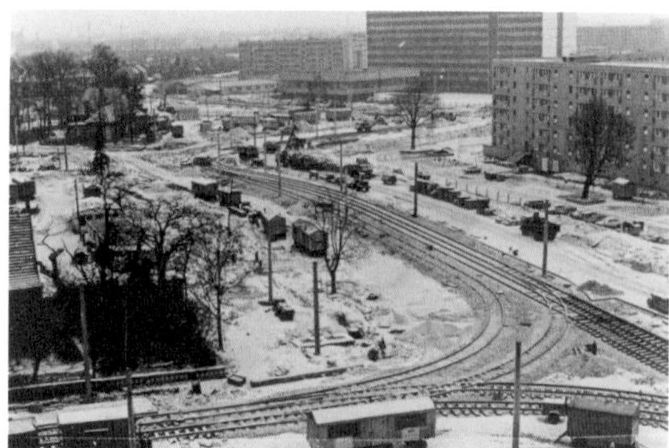

View of the GDR contract workers' housing complex "Gehrenseestrasse", seen from Hauptstrasse, circa 1980./
Blick auf das DDR-Vertragsarbeiter*innenwohnheim „Objekt Gehrenseestraße" von der Hauptstraße aus, circa 1980.

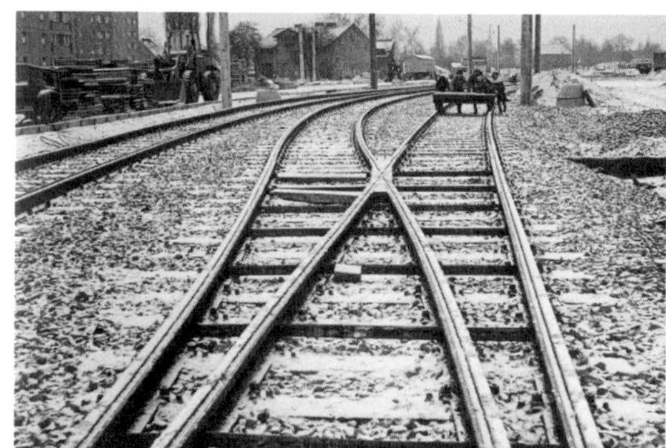

Track laying for the new tram line on Rhinstrasse, with the GDR contract workers' housing complex visible nearby, 1984./
Gleisbauarbeiten für die neue Straßenbahnverbindung an der Rhinstraße; im Hintergrund die DDR-Vertragsarbeiter*innenwohnheime, 1984.

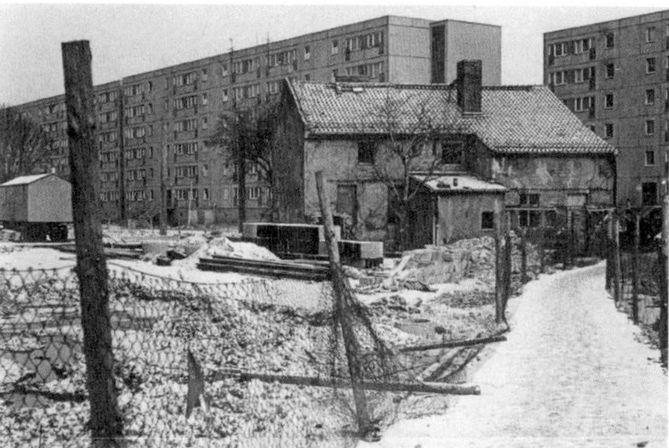

View of the GDR contract workers' housing complex and a bakery in a rural building, 1984./
Blick auf das DDR-Vertragsarbeiter*innenwohnheim und ihre Nebengebäude, unter anderem eine Bäckerei, 1984.

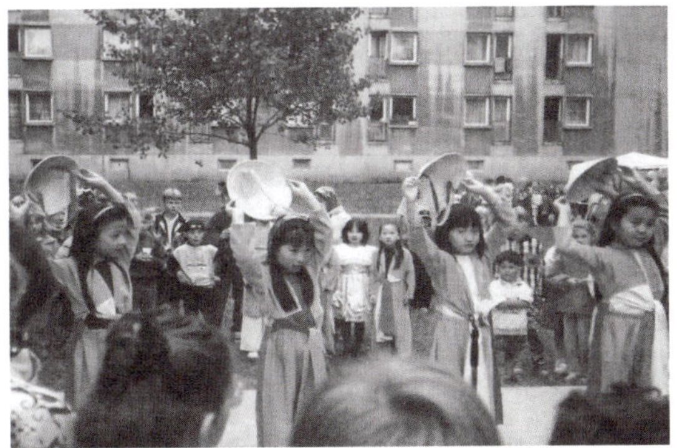
Children's celebration at the Gehrensee-strasse housing complex, circa 1991./
Kinderfest in der Wohnsiedlung Gehren-seestraße, circa 1991.

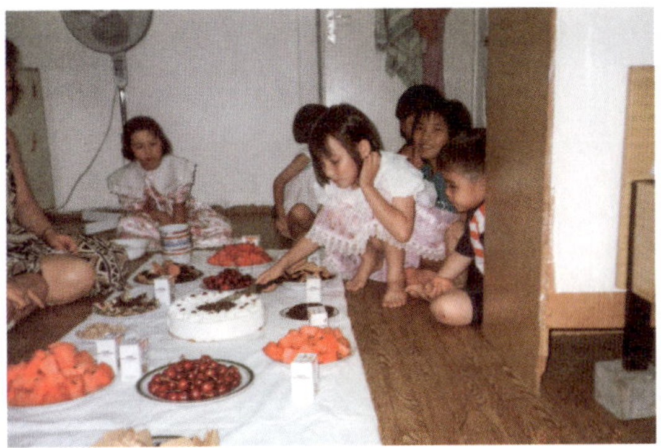
Group photo of Sung Tieu and her friends at home at the housing complex Gehrenseestrasse, circa 1995./
Gruppenfoto mit Sung Tieu und ihren Freund*innen zu Hause in der Wohnsied-lung Gehrenseestraße, circa 1995.

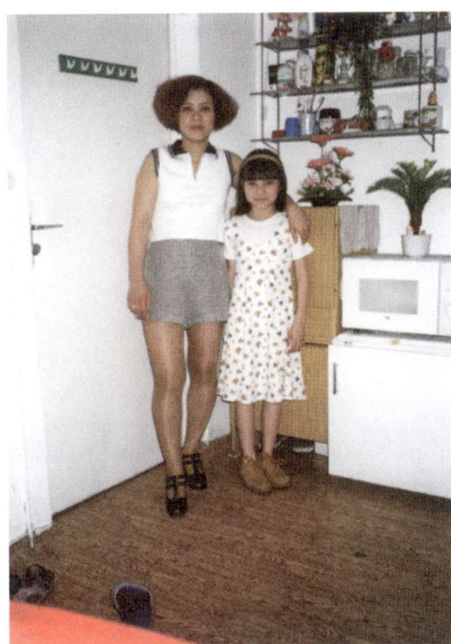
Sung Tieu and her mother, Vũ Thị Hạnh, in their room in Gehrenseestrasse, circa 1997.
Sung Tieu und ihre Mutter, Vũ Thị Hạnh, in ihrem Wohnheimzimmer in der Gehren-seestraße, circa 1997.

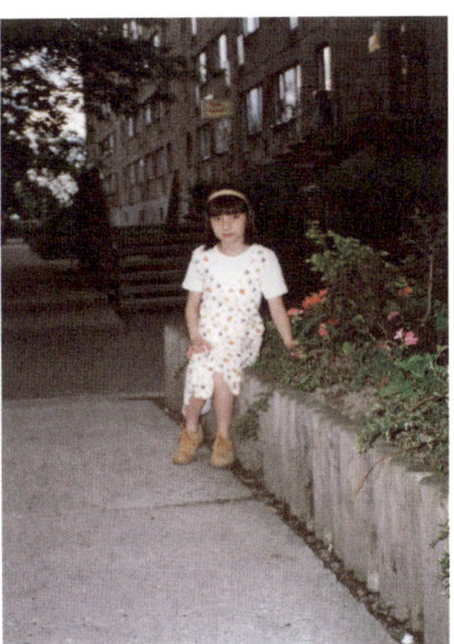
Sung Tieu in front of the entrance of the housing complex on Gehrenseestrasse, circa 1997./
Sung Tieu vor dem Eingang der Wohnsied-lung Gehrenseestraße, circa 1997.

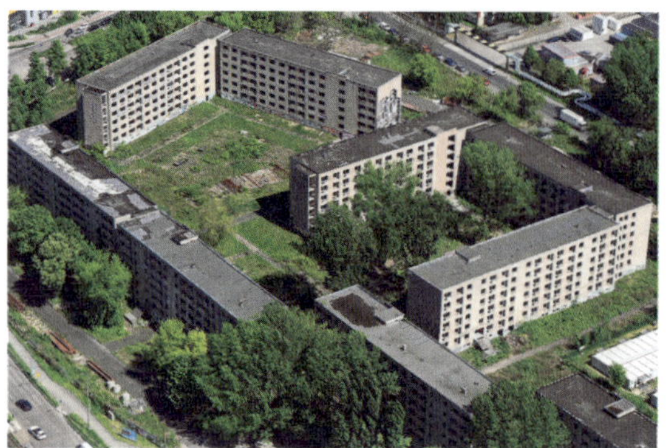

Aerial view of the vacant, gutted residential blocks, circa 2010./
Luftansicht der leerstehenden, entkernten Wohnblöcke, circa 2010.

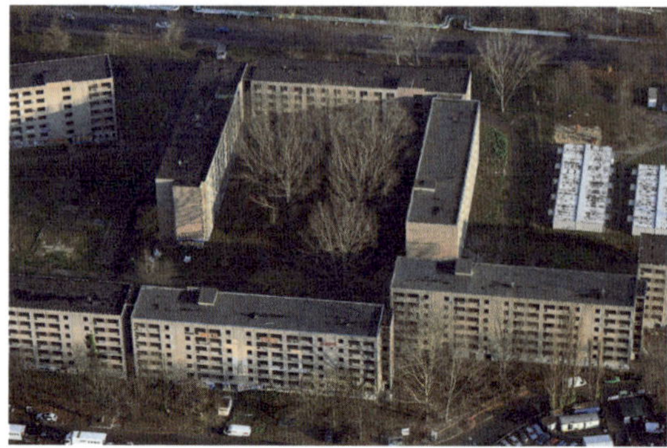

Aerial view of the vacant, gutted residential blocks, circa 2010./
Luftansicht der leerstehenden, entkernten Wohnblöcke, circa 2010.

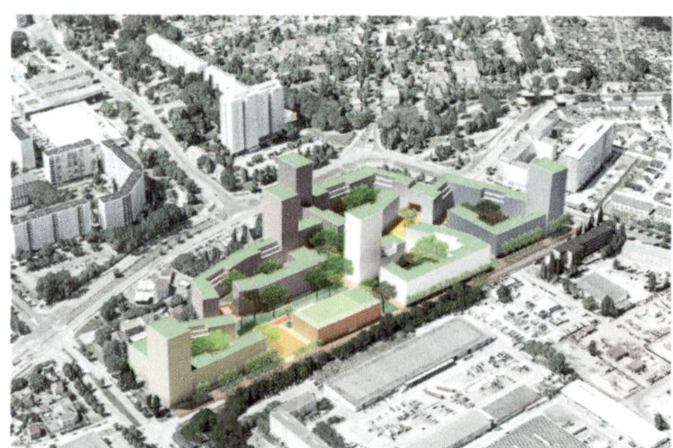

Proposal rendering for "Gehrensee Courts" for residential, commercial and private use./
Entwurfsvisualisierung für „Gehrenseehöfe" zur Wohn-, Gewerbe- und Privatnutzung.

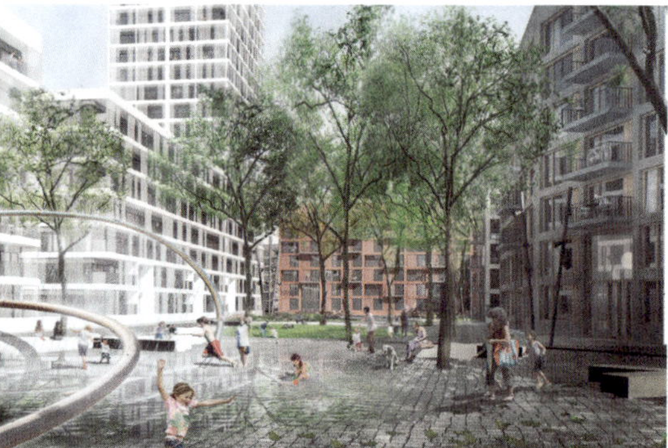

Proposal rendering for "Gehrensee Courts" for residential, commercial and private use./
Entwurfsvisualisierung für „Gehrenseehöfe" zur Wohn-, Gewerbe- und Privatnutzung.

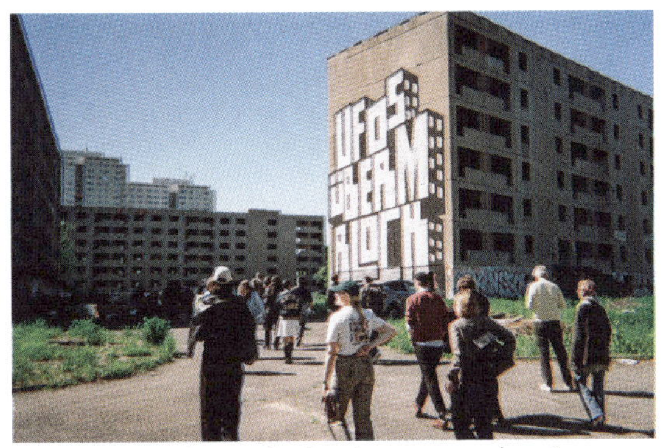

Documentation of the bus tour by Sung Tieu and Tamara Hentschel as part of the exhibition *Sung Tieu – 1992, 2025*, at Kunst-Werke, KW Institute for Contemporary Art, 2025./
Dokumentation der Bus Tour von Sung Tieu und Tamara Hentschel als Teil der Ausstellung *Sung Tieu – 1992, 2025*, in den Kunst-Werken, KW Institute for Contemporary Art, 2025.

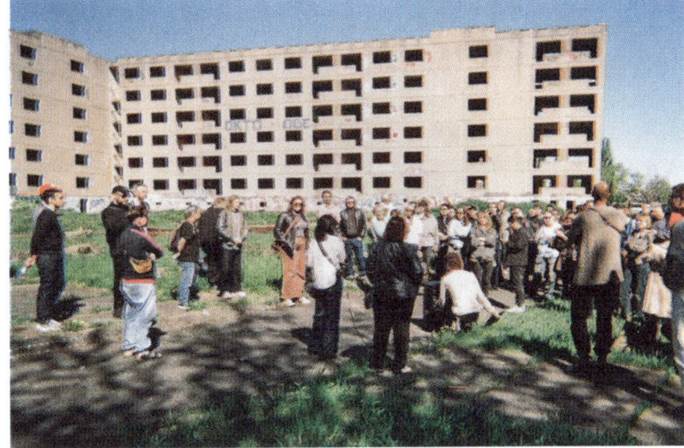

Documentation of the bus tour by Sung Tieu and Tamara Hentschel as part of the exhibition *Sung Tieu – 1992, 2025*, at Kunst-Werke, KW Institute for Contemporary Art, 2025./
Dokumentation der Bus Tour von Sung Tieu und Tamara Hentschel als Teil der Ausstellung *Sung Tieu – 1992, 2025*, in den Kunst-Werken, KW Institute for Contemporary Art, 2025.

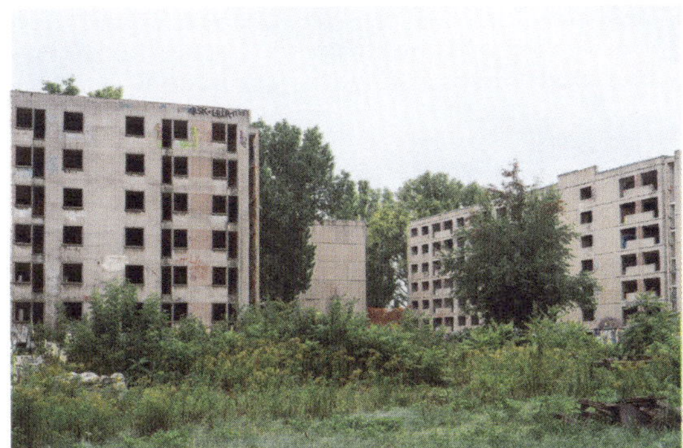

Sung Tieu, Documentation of Gehrenseestrasse, 2025./
Sung Tieu, Dokumentation der Gehrenseestraße, 2025.

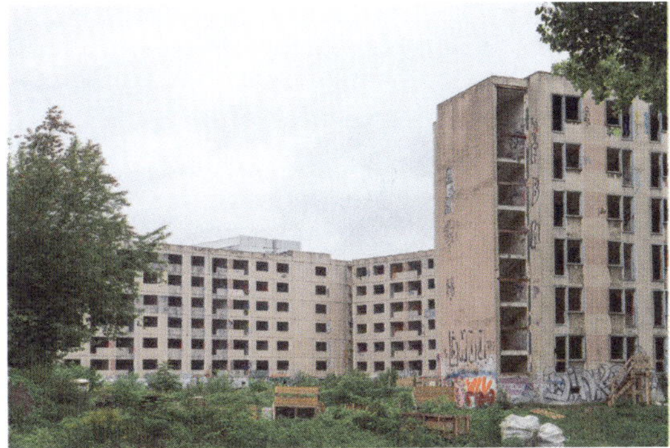

Sung Tieu, Documentation of Gehrenseestrasse, 2025./
Sung Tieu, Dokumentation der Gehrenseestraße, 2025.

*Die Ruine der Plattenbausiedlung in der Gehrenseestraße in Berlin-Alt-Hohenschönhausen war einst einer der größten Wohnkomplexe für Vertragsarbeiter*innen der DDR und von 1994 bis 1997 Wohnort der Künstlerin Sung Tieu und ihrer Mutter. Die Chronik zeichnet die Geschichte des Gebäudeensembles von 1970 bis heute nach und dokumentiert seinen tiefgreifenden Wandel.*

1970

Die Falkenberger Straße, 1980 in Gehrenseestraße umbenannt, liegt in Hohenschönhausen im Norden Ost-Berlins, am damaligen Stadtrand der Hauptstadt der Deutschen Demokratischen Republik (DDR, 1949–1990). Auf der Nordseite erstreckt sich eine großflächig landwirtschaftlich genutzte Fläche.

Zu dieser Zeit herrscht in der gesamten DDR ein massiver Wohnraummangel. Ursachen sind die Zerstörungen des Zweiten Weltkriegs, Reparationsleistungen sowie die politische Konzentration auf den Aufbau der Schwerindustrie unter Walter Ulbricht. Besonders in Ost-Berlin ist die Lage angespannt: Die Sanierung der bestehenden Altbausubstanz gilt als technisch aufwendig und wirtschaftlich kaum finanzierbar.

Für die rund 17 Millionen Bürger*innen der DDR bedeutet dies ein dauerhaft knappes und in vielerlei Hinsicht – etwa für Verfügbarkeit, Größe, Lage und Ausstattung – unzureichendes Wohnungsangebot. Der wachsende Mangel erhöht den politischen Druck, neue groß angelegte Wohnungsbauprojekte umzusetzen.

1971

Als Reaktion auf die anhaltende Wohnungsnot beschließt der VIII. Parteitag der Sozialistischen Einheitspartei Deutschlands (SED) unter dem neuen Generalsekretär Erich Honecker ein umfassendes Wohnungsbauprogramm im Sinne der propagierten „Einheit von Wirtschafts- und Sozialpolitik". Als Ziel wird gesetzt, die Wohnungsnot bis 1990 zu beseitigen.

Um dieses ambitionierte Vorhaben zu erreichen, setzt die staatliche Wohnraumpolitik auf den schnellen und massenhaften Bau von Großwohnsiedlungen in industrieller Plattenbauweise. Diese Gebäude bestehen aus vorgefertigten Betonplatten für Wände und Decken, wodurch Material-, Zeit- und Arbeitsaufwand deutlich reduziert werden. Zwar entstehen Wohnsiedlungen in dieser Bauweise bereits seit 1958, doch wird ihre Produktion nun erheblich ausgeweitet: Bis 1990 werden rund 1,5 Millionen Wohnungen errichtet, die meisten davon in neu angelegten Großsiedlungen an den Stadträndern. Diese Neubauten verkörpern das sozialistische Modernisierungsversprechen.

1973

Im Rahmen des Wohnungsbauprogramms beschließt die SED die Entwicklung der östlichen Randgebiete Berlins. Bis 1985 soll der neue Stadtbezirk Marzahn entstehen, während in Hohenschönhausen rund 30.000 neue Wohnungen geplant werden. Diese Projekte verändern das bislang dörflich geprägte Umland Ost-Berlins grundlegend. Auch die spätere Gehrenseestraße wird Teil dieser urbanen Großprojekte.

1975

Für die Errichtung der neuen Ost-Berliner Wohngebiete werden Arbeitskräfte aus der gesamten DDR zusammengezogen. Der entstehende Neubau an der späteren Gehrenseestraße wird zunächst für die temporäre Unterbringung dieser Arbeitskräfte konzipiert. Zu diesem Zweck soll die Fläche mit neun sechsgeschossigen Wohnblocks bebaut werden.

Die Grundrisse der Wohnheime orientieren sich vermutlich an Kasernenbauten. Die Anlage umfasst etwa 1000 Zimmer mit insgesamt 2160 Wohnheimplätzen in rund 16 Quadratmeter großen Räumen für jeweils drei bis vier Personen. Küchen und Sanitäranlagen sind als Gemeinschaftseinrichtungen auf den Etagen vorgesehen, während Räume für Erholung oder Freizeit nicht eingeplant sind.

1977

Die Bauphase der Wohnsiedlung beginnt. Träger des Projekts ist der VEB Hauptauftragsgeber Komplexer Wohnungsbau (VEB, „Volkseigener Betrieb", war in der DDR ein staatlicher Betrieb), im Auftrag des „Magistrats von Berlin, Hauptstadt der DDR". Als Hauptauftragnehmer wird der VEB Wohnungsbaukombinat Neubrandenburg verpflichtet. Die fertigen Plattenbauten an der späteren Gehrenseestraße sollen anschließend von der Arbeiterwohnheimverwaltung betreut werden, ebenfalls im Auftrag des Magistrats von Berlin.

1978

Die ersten Bauarbeiter*innen des Wohnungsbaukombinats Neubrandenburg beziehen die inzwischen fertiggestellten Wohnheimplätze, während die notwendigen Versorgungsleitungen für Strom, Abwasser und Telefon noch eingerichtet werden.

Trotz nahezu vollständiger Beschäftigung der Bevölkerung herrscht seit Ende der 1960er-Jahre in der DDR ein zunehmender Fachkräftemangel. Um diesem entgegenzuwirken, schließt die DDR-Regierung mit verschiedenen „sozialistischen Bruderstaaten" Abkommen über die Ausbildung und zeitlich befristete Beschäftigung ausländischer Arbeitskräfte. Die ersten Verträge werden mit Polen (1963), Ungarn (1967) und Algerien (1974) abgeschlossen. 1978 folgt ein weiteres Abkommen mit Kuba, auf dessen Grundlage bis 1989 rund 25.000 kubanische Staatsbürger*innen in die DDR kommen.

Die Unterbringung dieser Arbeitskräfte erfolgt meist innerhalb oder in unmittelbarer Nähe der Betriebsgelände, auf denen sie arbeiten sollen, und ist oftmals von den Wohngebieten der DDR-Bevölkerung abgeschottet. Kubanische Vertragsarbeiter*innen leben später auch in den Wohnheimen in der Gehrenseestraße.

1979

Die Wohnheime an der späteren Gehrenseestraße sind fertiggestellt.

Im Februar 1979 schließt die DDR-Regierung auch mit der Volksrepublik Mosambik einen „Vertrag über Freundschaft und Zusammenarbeit" ab. In diesem Zuge werden auch erste Arbeitskräfte von dort in die DDR geschickt. Insgesamt kommen bis 1989 fast 20.000 Mosambikaner*innen in die DDR. Einige von ihnen beziehen Zimmer in den Wohnheimen in der Gehrenseestraße.

1980

Im April wird das umfangreichste und politisch bedeutendste bilaterale Abkommen dieser Art mit der Sozialistischen Republik Vietnam unterzeichnet. In ihm wird „die zeitweilige Beschäftigung und Qualifizierung vietnamesischer Werktätiger in Betrieben der DDR" vereinbart.

Bis 1989 kommen rund 60.000–70.000 Vietnames*innen in die DDR und bilden damit die größte Gruppe ausländischer Arbeitskräfte. Viele von ihnen werden ab 1982 in der Gehrenseestraße untergebracht. In den folgenden Jahren werden weitere Vereinbarungen mit den sozialistischen „Bruderländern" Mongolei (1982), Angola (1985), China und Nordkorea (1986) geschlossen, allerdings mit deutlich geringerer Zahl der Entsandten.

Vor der Übersiedlung in die DDR werden die Vertragsarbeiter*innen in ihren Herkunftsländern im Rahmen sogenannter „Tauglichkeitsuntersuchungen" medizinisch auf ihre Eignung für die Arbeit geprüft. Nach ihrer Ankunft in der DDR müssen sie zudem verpflichtend weitere Gesundheitsuntersuchungen durchlaufen, die häufig ihre Privatsphäre verletzen und teilweise auch von der Stasi dokumentiert werden. Ab 1985 werden diese Untersuchungen auch auf HIV-Tests ausgeweitet.

Neben dem Grundlohn von etwa 600 Mark sind eine tägliche Trennungsentschädigung von vier Mark sowie je nach Herkunftsland Bekleidungsbeihilfen vorgesehen. Vietnamesische Arbeiter*innen müssen zwölf Prozent ihres Lohns an den vietnamesischen Staat abführen. Der Geld- und Warentransfer in die Heimat ist begrenzt.

Die Möglichkeiten für Bildung und Weiterbildung sind stark eingeschränkt: Die Dauer der Deutschsprachkurse variiert erheblich, liegt jedoch meist bei nur drei Monaten. Ab 1987 werden sie zudem häufig auf lediglich einen Monat verkürzt.

Vietnamesische Arbeitskräfte werden in fast 1000 Betrieben der DDR eingesetzt, vor allem in der Leicht- und Schwerindustrie sowie im Maschinenbau, meistens dort, wo die Bedingungen für DDR-Bürger*innen unattraktiv sind.

1982

Die meisten Bauarbeiter*innen ziehen aus den Wohnheimen in der Gehrenseestraße aus. Die Gebäude werden nun vor allem von Vertragsarbeiter*innen bewohnt, der Großteil kommt aus Vietnam, eine kleinere Anzahl aus Kuba, Angola und Mosambik. Es wird einer der größten Wohnkomplexe für Vertragsarbeiter*innen in der DDR.

Die Wohnbedingungen in den Wohnheimen sind durch strenge Vorschriften und Überwachung geregelt: In jedem Zimmer dürfen bis zu vier Personen untergebracht werden, denen jeweils etwa fünf Quadratmeter Wohnraum zustehen. Die Zimmer sind mit Bett, Nachttisch, Stuhl und grundlegenden Haushaltsgegenständen ausgestattet. Männer und Frauen werden grundsätzlich getrennt untergebracht. Die Miete für alle Vertragsarbeiter*innen soll laut Abkommen maximal 30 Mark im Monat betragen. In der Praxis sehen die Wohnverhältnisse oft schlechter aus: Die Zimmer bieten keine Privatsphäre und sind häufig überbelegt, Sanitär- und Küchenbereiche unzureichend ausgestattet – manchmal gibt es nur eine Kochgelegenheit für 50 Personen – und in vielen Räumen lassen sich die vorgesehenen Betten, Tische und Schränke kaum unterbringen.

Eine Ausgangssperre von 22–7 Uhr regelt die Nachtruhe. Regelmäßig werden die Zimmer von Mitarbeiter*innen der Abteilung des Inneren der Bezirke und von Gruppenleiter*innen kontrolliert. Jene kommen meist aus den jeweiligen Botschaften der Herkunftsländer der Vertragsarbeiter*innen. Sie fungieren als Bindeglied zur Betriebs- und Wohnheimleitung und überwachen Disziplin und Arbeitsmoral.

Die Freizeitangebote in den Wohnheimen beschränken sich auf Tanzabende in den Klubräumen. Sportmöglichkeiten sind aufgrund eines Mangels an Turnhallen oder Sportplätzen oft auf Tischtennis reduziert. Fernsehen und Lesen sind nur möglich, soweit fremdsprachliche Filme und Literatur zugänglich sind.

Gesellschaftliche Integration ist weder vorgesehen noch erwünscht. Die Kontakte zur DDR-Bevölkerung werden kontrolliert und häufig unterbunden. Paare, die gleichzeitig als Vertragsarbeiter*innen entsandt sind, werden in unterschiedlichen Städten bzw. Betrieben eingesetzt. Eheschließungen mit DDR-Bürger*innen werden weitestmöglich unterbunden. Schwangerschaften führen bis 1987 meist zum Jobverlust und der Rückführung oder werden durch erzwungene Abtreibungen abgebrochen.

1987

Der Vater von Sung Tieu, Tiêu Dũng Tiến, kommt als 27-Jähriger vietnamesischer Vertragsarbeiter nach Freital bei Dresden, wo er im VEB Edelstahlwerk Freital arbeitet.

Seine Ankunft fällt in eine Phase, in der die DDR verstärkt Arbeitskräfte aus Vietnam anwirbt, um einen angestrebten Produktivitätssprung zu unterstützen und dem anhaltenden Arbeitskräftemangel zu begegnen. In diesem Jahr allein reisen rund 50.000 weitere Vietnames*innen in die DDR ein – der mit Abstand größte Zuzug.

Mit zunehmender Zahl an Vertragsarbeiter*innen nehmen die strengen Kontrollen in den Wohnheimen ab. Diese schaffen sich zunehmend inoffizielle Erwerbsformen zur Aufbesserung des geringen Einkommens wie die Herstellung und den Verkauf von Jeanswaren, die in der Mangelwirtschaft der DDR sehr begehrt sind.

1989

Im letzten Jahr der DDR kommen weitere 9000 vietnamesische Vertragsarbeiter*innen ins Land.

Im Mai werden Kommunalwahlen abgehalten. Sie sind von massivem, erstmals nachgewiesenem Wahlbetrug überschattet und schüren die Unzufriedenheit der Bevölkerung weiter. Zwei Monate zuvor ist beschlossen worden, den in der DDR lebenden Ausländer*innen das aktive und passive Wahlrecht bei Kommunalwahlen zuzugestehen – eine Reform, die nicht umgesetzt wurde.

Im Sommer fliehen DDR-Bürger*innen zu Tausenden über die bundesdeutschen Botschaften in Prag und Warschau in den Westen. Zur selben Zeit werden in der DDR erste Oppositions- und Bürgerrechtsgruppen gegründet, welche demokratische Reformen, Meinungsfreiheit und das Ende des Führungsanspruchs der SED fordern. Die sich daraus entwickelnde Friedliche Revolution erreicht im Oktober mit den Montagsdemonstrationen in Leipzig ihren Höhepunkt. Zehntausende Menschen gehen auf die Straße.

Am 9. November werden die Berliner Mauer und die innerdeutsche Grenze für DDR-Bürger*innen geöffnet. Was zunächst auf den Versuch der SED-Führung zurückgeht, mit einem neuen Reisegesetz die Stimmung in der Bevölkerung zu beruhigen, wird zum Symbol für das Ende der DDR. Kurz darauf streicht die Volkskammer den Führungsanspruch der SED aus der Verfassung, während der Zentrale Runde Tisch seine Arbeit aufnimmt.

Die Öffnung der Grenzen markiert für die Menschen in der DDR einen tiefgreifenden Einschnitt. Während die Mehrheit der Bevölkerung diesen Moment als Befreiung erlebt, ist die Situation für zahlreiche Vertragsarbeiter*innen nun von zunehmenden Existenzängsten, Unsicherheit und Diskriminierung geprägt.

1990

Am 1. März wird die Treuhandanstalt gegründet, um das DDR-Volkseigentum treuhänderisch zu verwalten. Zentrale Aufgabe ist die Auflösung der großen Kombinate und die Umwandlung ihrer Nachfolgeunternehmen in Kapitalgesellschaften.

Am 18. März wird die letzte DDR-Regierung unter Führung der (Ost-)CDU gewählt. Damit ist der Weg zur deutschen Einheit nach der Volkskammerwahl demokratisch legitimiert.

Auf dem Arbeitsmarkt herrscht schon bald große Ungewissheit, da viele DDR-Betriebe in wirtschaftliche Schwierigkeiten geraten und Arbeitsplätze abbauen. Dies führt auch zu Konkurrenz zwischen einheimischen Werktätigen und ausländischen Vertragsarbeiter*innen. Letztere geraten zunehmend in eine existenzielle Notlage, denn obwohl ihre Arbeitsverträge eigentlich weiterlaufen – einige sind noch bis 1995 gültig –, werden zahlreiche Vertragsarbeiter*innen nun unrechtmäßig entlassen.

Viele der betrieblichen Wohnheime der Vertragsarbeiter*innen werden aus Kostengründen geschlossen. Der Standort Gehrenseestraße bleibt allerdings bestehen. Er wird zunächst weiterhin von der städtischen Arbeiterwohnheimverwaltung (AWHV) betreut, bis diese im August 1990 privatisiert und in ARWOGE umbenannt wird. Ohne kommunale Mittel steigen die Mieten in den Wohnheimen deutlich: 1992 werden Einzelzimmer bereits 280 D-Mark kosten. Bis 2002 liegen die Mieten für größere Zimmer zwischen 450 und bis zu 1070 D-Mark.

In Hohenschönhausen gründen sich infolge der unsicheren Situation für die ausländischen Vertragsarbeiter*innen erste Unterstützungsinitiativen und Vereine. Viele nutzen in den kommenden Jahren Räume in der Gehrenseestraße für ihre Tätigkeiten. Sie fördern interkulturellen Austausch, bieten Deutschkurse, Freizeitangebote sowie rechtliche und psychologische Unterstützung an.

Zur gleichen Zeit wird Diedrich Wulfert als Ausländerbeauftragter bis 1994 in Hohenschönhausen eingesetzt.

Am 18. Mai unterzeichnen die DDR und die Bundesrepublik Deutschland den ersten Staatsvertrag, wodurch die Währungs-, Wirtschafts- und Sozialunion am 1. Juli in Kraft tritt. Die D-Mark wird offizielles Zahlungsmittel und die in Westdeutschland praktizierte soziale Marktwirtschaft eingeführt. Dies löst einen tiefgreifenden Strukturwandel aus: Preise, Löhne und Renten werden neu berechnet, Subventionen abgebaut, und viele DDR-Betriebe verlieren schlagartig ihre Wettbewerbsfähigkeit.

Am 13. Juni beschließt die DDR-Regierung die Veränderung von Arbeitsverhältnissen mit Vertragsarbeiter*innen, die auf den bilateralen Regierungsabkommen basieren. Hiermit werden die vorfristigen Kündigungen in den Monaten zuvor nachträglich legalisiert. Die neuen Regelungen ermöglichen Betrieben vorzeitige Entlassungen aus wirtschaftlichen Gründen und führen dazu, dass die meisten Vertragsarbeiter*innen ihre Anstellung verlieren. Bis Ende 1990 haben beispielsweise rund 81 Prozent der mosambikanischen Vertragsarbeiter*innen keinen Arbeitsplatz mehr. Auch von den rund 4600 Vietnames*innen in den östlichen Berliner Bezirken sind zu dieser Zeit etwa 3800 – also mehr als 80 Prozent – arbeitslos. Die Verpflichtung zur Bereitstellung von betrieblichen Wohnheimen entfällt. Am 17. Juni wird die Treuhandanstalt per Gesetz neu ausgerichtet. Sie übernimmt nun nicht nur die Verwaltung der Betriebe, sondern bereitet sie gezielt auf den Verkauf an private Investoren vor.

Gleichzeitig ziehen zunehmend Asylsuchende aus verschiedenen Ländern in die Gehrenseestraße. In der zweiten Jahreshälfte verlassen viele ehemalige Vertragsarbeiter*innen das Land. Um dies zu fördern, wird ein Anreiz in Form einer „einmaligen Ausgleichszahlung" von 3000 D-Mark sowie eines Flugtickets in das jeweilige Herkunftsland eingeführt. Formal sollen diese Zahlungen von den DDR-Betrieben selbst getragen werden, von denen sich viele jedoch bereits in der Abwicklung befinden. In der Praxis wird die Auszahlung häufig von den lokalen Behörden organisiert und kurz vor der Abreise vorgenommen. Dennoch berichten viele ehemalige Vertragsarbeiter*innen, dass die Zahlungen verspätet, unvollständig oder überhaupt nicht geleistet wurden.

Einige ehemalige Vertragsarbeiter*innen entscheiden sich jedoch für ein Bleiben in den neuen Bundesländern – oft ohne rechtliche Absicherung –, während andere aus der noch bestehenden DDR in die BRD fliehen und dort Asyl beantragen. Zu diesem Zeitpunkt befinden sich nur noch rund 28.000 Vertragsarbeiter*innen im Land, der Großteil von ihnen aus Vietnam.

Am 3. Oktober tritt der Einigungsvertrag zwischen der BRD und der DDR in Kraft. Damit ist Deutschland wiedervereinigt. Berlin wird zur Hauptstadt des wiedervereinigten Deutschlands, allerdings wird es bis 1999 dauern, dass der größte Teil der Regierung von Bonn nach Berlin übergesiedelt ist. Für viele Vietnames*innen ist das Leben in Deutschland von wachsender Angst geprägt. Wiederholte, brutale Angriffe von Neonazis führen bei zahlreichen Betroffenen zu tiefer Verunsicherung.

1991

Am 1. Januar tritt das neue Ausländergesetz (AuslG) in Kraft und führt bundesweit einheitliche Regelungen für den Aufenthalt von Ausländer*innen ein. Die bisherigen Aufenthaltsrechte ehemaliger Vertragsarbeiter*innen werden in Genehmigungen nach § 5 AuslG überführt, was für viele erhebliche Einschränkungen bedeutet. Anders als die Arbeitsmigrant*innen der BRD erhalten sie zunächst keine Perspektive auf einen dauerhaften Aufenthalt, da ihre Aufenthaltsrechte nur bis zum Ende der ursprünglichen Arbeitsverträge gelten. Die meisten erhalten lediglich eine befristete Duldung, die zudem auf die fünf „neuen Bundesländer" beschränkt ist. Auch ein Wechsel in die Selbstständigkeit erweist sich häufig als schwierig, da Gewerbegenehmigungen vielfach verweigert werden.

Auch wegen fehlender Deutschkenntnisse und nicht anerkannter Berufsabschlüsse ist der Zugang zum Arbeitsmarkt schwierig, zumal jede Anstellung vom Arbeitsamt genehmigt werden muss. Deshalb suchen viele auf dem informellen Arbeitsmarkt, vor allem im Kleinhandel, neue Möglichkeiten: Sie eröffnen Imbisse, Blumen- oder Textilläden, arbeiten auf Märkten, in Reinigungsfirmen oder in Restaurants, oft ohne offizielle Genehmigung.

An der Rhinstraße 100 in Berlin-Lichtenberg entsteht ein Handelszentrum, in dem vietnamesische Großhändler*innen Waren an Straßenverkäufer*innen weitergeben – ein Versuch, wirtschaftlich unabhängig zu werden.

In das Wohnheim in der Gehrenseestraße ziehen auch deutschstämmige Spätaussiedler*innen aus den Staaten des ehemaligen Ostblocks ein. Ihre Einreisebedingungen sind erleichtert und sie erhalten die deutsche Staatsbürgerschaft bei ihrer Ankunft sowie Zugang zu Sprachkursen und staatlicher Unterstützung.

Außerdem werden jüdische Kontingentflüchtlinge in der Gehrenseestraße aufgenommen. Ihre Zuwanderung aus der ehemaligen Sowjetunion erfolgt auf Grundlage eines speziellen Kontingentstatus, der einen Aufenthalt ohne Asylverfahren ermöglicht. Im Unterschied zu den Spätaussiedler*innen erhalten sie jedoch nicht automatisch die deutsche Staatsbürgerschaft und ihre Sozialleistungen bleiben eingeschränkt.

Darüber hinaus lebt weiterhin eine erhebliche Zahl ehemaliger Vertragsarbeiter*innen und anderer Migrantinnen im Komplex, darunter etwa 212 Vietnames*innen, 160 Mosambikaner*innen, 103 Pol*innen sowie 165 Bewohner*innen anderer Nationalitäten.

Mit der Aufhebung der früheren Zugangskontrollen zu den Wohnheimen nimmt die Überbelegung in der Gehrenseestraße massiv zu. In manchen Zimmern leben nun fünf bis zehn Personen.

Innerhalb rechtsextremer Kreise gewinnt das Konzept der „national befreiten Zonen" zunehmend an Bedeutung und auch den breiteren öffentlichen Diskurs zu beeinflussen. Im selben Zeitraum wird ein vietnamesischer Bewohner vor seiner Wohnung in der Gehrenseestraße angegriffen, ein frühes Beispiel der eskalierenden rassistischen Gewalt in Berlin.

Von den ursprünglich rund 90.000 Vertragsarbeiter*innen der DDR waren bis Ende 1991 nur noch etwa 6670 beschäftigt.

1992

Tieu und ihre Mutter, Vũ Thị Hạnh, emigrieren von Vietnam nach Deutschland. Nach kurzen Aufenthalten in Halle und Leipzig ziehen sie nach Freital zum Vater. Tieu besucht dort den Kindergarten.

Die Vereinigung der Vietnames*innen gründet sich in Berlin. Sie entwickelt zahlreiche Initiativen, um ihre Forderung nach einem Bleiberecht für die ehemaligen Vertragsarbeiter*innen bekannt zu machen.

Am 24. März spricht sich die Bundeskonferenz der Ausländerbeauftragten in Bonn dafür aus, den ehemaligen Vertragsarbeiter*innen den Einstieg in einen Daueraufenthalt zu ermöglichen und Integrationsmaßnahmen zu unterstützen.

Am 24. April wird der ehemalige vietnamesische Vertragsarbeiter Nguyễn Văn Tú am Brodowiner Ring in Berlin-Marzahn, unweit der Gehrenseestraße, von Rechtsextremen ermordet. Er ist eines der ersten bekannten Todesopfer rechtsextremer Gewalt in Deutschland seit der Wiedervereinigung. Auch anlässlich des Trauermarsches von Nguyễn Văn Tú am 3. Mai wird die Forderung nach einem Bleiberecht der ehemaligen Vertragsarbeiter*innen lauter.

Auf dem Alexanderplatz in Berlin demonstrieren im Juni rund 500 Menschen und fordern ein Bleiberecht für die ehemaligen Vertragsarbeiter*innen.

Am 3. Juni befürwortet der Ausländerausschuss des Berliner Abgeordnetenhauses einen Antrag, sich gemeinsam mit den neuen Bundesländern für die Erteilung der Aufenthaltserlaubnis einzusetzen.

Gleichzeitig eskaliert die rassistische Gewalt. Zwischen dem 22. und 26. August verüben Rechtsextreme pogromartige Brandanschläge auf das sogenannte *Sonnenblumenhaus*, ein Wohnheim ehemaliger vietnamesischer Vertragsarbeiter*innen und zugleich Sitz der Zentralen Aufnahmestelle für Asylsuchende (ZASt) in Rostock-Lichtenhagen. Deutsche Bewohner*innen des Plattenbaugebiets und angereiste Neonazis formieren sich zu einem Mob, den die Polizei tagelang gewähren lässt.

Währenddessen planen in Berlin rund 500 Rechtsextreme für September einen Angriff auf die Wohnblöcke in der Gehrenseestraße. Lokale Bewohner*innen greifen jedoch ein und die Polizei kann den Angriff verhindern.

Im gleichen Zeitraum wird ein Brandanschlag auf ein Wohnkomplex in der Zingsterstraße, am Rand von Hohenschönhausen, wo überwiegend Vietnames*innen leben, verübt. Ein Straßenbahngleisarbeiter bemerkt schwarzen Rauch, der aus dem Hauseingang qualmt, und alarmiert Feuerwehr und Polizei. Anschließend ist das gesamte Treppenhaus über sechs Stockwerke bis unter das Dach verrußt.

In der Nähe der Gehrenseestraße verüben Unbekannte einen Brandanschlag auf den unter rechtsextremem Einfluss stehenden Jugendclub Wurzel. Antifaschistische Gruppen begründen die Tat damit, dass der Club als Treffpunkt für Skinheads dient.

Ab September organisiert die SOMAG, eine Tochterfirma der ARWOGE, die Unterbringung von Geflüchteten in der Gehrenseestraße und übernimmt die Verwaltung von zwei der neun Wohnblöcke.

Unweit der Gehrenseestraße eröffnet die dorthin verlegte Zentrale Anlaufstelle für Asylbewerber in Hohenschönhausen. Kurz darauf versammeln sich rechtsextreme Jugendliche vor den nahegelegenen Wohnheimen in der Gehrenseestraße und skandieren rassistische Parolen.

Unter Druck zahlreicher Vereine beauftragen Bund und Länder am 17. Dezember die Innenminister der Länder, eine Lösung für ehemalige Vertragsarbeiter*innen zu finden. Bis zum 30. April 1993 soll ein begrenzter Abschiebestopp gelten. Jener bietet Menschen einen gewissen Schutz vor der Rückkehr in Länder, die für sie als politisch oder wirtschaftlich unsicher gelten.

1993

In der Gehrenseestraße werden nun auch Kriegsflüchtlinge aus Bosnien-Herzegowina aufgenommen, überwiegend befristet und unter eingeschränkten Bedingungen. Gleichzeitig beauftragt die SOMAG eine Sicherheitsfirma, die rund um die Uhr die beiden von ihr verwalteten Wohnblöcke überwacht. Später werden die Kontrollgänge auch auf weitere Häuserblöcke ausgeweitet.

Inmitten dieser Spannungen wird Manuel T., ein ehemaliger Vertragsarbeiter aus Mosambik und Bewohner der Gehrenseestraße, von sechs rechtsextremen Jugendlichen mit Baseballschlägern in der Nähe der Wohnheime angegriffen und schwer verletzt. Als Reaktion auf die zunehmend prekäre Situation ziehen mehrere Initiativen und Bürgervereine in Räumlichkeiten der Gehrenseestraße ein, um den Bewohner*innen Unterstützung zu bieten.

Gleichzeitig geraten Vietnames*innen, die zur Bestreitung ihres Lebensunterhalts mit unverzollten Zigaretten handeln, zunehmend in den Fokus der medialen Berichterstattung. In diesem Zusammenhang nehmen Razzien in verschiedenen Wohnheimen zu. Für die Gehrenseestraße richtet die Polizei eine Sonderermittlungsgruppe zur Bekämpfung von Kriminalität ein.

Anfang der 1990er-Jahre steigt die Zahl der Asylbewerber*innen in Deutschland stark an. Dies führt zu intensiven öffentlichen und medialen Debatten sowie zu politischen Forderungen nach einer Einschränkung des Asylrechts. Am 26. Mai 1993 wird Artikel 16 des Grundgesetzes geändert und durch Artikel 16a ergänzt. Mit der Einführung der sogenannten Drittstaatenregelung wird der Anspruch auf Asyl neu geregelt und auf politisch Verfolgte beschränkt.

Trotz der Einschränkungen beschließen am 17. Juni die Innenminister der neuen Bundesländer in Abstimmung mit dem Bundesinnenminister eine Bleiberechtsregelung für ehemalige Vertragsarbeiter*innen aus Vietnam und Mosambik. Mit der Asylrechtsreform werden diese Bleiberechte auf zwei Jahre befristet und an strenge Voraussetzungen geknüpft: Die Betroffenen müssen nachweisen, dass sie ihren Lebensunterhalt eigenständig sichern können und keine Straftaten begangen haben.

Für viele ehemalige Vertragsarbeiter*innen bleibt somit die Situation weiterhin prekär, da ihr Aufenthaltsstatus weiterhin ungeklärt ist. Zugleich wird der Verein Reistrommel e. V. gegründet, der Migrationsberatung anbietet, insbesondere für vietnamesische Bewohner*innen in den östlichen Berliner Bezirken. In den 1990er-Jahren liegt der Schwerpunkt der Vereinstätigkeit auf der Wahrung der Mietrechte der Bewohner*innen in den Wohnheimen der ARWOGE. Darüber hinaus leistet Reistrommel e. V. einen wichtigen Beitrag zum Einsatz für das Bleiberecht ehemaliger Vertragsarbeiter*innen.

Der im Frühjahr 1993 eingeführte, begrenzte generelle Abschiebestopp für ehemalige Vertragsarbeiter*innen endet.

1994

Nach der Trennung ihrer Eltern ziehen Tieu und ihre Mutter nach Berlin Alt-Hohenschönhausen in die Gehrenseestraße. Tieu besucht dort die Grundschule, die in fußläufiger Entfernung vom Wohnheim gelegen ist. Ihre Mutter ist zunächst als Metzgerin und Obsthändlerin beschäftigt, anschließend arbeitet sie in einem Imbiss-Bus.

Zur gleichen Zeit wird Polizeigewalt gegen Vietnames*innen in einer Bernauer Polizeiwache öffentlich bekannt. Den Beamt*innen wird vorgeworfen, zwischen März 1993 und Juni 1994 Vietnames*innen gefoltert und misshandelt zu haben. Die Beteiligten werden vom Dienst suspendiert, rechtliche Konsequenzen bleiben jedoch aus.

In der Gehrenseestraße bereiten Flüchtlings- und Bürgerinitiativen eine symbolische Wahlaktion für Migrant*innen in Berlin vor. Damit wird auf die fehlende politische Mitbestimmung von Menschen, die in Deutschland leben, arbeiten und Steuern zahlen, aber nicht wählen dürfen, aufmerksam gemacht. In der Gehrenseestraße und an anderen bestimmten Orten können Migrant*innen symbolisch ihre Stimme abgeben.

In dieser Zeit werden die kommunalen Wohnungsunternehmen ARWOGE (Ost-Berlin) und ARWOBAU (West-Berlin) fusioniert und heißen nun ARWOBAU.

1995

Vermehrt werden in Wohnheimen in Hohenschönhausen Großrazzien durchgeführt. In diesem Zusammenhang diskutiert der Berliner Senat die Schließung der Heime in der Gehrenseestraße zur Kriminalprävention. Diese Forderung löst große Unsicherheit unter den Bewohner*innen aus. Um ihre Interessen zu vertreten, bestimmen rund 200 von ihnen Vertreter*innen, die dann das Gespräch mit den Behörden suchen, was dazu führt, dass der Standort bestehen bleibt. Zwei andere Wohnheime in Hohenschönhausen müssen allerdings schließen.

Nach dem Ablauf der befristeten Bleiberechtsregelung von 1993 stehen viele der ehemaligen Vertragsarbeiter*innen erneut vor rechtlicher Unsicherheit. Forderungen werden lauter, die Benachteiligung zu beenden, allen seit mehr als acht Jahren rechtmäßig in Deutschland lebenden Personen eine Aufenthaltserlaubnis zu erteilen und auch geringfügig straffällig gewordenen Betroffenen den Zugang zu einem Bleiberecht zu eröffnen.

Im April wird der 22-jährige Thái Văn Hương in der Gehrenseestraße von einem anderen vietnamesischen Bewohner ermordet. Der Fall kann nie endgültig aufgeklärt werden. In den Jahren häufen sich ähnliche Tötungsdelikte, viele von ihnen werden nicht angezeigt, da die Betroffenen der Polizei misstrauen.

Die Bewohner*innen der Wohnheime in der Gehrenseestraße müssen die Bewachungskosten ihrer Unterkünfte selbst tragen. Ein Drittel ihrer Miete fließt nun in Sicherheitsdienste, die ihr Kommen und Gehen kontrollieren.

Deutschland und Vietnam unterzeichnen im Juli nach einjährigen Verhandlungen den Vertrag zur Rückführung der ohne Aufenthaltsberechtigung in Deutschland lebenden Vietnames*innen. Das Abkommen sieht bis zum Jahr 2000 die schrittweise Abschiebung von mindestens 40.000 vietnamesischen Staatsangehörigen vor. Der Vertrag ist verbunden mit deutschen Finanzhilfen in Höhe von 25 Millionen Mark, außerdem der Freigabe von zuvor eingefrorener Entwicklungshilfe in Höhe von 75.000 Mark. Vertreter*innen von Betroffenenorganisationen üben heftige Kritik an diesem Abkommen, das die Rückführung von 2500 Personen noch in diesem Jahr vorsieht.

Nach dem Inkrafttreten des Rückübernahmeabkommen sind rund 1000 in der Gehrenseestraße lebende Vietnames*innen von Abschiebung bedroht. Durch ihre hohe Zahl in den Heimen können die Behörden dort großangelegte Kontrollen und Abschiebungen durchführen. Viele Bewohner*innen bereiten sich daher auf einen illegalen Aufenthalt vor, da die Rückkehr nach Vietnam mit unsicheren Lebensbedingungen und rechtlichen Risiken verbunden ist.

Nach umfassenden Abschiebungen leben am Ende des Jahres nur noch ein Viertel, circa 22.500, der ehemaligen rund 90.000 Vertragsarbeiter*innen aus Vietnam, Angola, Mosambik, Kuba und anderen Staaten in den neuen Bundesländern.

1997

Der ehemalige Vertragsarbeiter Phan Văn Toản wird am 31. Januar am brandenburgischen S-Bahnhof Fredersdorf unweit von Hohenschönhausen von Rechtsradikalen lebensgefährlich verletzt und stirbt drei Monate später an den Folgen im Krankenhaus. Im Jahr 2020 organisieren Vertreter*innen der Zivilgesellschaft die erste Gedenkkundgebung, woraufhin die Gründung der Gedenkinitiative Phan Văn Toản folgt, die sich für die Schaffung eines öffentlichen Gedenkorts für ihn in Fredersdorf einsetzt.

Seit Unterzeichnung des Abkommens zur Rückführung von Vietnames*innen von 1995 sind etwa 2800 Vietnames*innen ohne Bleiberecht abgeschoben worden.

Nach jahrelangem Kampf um das Bleiberecht beschließt die Bundesregierung im November die rechtliche Gleichstellung der ehemaligen DDR-Vertragsarbeiter*innen mit den Arbeitsmigrant*innen der (westdeutschen) Bundesrepublik. Nachdem 1993 eine befristete Bleiberechtsregelung für ehemalige Vertragsarbeiter*innen in Kraft getreten war, blieb die Hürde für ein unbefristetes Aufenthaltsrecht zunächst hoch: Erforderlich war eine achtjährige Aufenthaltsdauer, wobei anfangs nur die Jahre ab 1993 angerechnet wurden. Die in der DDR verbrachten Jahre blieben somit unberücksichtigt. Erst die Rechtsangleichung 1997 korrigiert dies und rechnet die vorherigen Aufenthaltszeiten rückwirkend an. Ein dauerhaftes Bleiberecht erhalten diejenigen, die ihren Lebensunterhalt selbst sichern können und nicht strafrechtlich auffällig geworden sind. Wesentliche Beiträge zu dieser Anpassung leisteten diverse Vereine und Initiativen, darunter Reistrommel e.V.

Mit der Klärung ihres Aufenthaltsstatus erhalten die ehemaligen Vertragsarbeiter*innen erstmals Anspruch auf staatliche Sozialleistungen und eine langfristige Perspektive in Deutschland.

Zur gleichen Zeit ziehen Tieu und ihre Mutter aus der Gehrenseestraße aus und wohnen anschließend in Berlin-Friedrichshain. Ihre Mutter beginnt, als Fabrikarbeiterin bei der Großwäscherei Larosé GmbH in Berlin-Grünau zu arbeiten.

1998

Im Februar beginnt der Kosovo-Krieg. In der Gehrenseestraße kommt es zu nächtlichen Polizeieinsätzen gegen bosnische Geflüchtete, trotz Abschiebeschutz. Die Maßnahmen lösen Angst, Proteste und politische Kritik aus.

1999

In Berlin werden im Rahmen des bundesdeutschen Verteilungsschlüssels zunächst 220 Geflüchtete aus dem Kosovo aufgenommen. Rund 100 von ihnen werden in dem von der SOMAG verwalteten Wohnblock in der Gehrenseestraße untergebracht. Dort sind für sie Ein- bis Fünf-Bett-Zimmer vorbereitet. Sie erhalten eine ärztliche

Erstuntersuchung und Verpflegung. Ihre Aufenthaltsgenehmigung gilt zunächst für drei Monate.

Am 10. Juni endet der Kosovo-Krieg. Trotz der Friedenshoffnung bleiben viele der in der Gehrenseestraße lebenden Geflüchteten aus dem Kosovo skeptisch. Viele sind stark traumatisiert und unsicher, ob sie zurückkehren können.

2001

In Berlin-Hohenschönhausen findet am 1. Mai unweit der Gehrenseestraße eine von der rechtsextremen Nationaldemokratischen Partei Deutschlands (NPD) organisierte Demonstration unter dem Motto „Arbeit zuerst für Deutsche" statt.

Viele der vor dem Krieg im Kosovo Geflüchteten verlassen die Heime der Gehrenseestraße und reisen in andere Länder aus. Die ARWOBAU beginnt mit der vollständigen Räumung der Unterkünfte von allen Bewohner*innen.

2003

Die letzten Bewohner*innen der Gehrenseestraße erhalten Kündigungen und der Leerstand des Gebäudes beginnt. Die ARWOBAU erhält eine Genehmigung zum Abriss der Wohnblöcke, verkauft das Grundstück aber stattdessen an einen privaten Nutzer. Obwohl ein Umbau der Gebäude vorgesehen ist, werden sie in den folgenden Jahren mehrfach weiterverkauft, ohne dass Sanierungsmaßnahmen stattfinden.

2006

Das Schul-Nebengebäude auf dem Gelände wird abgerissen.

2007

Das Grundstück an der Gehrenseestraße wird an einen Investor aus Neuss in Nordrhein-Westfalen verkauft. Dieser plant die Sanierung der neun Plattenbauten und die Entwicklung von insgesamt 625 unterschiedlich großen Wohnungen zu erschwinglichen Mieten.

2008

Die Gebäude in der Gehrenseestraße werden entkernt. Alle Rohrleitungen und Sanitäranlagen sowie Fenster und Türen werden entfernt. Da sich das Grundstück in Privateigentum befindet, hat das Bezirksamt Lichtenberg kaum Einfluss auf Rekonstruktion, Rückbau oder die künftige Nutzung der Bauten. In den folgenden Jahren verfallen die Gebäude zunehmend.

2010

Das Gelände bleibt weiterhin ungenutzt, während die Eigentümer mehrfach wechseln.

2013

Zwei wohnungslose Menschen sterben in den leerstehenden Gebäuden in der Gehrenseestraße. Die Todesursache bleibt ungeklärt.

2015

Der seit 2011 andauernde Syrien-Konflikt entwickelt sich zu einer humanitären Katastrophe, die bis 2016 etwa 6 Millionen Menschen zur Flucht zwingt. Zusammen mit Schutzsuchenden aus dem Irak und Afghanistan erreicht die Zahl der Asylsuchenden in der EU in diesem Zuge eine neue Dimension, wobei Hunderttausende die gefährliche und strapaziöse Route über den Balkan wählen. Als sogenannte „Flüchtlingskrise" werden diese Entwicklungen europaweit in den Fokus gerückt und führen bezüglich der Lastenverteilung zu einer tiefen politischen Spaltung innerhalb der EU. In Deutschland steht man vor administrativen und logistischen Herausforderungen, um zeitnah Unterbringung und Versorgung von rund 1 Million Syrer*innen sicherzustellen. Gleichzeitig offenbart die Situation eine tiefgreifende gesellschaftliche Polarisierung, die mit einem massiven Anstieg rassistischer Übergriffe einhergeht. Allein im Jahr 2015 sind 528 solcher Angriffe dokumentiert, darunter 126 Brandanschläge. Statistisch gesehen brennt damit fast alle drei Tage eine Unterkunft für Geflüchtete in Deutschland.

Auf dem benachbarten, zunehmend verfallenden Gelände der Gehrenseestraße wird eine leerstehende Turnhalle vorübergehend zur Unterbringung von Geflüchteten genutzt. Auch hier kommt es zu rassistischen Angriffen.

Die Wohnungsnot in Berlin hat sich in den vergangenen Jahren verschärft und die Immobilienpreise steigen. Dadurch werden auch die lange Zeit gering geschätzten östlichen Randbezirke mit den großen Plattenbauvierteln als Standorte immer gefragter. Das kommunale Wohnungsunternehmen HOWOGE kauft über 1000 Wohnungen im Umfeld der Gehrenseestraße und markiert damit den Beginn einer neuen städtebaulichen Entwicklungsphase.

2016

Auf dem Nachbargrundstück der Gehrenseestraße, neben der Turnhalle, wird eine Containersiedlung mit rund 200 Plätzen zur Unterbringung von Geflüchteten errichtet. Der Betreiber Albatros übernimmt die Betreuung. Für viele Geflüchtete bedeutet der Umzug von der Turnhalle in die Containerunterkünfte eine deutliche Verbesserung ihrer Lebensbedingungen.

Der nordöstliche Nebentrakt der ehemaligen Wohnanlage wird abgerissen.

Das Gelände geht an den Immobiliendienstleister Accentro über, der dort 675 Wohnungen mit insgesamt 40.000 Quadratmeter Wohnfläche plant. Ab 2017 sollen die leerstehenden Plattenbauten saniert und neu vermarktet werden.

2018

Anstatt die Häuser in der Gehrenseestraße zu sanieren, verkauft Accentro das Grundstück an die Berliner Investorengruppe Belle Époque, die bis heute die Besitzer der Anlage sind.

Im April wird ein neues Baukonzept entwickelt. Die Belle Époque plant, gemeinsam mit der HOWOGE ein neues Stadtquartier auf 6,3 Hektar mit rund 2200 Wohnungen zu bauen. Während die Belle Époque 80 Prozent des Areals bebauen will, soll die HOWOGE die restlichen 20 Prozent bespielen. Das neu eingeleitete Projekt der HOWOGE und Belle Époque markiert eine wichtige Wandel. Statt den baufälligen Bestand der ehemaligen Arbeiterwohnheime zu sanieren, sieht das Konzept nun den Abriss und eine vollständige städtebauliche Neuordnung vor. Geplant ist eine Mischung aus Miet- und Eigentumswohnungen im Geschosswohnungsbau. Vorgesehen dabei sind Ein- bis Fünf-Zimmer-Wohnungen, wobei insgesamt 137 Einheiten durch kommunale Förderung entstehen würden.

Acht Planungsteams nehmen am Wettbewerb teil. In mehreren Werkstattrunden setzen sich zwei Favoriten durch. Das Büro MLA+/Studio M³ erhält den ersten Platz und bildet nun die Grundlage für den Masterplan „Gehrensee-Höfe".

2019

Belle Époque und HOWOGE ersuchen das Bezirksamt, um das bestehende Bebauungsplanverfahren einzustellen und den Masterplan „Gehrenseehöfe" einzuleiten, der besser an die Bedürfnisse der Bevölkerung und städtebaulichen Anforderungen angepasst ist.

2020

Das neue Bebauungsplanverfahren wird offiziell eingeleitet. Belle Époque führt hierzu eine Bürgerinformationsveranstaltung durch.

2021

Ein Bezirksamtsbeschluss legt fest, dass das Bauerfahren erst weitergeführt werden kann, wenn gesunde Wohnverhältnisse und ausreichend Freiräume nachgewiesen werden können. Ein städtebauliches Gutachten empfiehlt daraufhin, die massive Baumasse deutlich zu reduzieren . Um diese neuen Anforderungen zu erfüllen, werden umfassende Untersuchungen zu Verschattung, Mobilität und Schulplanung eingeleitet.

Bis zum Abriss soll das Areal an der Gehrenseestraße für ein temporäres Graffitikunstprojekt geöffnet werden. In Zusammenarbeit mit *Street Art Berlin* soll der Standort als touristischer Anziehungspunkt genutzt werden, wobei auch der Vorschlag, ausgewählte Graffitikunst nach Möglichkeit in den späteren Neubau zu integrieren, vorgestellt wird.

2023

Verbleibende Differenzen zwischen den Entwickler*innen und dem Bezirksamt unter Einbeziehung der Senatskommission werden geklärt und eine abschließende Einigung über die zulässige Baumasse erzielt. gemeinsam mit den Fachbehörden wird eine neue Strategie für die Freiflächen und Mobilität um die Gehrenseestraße finalisiert.

Vom Sommer 2023 bis 2025 bietet Tieu regelmäßig an Wochenenden informelle Führungen durch das Gelände des ehemaligen Vertragsarbeiterwohnheims an. Die Führungen reflektieren die Komplexität des Migrationsgeschehens sowie den einhergehenden politischen Wandel an diesem Ort.

2024

Eine konkreten Erarbeitung des Bebauungsplans sowie der Fertigstellung aller notwendigen Fachgutachten wird vorangetrieben.

2025

Im Rahmen der Ausstellung *Sung Tieu – 1992, 2025,* in den Kunst-Werken, KW Institute for Contemporary Art in Berlin-Mitte, veranstalten Sung Tieu und Tamara Hentschel eine fünfstündige Bustour durch Berlin-Marzahn und Lichtenberg. Die Route führt zum ehemaligen rechten Jugendclub Wurzel sowie zum Brodowiner Ring – wo 1992 Nguyễn Văn Tú ermordet wurde. Auch der Wohnkomplex in der Gehrenseestraße ist Teil der

Tour. Bis Ende 2025 nehmen mehr als 1000 Menschen an Tieus Führungen teil, welche die komplexe Geschichte des Gebäudes reflektieren und öffentlich sichtbar machen.

Die Containerunterkünfte neben den ehemaligen Wohnheimen in der Gehrenseestraße werden geschlossen und bleiben ungenutzt.

Der Anbieter Bairsoft nutzt die leerstehenden Gebäude und das Areal der Gehrenseestraße als Airsoft-Feld. Dort können Teilnehmer*innen mit Attrappenwaffen Kriegssituationen simulieren.

Im Sommer leitet das Amtsgericht Charlottenburg ein vorläufiges Insolvenzverfahren gegen die Gesellschaften der Projektentwicklergruppe Belle Époque ein. Eine von ihnen ist die Belle Époque Quartier Gehrenseestraße GmbH, welche ebenfalls betroffen ist. Der Insolvenzantrag, der auf einer falschen steuerlichen Einschätzung basiert, wird Ende Juli zurückgenommen. Es ist jedoch weiterhin unklar, wann und in welcher Form das Bauprojekt fortgesetzt wird.

Die Zwischennutzung des Geländes durch den Anbieter Bairsoft endet.

Nach anfänglicher Verzögerung soll der Baubeginn der „Gehrenseehöfe" im Oktober 2028 erfolgen, die Fertigstellung ist für September 2032 vorgesehen. Inzwischen liegt die Projektentwicklung des Quartiers nun bei der BE Development GmbH und nicht mehr bei der Belle Époque.

2026

Anfang März beginnen die Abrissarbeiten an den Gebäuden im östlichen Bereich der Anlage. Damit soll Platz für den Bau einer Schule geschaffen werden, die im Bebauungsplanverfahren vorgesehen ist.

Während die Plattenbauten der Gehrenseestraße verschwinden, lässt Sung Tieu den Wohnkomplex als großformatiges Mosaik neu erstehen. In Originalgröße rekonstruiert das Werk den heutigen ruinösen Zustand des Wohnkomplexes, der einst ihr Zuhause war, und bespielt die Fassade des Deutschen Pavillons auf der 61. Kunstbiennale in Venedig.

REFERENCES

"15 Anzeigen gegen Polizisten." In: *taz, die tageszeitung*, 5.7.1994. https://taz.de/15-Anzeigen-gegen-Polizisten/!1554762&s=bernauer%2Bpolizei

"2015: Dramatischer Anstieg von Gewalt gegen Flüchtlinge." *Pro Asyl*, 13.1.2016. https://www.proasyl.de/news/2015-dramatischer-anstieg-von-gewalt-gegen-fluechtlinge

ACCENTRO Real Estate AG: "ACCENTRO kauft 675 Wohnungen in Berlin und tritt im Gegenzug wertgleiche Mehrheit an bestandshaltender Gesellschaft ab." *Ad-Hoc-Meldung*, 28.12.2016. https://investors.accentro.de/news/ad-hoc/accentro-kauft-675-wohnungen-in-berlin-und-tritt-im-gegenzug-wertgleiche

"Alt-Hohenschönhausen wird zum Graffiti-Kunst-Mekka." In: *Berlin Boxx BusinessMagazin*, 24.9.2021. https://berlinboxx.de/alt-hohenschoenhausen-wird-zum-graffiti-kunst-mekka.html

Amadeu Antonio Stiftung: "Angolanische Vertragsarbeiter*innen in der DDR." https://www.amadeu-antonio-stiftung.de/amadeu-antonio/die-ausgebeuteten-brueder-angolanische-vertragsarbeiterinnen-in-der-ddr

Arbeitskreis gegen Fremdenfeindlichkeit: "Erteilung von Aufenthaltsbefugnissen an ehemalige DDR-Vertragsarbeitnehmer aus Angola, Mosambik und Vietnam – Bleiberechtsregelung vom 17.6.1993." *Hintergründe*, 1993.

Bairsoft.de. https://bairsoft.de

Belkin, Dmitrij: "Russlanddeutsche und andere postsozialistische Migranten: Jüdische Kontingentflüchtlinge und Russlanddeutsche." Bonn: *Bundeszentrale für politische Bildung*, 2017. https://www.bpb.de/themen/migration-integration/kurzdossiers/252561/juedische-kontingentfluechtlinge-und-russlanddeutsche

Bobey Rodríguez, Liz / Mücke, Ulrich / Waziri, Miene: "Kubanische Vertragsarbeiter:innen erinnern ihr Leben in der DDR." In: *Arbeit – Bewegung – Geschichte: Zeitschrift für historische Studien*, 24.5.2024. https://www.arbeit-bewegung-geschichte.de/kubanische-vertragsarbeiterinnen-erinnern-ihr-leben-in-der-ddr

Bois, Marcel / Mentz, Milan: "Im Rahmen unserer Möglichkeiten sollten wir ihnen helfen: Die DGB-Gewerkschaften und die ehemaligen Vertragsarbeiter*innen der DDR." In: Brunner, Detlev / Kuhnhenne, Michaela (Hg.): *Gewerkschaften und ostdeutsche Transformation. Mitgestaltung – Mitbestimmung?* Bielefeld: Transcript, 2025.

Braun, Juri: "Gericht hebt Insolvenzverfahren gegen Belle Époque Quartier auf." *Entwicklungsstadt*, 28.7.2025. https://entwicklungsstadt.de/gericht-hebt-insolvenzverfahren-gegen-belle-epoque-quartier-gehrensee-auf

Braun, Juri: "Insolvenzverfahren Belle Époque: Diese Bauprojekte sind betroffen." *Entwicklungsstadt*, 23.7.2025. https://entwicklungsstadt.de/insolvenzverfahren-die-lage-beim-projektentwickler-belle-epoque

Bröskamp, Bernd: "Vom Auswanderungs- zum Einwanderungsland: die DDR, ihre Ausländer, die deutsche Wiedervereinigung und die Folgen." In: Bröskamp, Bernd / Farah, Ahmed / Engelhardt, Eva (Hg.): *Schwarz-Weiße Zeiten. AusländerInnen in Ostdeutschland vor und nach der Wende. Erfahrungen der Vertragsarbeiter aus Mosambik. Interviews – Berichte – Analysen.* Bremen: Informationszentrum Afrika e.V. (IZA), 1993, pp. 13–34.

Bundesstiftung zur Aufarbeitung der SED-Diktatur (ed.): *Chronik 1989/90 – Friedliche Revolution, deutsche Einheit und Transformation. Online-Dossier*, Bundesstiftung zur Aufarbeitung der SED-Diktatur. https://www.bundesstiftung-aufarbeitung.de/de/recherche/dossiers/198990-friedliche-revolution-und-deutsche-einheit/chronik

"Das Jahr 2015: Flucht und Flüchtlinge im Fokus – ein Rückblick." *Bundeszentrale für politische Bildung*, 15.12.2025. https://www.bpb.de/themen/migration-integration/kurzdossiers/217367/das-jahr-2015-flucht-und-fluechtlinge-im-fokus-ein-rueckblick

Deutscher Bundestag (1996): Minor interpellation by representative Ulla Jelpke and the PDS Group: "Stand der Umsetzung des deutsch-vietnamesischen Rückübernahmeabkommens," *Drucksache 13/4738*, 13th legislative period, May 23, 1996, Deutscher Bundestag. https://dserver.bundestag.de/btd/13/047/1304738.pdf.

Deutscher Bundestag (1997): Federal government's response to the minor interpellation by representatives Christa Nickels, Cem Özdemir, Amke Dietert-Scheuer, and the BÜNDNIS 90/DIE GRÜNEN faction: *Drucksache 13/8053: Umsetzung des deutsch-vietnamesischen Rückübernahmeabkommens vom 21. Juli 1995. Drucksache 13/8230*, Deutscher Bundestag, 13th legislative period, July 15, 1997. https://dserver.bundestag.de/btd/13/082/1308230.pdf.

DOMiD – Dokumentationszentrum und Museum über die Migration in Deutschland (ed.): "Vertragsarbeiter in der DDR." Online: https://domid.org/news/vertragsarbeit-in-der-ddr

"Ehemalige DDR-Vertragsarbeitnehmer: Zur sozialen und aufenthaltsrechtlichen Situation." *Hintergründe 4*, 1996.

Eigensinn im Bruderland (ed.): "Nach Feierabend." Online episode of the web documentation *Eigensinn im Bruderland.* https://bruderland.de/episodes/nach-feierabend
Elsner, Eva-Maria / Elsner, Lothar (1994): "Ausländerpolitik und Ausländerfeindschaft in der DDR (1949–1990)." In: Rosa-Luxemburg-Verein e.V. (ed.), *Texte zur politischen Bildung,* vol. 13, Leipzig 1994. https://www.rosalux.de/fileadmin/ls_sachsen/dokumente/Publikationen/Texte_zur_politischen_Bildung/Texte_zur_politischen_Bildung_13_1994.pdf
"Ermittlungsgruppe Gehrenseestrasse meldet Erfolg." In: *Neues Deutschland,* 24.2.1994. https://www.nd-aktuell.de/artikel/471481.ermittlungsgruppe-gehrenseestrasse-meldet-erfolg.html?sstr=Gehrensee stra%C3%9Fe
Europäisches Institut für Migrationsstudien: "efms – Migration Report", 1994–97. https://www.efms.uni-bamberg.de/dapr98_d.htm
"Falschaussagen halfen nichts: Prügelpolizisten verurteilt." In: *taz, die tageszeitung,* 5.5.1998. https://taz.de/Falschaussagen-halfen-nichts-Pruegelpolizisten-verurteilt/!1346354&s=bernauer%2Bpolizei
Gaserow, Vera: "Die Ungewissheit beginnt von neuem." In: *taz, die tageszeitung,* 30.3.1995. https://taz.de/Die-Ungewissheit-beginnt-von-neuem/!1514499
"Geflüchtetenfeindliche Pöbelei an Unterkunft in Alt-Hohenschönhausen." *Berliner Register,* 21.9.2021. https://berliner-register.de/vorfall/61f16b69-af13-4e33-90e6-54cbf8f383bd
"Gegen rechte Gewalt die Solidarität der Demokraten." In: *taz, die tageszeitung,* 31.12.1992. https://taz.de/!1637320
"Gesetz zur Änderung ausländer- und asylverfahrensrechtlicher Vorschriften." In: *Bundesgesetzblatt,* part I, no. 72, October 31, 1997, pp. 2584 ff., published on Bundesgesetzblatt https://www.bgbl.de/xaver/bgbl/start.xav?start=%2F%2F*%5B@attr_id%3D%27bgbl197s2584.pdf%27%5D
Goddar, Jeannette: "Die Opferrolle hilft den Vietnamesen wenig." In: *taz, die tageszeitung,* 2.5.1992. https://taz.de/Die-Opferrolle-hilft-den-Vietnamesen-wenig/!1671935
Grundmann, Siegfried / Müller-Hartmann, Irene / Schmidt, Ines: *Vietnamesen in Ostdeutschland: ihre Lage und ihre Perspektiven,* Berlin: Berliner Institut für Sozialwissenschaftliche Studien (BISS), 1990
Gural, Toja: „Gehrenseestraße in Lichtenberg: Abriss der Vertragsarbeitersiedlung startet." In: Entwicklungsstadt, 5.3.2026. https://www.entwicklungsstadt.de/gehrenseestrasse-in-lichtenberg-abriss-der-vertragsarbeitersiedlung-startet/#google_vignette
"Hinrichtung im Ausländerwohnheim." In: *taz, die tageszeitung,* 09.01.1995. https://taz.de/Hinrichtung-im-Auslaenderwohnheim/!1525843
Hopfmann, Karin: "Der Kampf um das Bleiberecht in den 1990er Jahren – oder 'Das Private ist das Politische.'" Berlin: *Heinrich-Böll-Stiftung,* 2020. https://www.boell.de/de/2020/05/19/der-kampf-um-das-bleiberecht-den-1990er-jahren-oder-das-private-ist-das-politische
HOWOGE: "1. Rang – MLA+ Architecture, Planning and Consultancy." https://unternehmen.howoge.de/quartiersentwicklung/wettbewerbe/quartier-gehrenseestrasse-wollenberger-strasse/ergebnisse/mla-architecture.html
HOWOGE Wohnungsbaugesellschaft mbH (ed.): *Werkstattverfahren Quartier Gehrenseestrasse/ Wollenberger Strasse.* Online: https://unternehmen.howoge.de/quartiersentwicklung/wettbewerbe/quartier-gehrenseestrasse-wollenberger-strasse.html
Humboldt-Universität zu Berlin: "Vietnamesische Vertragsarbeit in der DDR." https://www.projekte.hu-berlin.de/de/migrationddr/migration-in-die-ddr-und-brd/projekte/jungewelt/copy_of_vertragsarbeit
Leffler, Björn: "Hohenschönhausen: 1.000 neue Wohnungen an der Gehrenseestrasse." *Entwicklungsstadt,* 06.05.2022. https://entwicklungsstadt.de/hohenschoenhausen-1-000-neue-wohnungen-an-der-gehrenseestrasse
Mai, Marina: "Keine neue Fristen für Vietnamesen." In: *taz, die tageszeitung,* 29.5.1997 https://taz.de/Keine-neue-Fristen-fuer-Vietnamesen/!1398676
"Menschenkette gegen Abschiebung." In: *taz, die tageszeitung,* 11.6.1992. https://taz.de/!1666811
Meyerhöfer, Rolf: "Obdach auf Zeit: Zur Geschichte der Ausländerwohnheime in der Gehrenseestrasse in Berlin-Hohenschönhausen." In: *Hohenschönhausen Gestern und Heute,* Berlin: Förderverein Schloss Hohenschönhausen e.V., 2012
ModernRuins.de (ed.): "Wohnheim für Vertragsarbeiter." https://www.modernruins.de/index.php/lost-places/freizeit-und-erholung/hotel-und-wohnheim/wohnheim-fuer-vertragsarbeiter
Müggenburg, Andreas: "Die ausländischen Vertragsarbeitnehmer in der ehemaligen DDR – Darstellung und Dokumentation." *Mitteilungen der Beauftragten der Bundesregierung für die Belange der Ausländer,* 1996, pp. 13–27
Nitzsche, Anja: "Zurück gehe ich auf keinen Fall!" In: *taz, die tageszei-*

tung, 29.9.1995. https://taz.de/Zurueck-gehe-ich-auf-keinen-Fall/!1490841
"Opferperspektive – Solidarisch gegen Rassismus, Diskriminierung und rechte Gewalt e. V.: Phan Văn Toàn." In: *Todesopfer rechter Gewalt in Brandenburg*. Online: https://todesopfer-rechter-gewalt-in-brandenburg.de/phan-van-toan
Panagiotidis, Jannis: "Ankunft und Integration in Deutschland." In: Hesse, Christine (ed.): *(Spät-)Aussiedler in der Migrationsgesellschaft. Informationen zur politischen Bildung*, Nr. 340. Bonn: Bundeszentrale für politische Bildung, 2019, pp. 21–25.
Petschow, Annabelle: "Montagsdemonstrationen." In: *Lebendiges Museum Online*, Stiftung Haus der Geschichte der Bundesrepublik Deutschland. https://www.hdg.de/lemo/kapitel/deutsche-einheit/friedliche-revolution/montagsdemonstrationen.html
Phạm, Vũ Vân: "Vertragsarbeiterinnen in der DDR: Frauen aus Vietnam im Blick." Bonn: *Bundeszentrale für politische Bildung*, 2024. https://www.bpb.de/themen/deutschlandarchiv/548449/vertragsarbeiterinnen-in-der-ddr
Philippi, Hanh Trinh-Lukas: "Zehn Quadratmeter Deutschland." In: *taz, die tageszeitung*, 27.3.1991. https://taz.de/Zehn-Quadratmeter-Deutschland/!1726258&s=Gehrenseestra%C3%9Fe
Plarre, Plutonia: "Wir haben die ganze Nacht vor Angst gezittert." In: *taz, die tageszeitung*, 11.9.1992. https://taz.de/Wir-haben-die-ganze-Nacht-vor-Angst-gezittert/!1653508
Poutrus, Patrice G.: "Ausländische Arbeitsmigrant*innen im 'Arbeiter-und-Bauern-Staat.'" In: Berger, Stefan / Jäger, Wolfgang / Teichmann, Ulf (eds.): *Gewerkschaften im Gedächtnis der Demokratie. Welche Rolle spielen soziale Kämpfe in der Erinnerungskultur?* Bielefeld: Transcript, 2022, pp. 227–46
Poutrus, Patrice G.: *Umkämpftes Asyl. Vom Nachkriegsdeutschland bis in die Gegenwart*, Berlin: Ch. Links, 2019
Schulz, Gesa: "Angst vor der Mafia." In: *taz, die tageszeitung*, 23.4.1995. https://taz.de/Angst-vor-der-Mafia/!1515371
Seefeld, Kathi: "Endstation Vietnam?" In: *taz, die tageszeitung*, 26.7.1995. https://taz.de/Endstation-Vietnam/!1499576
Seefeld, Kathi: "Symbolisches Wahlrecht für MigrantInnen." In: *taz, die tageszeitung*, 20.8.1994. https://taz.de/Symbolisches-Wahlrecht-fuer-MigrantInnen/!1547361
SPD Fraktion Lichtenberg: "Aktueller Status zum Bauvorhaben Gehrensee-Höfe", 11.6.2024. https://spd-fraktion-lichtenberg.de/aktueller-status-zum-bauvorhaben-gehrenseehoefe
"Vertragsarbeiter der Ex-DDR sollen bleiben." In: *taz, die tageszeitung*, 16.12.1992. https://taz.de/Vertragsarbeiter-der-Ex-DDR-sollen-bleiben/!1638935
"Vietnamesen sollen für Sicherheit zahlen." In: *taz, die tageszeitung*, 29.11.1995. https://taz.de/Vietnamesen-sollen-fuer-Sicherheit-zahlen/!1482549&s=Ausl%C3%A4nderwohnheim
"Was ist los im Osten? Teil 1: Situation der Ausländer in den neuen Ländern." In: *VIA Magazin*, 1992
"Wegweiser zum Bleiberecht für ehemalige Vertragsarbeitnehmer und Vertragsarbeitnehmerinnen." *Hintergründe 2*, 1993
Weiss, Karin: "Migrantische Perspektiven: Zwischen Rückkehr in die Heimatländer und Existenzsicherung vor Ort – Die Situation vietnamesischer Vertragsarbeiter 1989/90." Bonn: *Bundeszentrale für politische Bildung*, 2021. https://www.bpb.de/themen/deutsche-einheit/migrantische-perspektiven/325194/zwischen-rueckkehr-in-die-heimatlaender-und-existenzsicherung-vor-ort
Wildt, Dirk: "Polizei verhindert rassistische Überfälle." In: *taz, die tageszeitung*, 07.09.1992. https://taz.de/Polizei-verhindert-rassistische-Ueberfaelle/!1654162&s=razzia%2Bausl%C3%A4nderwohnheim
"Zwei Obdachlose tot in Lichtenberger Abrisshaus entdeckt." In: *Berliner Morgenpost*, 18.3.2013. https://www.morgenpost.de/printarchiv/berlin/article114526118/Zwei-Obdachlose-tot-in-Lichtenberger-Abrisshaus-entdeckt.html
Wikipedia: "Kommunalwahlen in der DDR 1989." In: *Wikipedia – Die Freie Enzyklopädie*. https://de.wikipedia.org/wiki/Kommunalwahlen_in_der_DDR_1989#
Europäisches Institut für Migrationsstudien: "efms – Migration Report," 1994–97. https://www.efms.uni-bamberg.de/dapr98_d.htm

SABETH BUCHMANN is an art historian and critic. Since 2004, she has held the professorship for Modern and Postmodern Art at the Academy of Fine Arts Vienna. Buchmann regularly contributes writing to scholarly essay collections, exhibition catalogs, and art journals. In addition, she is co-editor of *PoLyPen*—a series on art criticism and political theory (b_books, Berlin). She is a member of the advisory boards of *Texte zur Kunst*, *The European Kunsthalle*, and *Documenta Institut*. Buchmann's recent publications include *Art as Infrastructure* (2022); *Broken Relations: Infrastructure, Aesthetic, and Critique* (2022, edited with Martin Beck, Beatrice von Bismarck, and Ilse Lafer); and *Putting Rehearsals to the Test: Practices of Rehearsal in Fine Arts, Film, Theater, Theory, and Politics* (2016, edited with Constanze Ruhm and Ilse Lafer). Earlier publications include *Textile Theories of Modernity: Alois Riegl in Art Criticism* (2015, edited with Rike Frank); *Hélio Oiticica, Neville D'Almeida and Others: Block-Experiments in Cosmococa* (2013, written with Max Jorge Hinderer Cruz); *Film Avant-Garde Biopolitics* (2009, edited with Helmut Draxler and Stephan Geene); *Thinking Against Thinking: Production – Technology – Subjectivity in Sol LeWitt, Yvonne Rainer, and Hélio Oiticica* (2007, revised doctoral dissertation); and *Art After Conceptual Art* (2006, edited with Alexander Alberro).

The work of HENRIKE NAUMANN (1984 Zwickau, GDR–2026 Berlin, Germany) reflects on socio-political issues at the level of design and interior design, exploring the friction between opposing political opinions in relation to taste and personal everyday aesthetics. In her installations, she arranged furniture and objects to create scenographic spaces into which she integrated video, sound, and performance. Naumann's work probes the mechanisms of radicalization and their entanglement with personal experience. Her artistic practice expanded into a broad range of lectures and interdisciplinary collaborations. Naumann received numerous prizes, including the Karl Schmidt-Rottluff Scholarship, the Max Pechstein Prize of the City of Zwickau, the Leipziger Volkszeitung Art Prize, and the Scholarship of Villa Aurora / Thomas Mann House in Los Angeles. Her work has been presented in major exhibitions at SculptureCenter, New York; the Busch-Reisinger Museum, Harvard University; the Museum of Modern Art Warsaw; and the Wall Memorial of the German Bundestag, as well as the Ghetto Biennale (2015) and the Kyiv Biennale (2023). Naumann was a fellow at the Berlin Artistic Research Program 2024/25, where she researched the relationship between art and war.

KATHLEEN REINHARDT is the director of the Georg Kolbe Museum in Berlin. Her curatorial practice engages German and international contexts, with a focus on contemporary art, art under state socialism and post-socialist practices, and the discursive potential of collections in relation to ideology, memory, and identity. She is particularly interested in the museum as a space for artistic research and production, as well as the role of feminist thought in rethinking institutional frameworks. At the Georg Kolbe Museum, Reinhardt has developed a program combining historical inquiry with contemporary practice, including exhibitions such as *Lin May Saeed. The Snow Falls Slowly in Paradise*, *A Dialogue with Renée Sintenis* (2023), *Noa Eshkol. No Time to Dance* (2024) and *David Hartt. Metabolic Rift* (2025). From 2016 to 2022, she was curator for contemporary art at the Albertinum (Dresden State Art Collections), overseeing acquisitions, solo and group exhibitions, and publications including *Slavs and Tatars. Made in Dschermany* (2018) and *For Ruth, the Sky in Los Angeles. Ruth Wolf-Rehfeldt and David Horvitz* (2019). In 2020/21, she curated *1 Million Roses for Angela Davis* and initiated the research and exhibition project *Revolutionary Romances? Transcultural Art Histories in the GDR* (2019–2024). A scholar of African American art and socially engaged practices, Reinhardt holds a PhD from Freie Universität Berlin in Global Art Histories. She teaches internationally and publishes in exhibition catalogues, scholarly volumes, and journals including *African Arts*, *Art Margins*, *Contemporary And*, and *Kaleidoscope*.

KERSTIN STAKEMEIER is a writer and educator at the Academy of Fine Arts Nuremberg, whose work is dedicated to what—and who—has been disfigured through being rendered obscene. She co-authored *Universal Receptivity* (2021) with Bill Dietz and *Reproducing Autonomy* (2016) with Marina Vishmidt. Stakemeier wrote *Entgrenzter Formalismus. Verfahren einer antimodernen Ästhetik* (b_books, 2017), and a special issue of the journal *Selva* dedicated to the work of Peter Gorsen will continue this line of inquiry in 2026. Between 2021–2023, she curated *Illiberal Arts/Lives* (Haus der Kulturen der Welt Berlin/Ludwig Forum Aachen) together with Anselm Franke. She is currently writing a joint essay with Devin Fore, as well as a series of introductions for a set of conversations dedicated to "The Fantasies of the People" for *e-flux*.

SUNG TIEU, (b. 1987, Hải Dương, Vietnam) is a Berlin-based artist. Having been raised between political systems, Tieu's work unfolds at the intersection of biography and geopolitics. Her practice examines the enduring aftershocks of the Cold War and observes colonial entanglements and the subtle mechanisms of institutional power and sociopolitical agendas. Through sculpture, found objects, sound, video, photography, text, and archival material, Tieu constructs spatially dense, immersive installations, creating environments that unpack the social and psychological effects of migration, bureaucracy, and control. Her work has been the subject of major solo exhibitions held at Kunsthalle Bern; KW Institute for Contemporary Art, Berlin; Museum für Gegenwartskunst Siegen; Kunsthalle Nürnberg; Amant, New York; Neuer Berliner Kunstverein (n.b.k.); Mudam—Musée d'Art Moderne Grand-Duc Jean, Luxembourg; and Haus der Kunst, Munich, among others. She has also participated in the Taipei Biennial (2025), Gwangju Biennale (2024), Shanghai Biennale (2023), Bienal de São Paulo (2021), and the Kyiv Biennial (2021). Tieu has received numerous awards, including the Schering Stiftung Award for Artistic Research (2024), the Rubens Promotional Award of the City of Siegen (2024), and the Audience Award of the Preis der Nationalgalerie (2021).

SABETH BUCHMANN ist Kunsthistorikerin und Kritikerin. Seit 2004 ist sie Professorin für Kunst der Moderne und Nachmoderne an der Akademie der bildenden Künste Wien. Sie schreibt regelmäßig für wissenschaftliche Aufsatzbände, Ausstellungskataloge und Kunstzeitschriften. Darüber hinaus ist sie Mitherausgeberin von *PoLyPen* – einer Reihe zu Kunstkritik und politischer Theorie (b_books, Berlin). Sie ist Beiratsmitglied von *Texte zur Kunst*, The European Kunsthalle und des documenta Instituts. Zu ihren zuletzt erschienenen Publikationen zählen *Kunst als Infrastruktur*, 2022, *Broken Relations: Infrastructure, Aesthetic, and Critique*, 2022 (hg. mit Martin Beck, Beatrice von Bismarck und Ilse Lafer), *Putting Rehearsals to the Test. Practices of Rehearsal in Fine Arts, Film, Theater, Theory, and Politics*, 2016 (hg. mit Constanze Ruhm und Ilse Lafer). Zu früheren Publikationen zählen *Textile Theorien der Moderne. Alois Riegl in der Kunstkritik*, 2015, (hg. mit Rike Frank), *Hélio Oiticica, Neville D'Almeida and others: Block-Experiments in Cosmococa*, 2013 (verfasst mit Max Jorge Hinderer Cruz) und *Film Avantgarde Biopolitik*, 2009 (hg. mit Helmut Draxler und Stephan Geene), *Denken gegen das Denken. Produktion – Technologie – Subjektivität bei Sol LeWitt, Yvonne Rainer und Hélio Oiticica*, 2007 (überarbeitete Dissertationsschrift), *Art After Conceptual Art*, 2006 (hg. mit Alexander Alberro).

Die Werke von HENRIKE NAUMANN (1984 Zwickau, DDR–2026 Berlin, Deutschland) reflektieren gesellschaftspolitische Probleme auf der Ebene von Design und Interieur und das Reibungsverhältnis entgegengesetzter politischer Meinungen im Umgang mit Geschmack und persönlicher Alltagsästhetik. In ihren Installationen arrangierte sie Möbel und Objekte zu szenografischen Räumen, in welche sie Video- und Soundarbeiten integrierte. Naumanns Arbeiten untersuchen die Mechanismen der Radikalisierung und deren Zusammenhang mit persönlicher Erfahrung. Ihre künstlerische Praxis war von einer Vielzahl von Vorträgen und interdisziplinären Kooperationen begleitet. Sie wurde mit zahlreichen Preisen ausgezeichnet, darunter das Karl Schmidt-Rottluff-Stipendium, der Max-Pechstein-Preis der Stadt Zwickau, der Kunstpreis der Leipziger Volkszeitung sowie das Villa-Aurora-Stipendium/Thomas Mann House, Los Angeles. Wichtige Ausstellungen ihrer Werke fanden unter anderem im SculptureCenter in New York, im Busch-Reisinger-Museum in Harvard, im MoMA in Warschau, im Deutschen Bundestag sowie im Rahmen der Ghetto Biennale (2015) und der Kyiv Biennale (2023) statt. 2024 erschien ihr Künstlerbuch *CONCEPTS*, das Konzeptpapiere zu Arbeiten der vorangegangenen zehn Jahre versammelt.

KATHLEEN REINHARDT ist Direktorin des Georg Kolbe Museums in Berlin. Ihre kuratorische Praxis in deutschen und internationalen Kontexten legt Schwerpunkte auf zeitgenössische Kunst, Kunst in sozialistischen Systemen und post-sozialistischen Praktiken sowie dem diskursiven Potenzial von Sammlungen im Kontext von Ideologie, Erinnerung und Identität. Sie versteht das Museum als Ort künstlerischer Forschung und Produktion und befasst sich mit der Rolle feministischer Perspektiven für die Neugestaltung institutioneller Strukturen. Am Georg Kolbe Museum verbindet ihr Programm historische Fragestellungen mit zeitgenössischer Praxis, etwa in den Ausstellungen *Lin May Saeed. The Snow Falls Slowly in Paradise*, *A Dialogue with Renée Sintenis* (2023), *Noa Eshkol. No Time to Dance* (2024) und *David Hartt. Metabolic Rift* (2025). Von 2016 bis 2022 war sie Kuratorin für zeitgenössische Kunst am Albertinum (Staatliche Kunstsammlungen Dresden), wo sie Sammlungsankäufe, Einzel- und Gruppenausstellungen sowie Publikationen verantwortete, darunter *Slavs and Tatars. Made in Dschermany* (2018) und *For Ruth, the Sky in Los Angeles. Ruth Wolf-Rehfeldt and David Horvitz* (2019). 2020/2021 kuratierte sie die Gruppenausstellung *1 Million Rosen für Angela Davis* und initiierte das Forschungs- und Ausstellungsprojekt *Revolutionary Romances? Transkulturelle Kunstgeschichten in der DDR* (2019–2024). Reinhardt forscht und promovierte zu afroamerikanischer Kunst und sozial-engagierten künstlerischen Praktiken an der Freien Universität Berlin im Fachbereich Global Art Histories. Sie lehrt international und veröffentlicht in Ausstellungskatalogen, wissenschaftlichen Sammelbänden sowie Fachzeitschriften, darunter *African Arts*, *Art Margins*, *Contemporary And* und *Kaleidoscope*.

KERSTIN STAKEMEIER ist Autorin und Lehrende an der Akademie der Bildenden Künste Nürnberg. Ihre Arbeit widmet sich dem, was – und wem – durch die Herstellung von Obszönität entstellt worden ist. Gemeinsam mit Bill Dietz verfasste sie *Universal Receptivity* (2021) sowie mit Marina Vishmidt *Reproducing Autonomy* (2016). Stakemeier veröffentlichte *Entgrenzter Formalismus. Verfahren einer antimodernen Ästhetik* (b_books, 2017). Diese Untersuchungslinie wird 2026 in einer Sonderausgabe der Zeitschrift *Selva* fortgeführt, die dem Werk von Peter Gorsen gewidmet ist. Zwischen 2021 und 2023 kuratierte sie gemeinsam mit Anselm Franke *Illiberal Arts/Lives* (Haus der Kulturen der Welt Berlin/Ludwig Forum Aachen). Derzeit arbeitet sie an einem gemeinsamen Essay mit Devin Fore sowie an einer Reihe von Einleitungen zu einer Gesprächsreihe mit dem Titel „The Fantasies of the People" für *e-flux*.

SUNG TIEU (*1987, Hải Dương, Vietnam) ist eine vietnamesisch-deutsche Künstlerin, die in Berlin lebt und arbeitet. Das Aufwachsen zwischen politischen Systemen bildet die Grundlage für ein Werk im Spannungsfeld von Biografie und Geopolitik. Tieu verbindet Skulptur, Fundstücke, Klang, Video, Fotografie, Text und Archivmaterial zu immersiven Installationen, die Räume schaffen, in denen die sozialen und psychologischen Folgen von Migration, Bürokratie und Kontrolle erfahrbar werden. Ihre Praxis untersucht die Nachwirkungen des Kalten Krieges, koloniale Verflechtungen sowie die subtilen Mechanismen institutioneller Gewalt und gesellschaftspolitischer Agenden. Tieus Arbeiten wurden in bedeutenden Einzelausstellungen gezeigt, unter anderem in der Kunsthalle Bern; dem KW Institute for Contemporary Art, Berlin; dem Museum für Gegenwartskunst Siegen; der Kunsthalle Nürnberg; der Amant, New York; dem Neuer Berliner Kunstverein (n.b.k.); dem Mudam – Musée d'Art Moderne Grand-Duc Jean, Luxemburg; und dem Haus der Kunst, München. Darüber hinaus nahm sie an der Taipei Biennale (2025), der Gwangju Biennale (2024), der Shanghai Biennale (2023), der Bienal de São Paulo (2021) und der Kyiv Biennale (2021) teil. Tieu erhielt zahlreiche Auszeichnungen, darunter den Schering Stiftung Award for Artistic Research (2024), den Rubens-Förderpreis der Stadt Siegen (2024) sowie den Publikumspreis des Preis der Nationalgalerie (2021).

The German Pavilion at the 61ST International Art Exhibition—La Biennale di Venezia is realized by ifa – Institut für Auslandsbeziehungen on behalf of and funded by the German Federal Foreign Office./

Der Deutsche Pavillon zur 61. Internationalen Kunstausstellung – La Biennale di Venezia wird realisiert durch das ifa – Institut für Auslandsbeziehungen in Kooperation mit und gefördert vom Auswärtigen Amt der Bundesrepublik Deutschland.

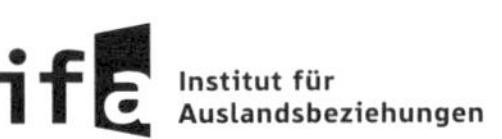

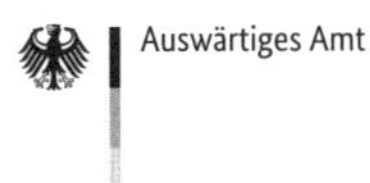

INITIAL PARTNER / INITIALPARTNER

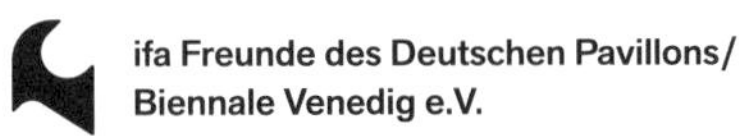

PARTNER

Sparkassen-Finanzgruppe in association with Sparkassen-Kulturfonds of Deutscher Sparkassen- und Giroverband, Ostsächsische Sparkasse Dresden, Ostdeutscher Sparkassenverband and DekaBank Deutsche Girozentrale/

Die Sparkassen-Finanzgruppe mit dem Sparkassen-Kulturfonds des Deutschen Sparkassen- und Giroverbandes, der Ostsächsischen Sparkasse Dresden, dem Ostdeutschen Sparkassenverband sowie der DekaBank Deutsche Girozentrale

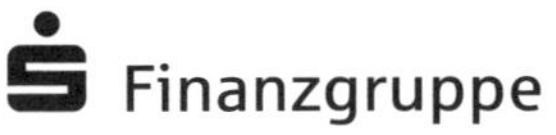

SUPPORTERS / FÖRDERER

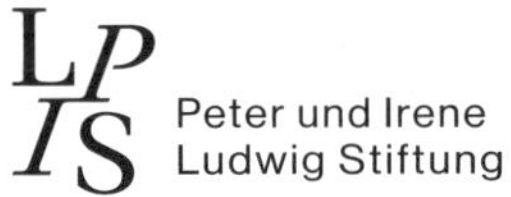

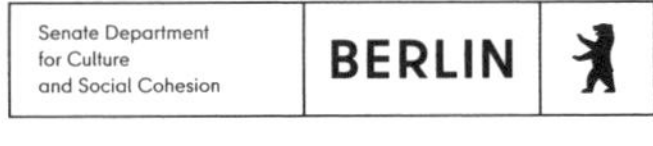

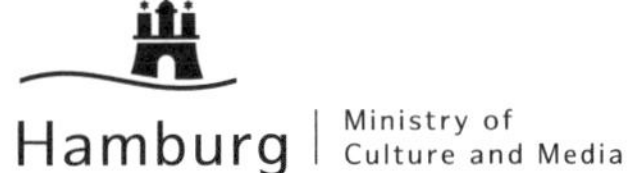

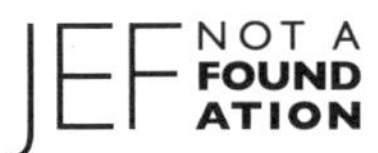

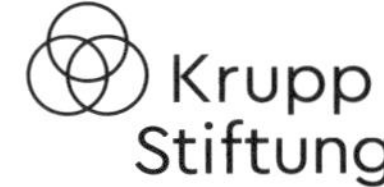

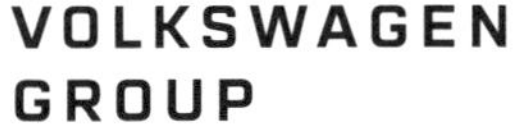

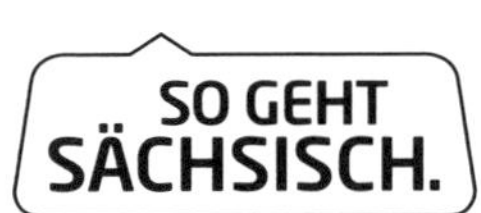

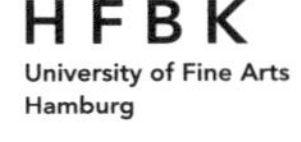

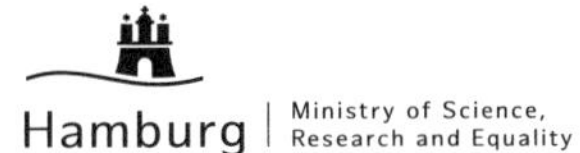

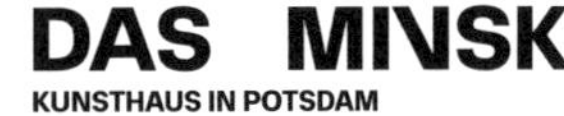

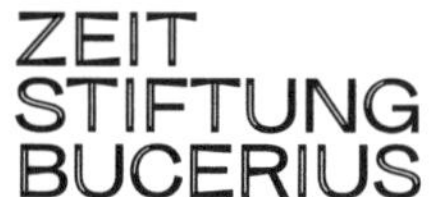

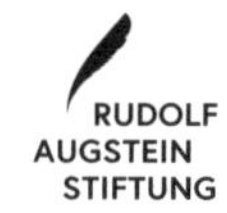

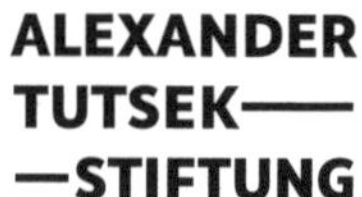

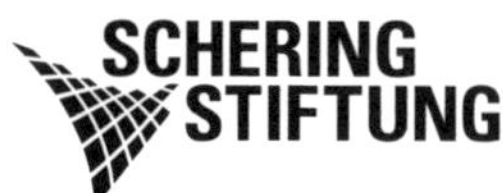

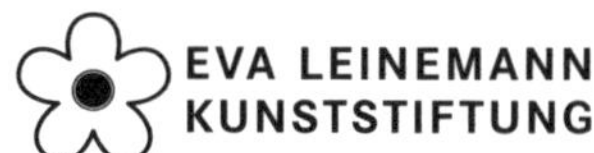

CONCRETE
PROJECTS

DANKSAGUNG / SPECIAL THANKS

Sammlung Becker
Emanuel Bodman
Lilli von Bodman
Boros Foundation
Burger Collection, Hong Kong
Dr. Hella Dierking
Emalin, London
Nicoletta Fiorucci Foundation
Carola & Jeremy Golding
Sammlung Gräfling
Barbara & Axel Haubrok
Sammlung Haus N
Carlos & Johanna von Hardenberg, München
Karin und Uwe Hollweg Stiftung
Korinna von Kempski, Halina von Kempski & Dr. Sebastian Baden
Ludwig Koehne
Koko Mosaico
F. Niemann Kronshagen
Kuhn & Bülow
Kirsten & Stephan Landwehr
Sammlung Andra Lauffs-Wegner
Clemens Leopold
Saskia Leopold
Hans-Dieter Lochmann
Private Collection, Liebaert Projects, Belgium
Robert Müller-Grünow
Brigitte und Arend Oetker
Perić Collection
Ravennae Mosaico Ori e Smalti S.r.l.
Collection Enea Righi, Bologna, Italy
Julie Schemann, München
Kunststiftung Christa & Nikolaus Schües
Dr. Karsten & Sandra Stein
Nicos Steratzias
Andrée Sfeir-Semler
Sfeir-Semler Gallery Beirut/Hamburg
Trautwein Herleth Berlin
Villa Massimo
Visit Berlin
Prof. Carsten Wiewiorra
Alexander Zuckowski
3548 Collection

My deepest thanks go to the artists Sung Tieu and Henrike Naumann for their vision and persistence in pursuing this project, as well as to their studios, galleries, and circle of supporters.

To the Friends of the German Pavilion, whose steadfast support has sustained this project and who always move forward with pragmatism and generosity, even in the face of the greatest complications.

Heartfelt thanks to all supporters and patrons of this project—for their openness, curiosity, and enthusiasm for art and artists who are demanding and challenging, resist fixed categorizations and linear narratives, and thereby open up other layers of meaning to us—thank you for embarking on this journey with us.

Extraordinary thanks go to all the scholars and researchers who have accompanied this project, for their knowledge as well as for their sensitivity, patience, and generosity in entering into dialogue with us: Eva Bentcheva, Matteo Bertelé, Sabeth Buchmann, Lutz Klinkhammer, Doreen Mende, Kerstin Stakemeier, Clemens Villinger, and many others whose scholarly and curatorial work has influenced us over the years on the path toward the German Pavilion.

Many thanks to Dan Solbach for his clear design vision, which shaped the visual identity of the project in keeping with the artists' way of thinking and ensured its impact. My deep gratitude also goes to Jesi Khadivi for her editorial vision, patience, and joy throughout—she has accompanied my texts for many years with precision and intelligence. Special thanks also go to DISTANZ Verlag. Heartfelt thanks to the wonderful team at the Georg Kolbe Museum, as well as to my excellent foundation board, for their trust and support in these challenging times.

Furthermore, I would like to thank everyone who has encouraged, supported, advised, and accompanied me in very different ways over the past year on this project: Elena Agudio, Heidi Ballet, Lilli von Bodman, Jakob Braeuer, Friederike von Brühl, Karl Dipti, Julia Draganović, Alexander Farenholtz, Rike Frank, Gabriela Galati, Annie Claire Geisinger, Natasha Ginwala, Monika Grütters, David Hartt, Aline Hollstein, David Horvitz, Ruth Lecher, Gregor Lersch, Karolina Majewska-Güdde, Ayumi Paul, Sebastian Pflum, Carmen Reinhardt, Heidi Reinhardt, Katharina von Ruckteschell-Katte, Annette Schemmel, Eva Schmitt, Alya Sebti, Nina Tesenfitz, Peter Vasil, Xiaoyu Weng, Amy Zion, Franciska Zólyom, and others who prefer to remain unnamed.

Last but not least, a deep bow to Anaïs Nyffeler and the brilliant Katharina Heise, who, even in complex situations and the most intense phases of the project, always kept a cool head and supported, shaped, and realized this project with great enthusiasm, patience, communication skills, and solutions—and in the process never lost their professionalism, humor, or sensitivity.

Tiefer Dank gilt den Künstlerinnen Sung Tieu und Henrike Naumann, ihrer Vision und Hartnäckigkeit für dieses Projekt sowie ihren Studios, Galerien und Unterstützer*innenkreis.

Den ifa Freunden des Deutschen Pavillons, welche wunderbar begleiten und immer pragmatisch und großzügig voranschreiteten, auch in den größten Komplikationen.

Allen Unterstützer*innen und Förderer*innen für dieses Projekt ein herzlicher Dank – für ihre Offenheit, Neugier und Begeisterung für eine Kunst und ihre Protagonistinnen, die anspruchsvoll und herausfordernd ist, die fixen Kategorisierungen und linearen Erzählungen widersteht und uns so andere Bedeutungsebenen eröffnen kann – danke, dass Sie mit uns auf diese Reise gegangen sind!

Allen dieses Projekt begleitenden Wissenschaftler*innen und Forschenden gilt außerordentlicher Dank für ihr Wissen sowie ihre Sensibilität, Geduld und Großzügigkeit, den Dialog mit uns einzugehen: Eva Bentcheva, Matteo Bertelé, Sabeth Buchmann, Lutz Klinkhammer, Doreen Mende, Kerstin Stakemeier, Clemens Villinger und vielen weiteren, deren wissenschaftliche und kuratorische Arbeit uns jeweils auf dem Weg zum Deutschen Pavillon über die Jahre beeinflusst hat.

Der klaren Gestaltungsvision von Dan Solbach, die im Sinne des künstlerischen Denkens der Künstlerinnen die visuelle Identität des Projekts geprägt und für seine Wirksamkeit gesorgt hat – vielen Dank. Jesi Khadivi gilt für ihre editorische Vision und die Geduld und Freude, die sie diesem Projekt durchweg entgegengebracht hat, mein tiefer Dank – seit vielen Jahren begleitet sie meine Texte mit Präzision und Intelligenz. Dem DISTANZ Verlag gilt zudem großer Dank.

Ein herzlicher Dank dem großartigen Team des Georg Kolbe Museums, sowie meinem tollen Stiftungskuratorium für das Vertrauen und die Unterstützung in diesen herausfordernden Zeiten. Desweiteren danke ich allen, die mich über das letzte Jahr bei diesem Projekt in ganz unterschiedlicher Weise ermutigt, unterstützt, beraten und begleitet haben: Elena Agudio, Heidi Ballet, Lilli von Bodman, Jakob Braeuer, Friederike von Brühl, Karl Dipti, Julia Draganović, Alexander Farenholtz, Rike Frank, Gabriela Galati, Annie Claire Geisinger, Natasha Ginwala, Monika Grütters, David Hartt, Aline Hollstein, David Horvitz, Ruth Lecher, Gregor Lersch, Karolina Majewska-Güdde, Ayumi Paul, Sebastian Pflum, Carmen Reinhardt, Heidi Reinhardt, Katharina von Ruckteschell-Katte, Annette Schemmel, Eva Schmitt, Alya Sebti, Nina Tesenfitz, Peter Vasil, Xiaoyu Weng, Amy Zion, Franciska Zólyom und weitere, die anonym bleiben möchten.

Last but not least eine große Verbeugung vor Anaïs Nyffeler und der brillanten Katharina Heise, die auch in den komplexesten Situationen und heißesten Projektphasen immer einen kühlen Kopf bewahrt haben, mit viel Elan, Geduld, Kommunikationskompetenz und Lösungsideen dieses Projekt getragen, gestaltet und umgesetzt und dabei nie ihre Professionalität, ihren Humor und ihre Sensibilität verloren haben.

STUDIO HENRIKE NAUMANN

Your family, friends, and colleagues thank you, dearest Henrike, for taking us along on your journey to the German Pavilion with such generosity, love, and appreciation over the years. We will never forget you!

Deine Familie, deine Freund:innen und deine Kolleg:innen danken dir, liebste Henrike, dass du uns alle über viele Jahre so großzügig, liebevoll und wertschätzend auf deinem Weg zum Deutschen Pavillon mitgenommen hast. Wir werden dich nie vergessen!

My deepest gratitude goes to my visionary curator, Kathleen Reinhardt. With her sharp intellect, she opened the framework within which Henrike and I were able to come together. Dear Henrike, our artistic dialogue is inscribed in the texture of every work and continues to resonate. I am thinking of you.

To my irreplaceable team and partner, I offer my admiration and gratitude for your belief in my vision.

Woven into the very heart of this project is my mother, Vũ Thị Hạnh. This work is dedicated to her, with all my love.

Finally, my thanks go to all those who have accompanied me over the years on my path. You have given meaning to my work and to me. My heartfelt thanks go to:

Mein tief empfundener Dank gilt meiner visionären Kuratorin Kathleen Reinhardt. Mit ihrem scharfen Intellekt hat sie jenen Rahmen eröffnet, in dem Henrike und ich zusammenfinden durften. Liebe Henrike, unser künstlerischer Dialog ist in jede Textur der Werke eingeschrieben und wirkt fort. Ich denke an dich.

Meinem unersetzlichen Team und Partner, gilt meine Bewunderung und mein Dank für euren Glauben an meine Vision.

Im Herzen dieses Projekts ist meine Mutter, Vũ Thị Hạnh, gegenwärtig. Dieses Werk ist ihr in Liebe gewidmet.

Mein Dank gilt schließlich all jenen, die mich über die Jahre hinweg auf meinem Weg begleitet haben. Ihr habt mich und meine Arbeit mit Sinn erfüllt, von Herzen danke ich:

Liberty Adrian, Patrick Armstrong, Nick Ash, Kader Attia, Mirela Baciak, Pedro Barbosa, Luca Barberini, Sam Bardaouil, Ute Meta Bauer, Martin Beck, Natalie Bell, Eva Bentcheva, Vincent Bevins, Giampaolo Bianconi, Juliane Bischoff, Konrad Bitterli, Nicolas Bourriaud, Sabeth Buchmann, Carina Bukuts, Monique & Max Burger, Sol Calero, Enzo Camacho, Adam Carr, Stefano Cernuschi, Alexis Chan, Carson Chan, Daniel Chew, Pamela Corey, Michelle Cotton, Lucy Cowling, Giuseppe Cristoferi, Jacopo Crivelli Visconti, Josef Dalle Nogare, Patrizia Dander, Phuong Dan, Saim Demircan, Maurin Dietrich, Udo Engel, Emma Enderby, Ruth Estevez, Marco Falcioni, Andrea Faraguna, Cédric Fauq, Jeanne Faust, Timo Feldhaus, Till Fellrath, Elena Filipović, Thomas Flierl, iLiana Fokianaki, Linda Franken, Goshka Gawlik, Anna-Catharina Gebbers, Vitali Gelwich, Martin Germann, Anna Roberta Götz, Friedrich & Johanna Gräfling, Anna Gritz, Marcela Guerrero, Adam Harrison, Gloria Hasnay, Bill Jingwen He, Bart van der Heide, Tamara Hentschel, Gerd Hessel, Adam Hines-Green, Hans Holm, Karin Hopfmann, Johannes Hörning, Uta Jankowsky, Malcolm Jayne, Meret Kaufmann, Morag Keil, Erika Keitzel, Nina Kettiger, Jesi Khadivi, Christopher Kline, Josh Kline, Brigitte Kölle, Wojciech Kosma, Martin Köttering, Janina Krepart, Léon Kruijswijk, Annie Kwan, Erika Landström, Pablo Larios, Gunar Laube, Lawrence Leaman, Dominick Lee, Damian Lentini, Sam Lewitt, Ami Lien, Do Tuong Linh, Phuong Linh, Elisa R. Linn, Andrea Lissoni, Emalin, Francesco Manacorda, Dan Meththananda, Barbara Mewis, Daniel Milnes, Dirk Moldt, Charlotte Mourgue d'Algue, Olivier Mourgue d'Algue, Christian Naujoks, Kito Nedo, Nam Nguyen, Tin Nguyen, Anaïs Nyffeler, Kadeem Oak, Shaolian Ouyang, Diana Pfammatter, Susanne Pfeffer, Picot Chapman, Gregor Quack, Veronika Radulovic, Kathleen Rahn, Asad Raza, Dan Rees, Willem de Rooij, Lynette Roth, Drew Sawyer, Anna Schneider, Fabian Schöneich, Alexander Schröder, Micky Schubert, Cory John Scozzari, Noam Segal, Anna Lena Seiser, Teresa Serafini, Andrée Sfeir-Semler, Sfeir-Semler Gallery, Ana Siler, Andreas Slominski, Dan Solbach, Chloe Stead, Tim Steer, Stefan Strobl, Sam Talbot, Milan Ther, Sarah Johanna Theurer, Thomas Thiel, Constantin Thun, Leopold Thun, Sam Thorne, Trautwein Herleth, Tuan Mami, Aurelia & Carlos Usandizaga, Jan Vorisek, Danh Võ, Angelina Volk, Jason Waite, Pip Wallis, Jonas Wendelin, Oliver Williams, Christopher Williams-Wynn, Benedict Winkler, Vincent Wolf, Haegue Yang, Harriet Zilch.

This catalogue is published in conjunction with the German Pavilion at the 61ST International Art Exhibition—La Biennale di Venezia. /

Dieser Katalog erscheint anlässlich des Deutschen Pavillons auf der 61. Internationalen Kunstausstellung – La Biennale di Venezia.

RUIN
61ST International Art Exhibition
La Biennale di Venezia
German Pavilion
May 9 – November 22, 2026

61. Internationale Kunstausstellung
La Biennale di Venezia
Deutscher Pavillon
9. Mai – 22. November 2026

EXHIBITION / AUSSTELLUNG

Artists / Künstlerinnen: Henrike Naumann, Sung Tieu
Curator / Kuratorin: Dr. Kathleen Reinhardt
Commissioner / Kommissar: ifa – Institut für Auslandsbeziehungen
General Secretary / Generalsekretärin: Gitte Zschoch
Head of Art Department / Leitung Kunstabteilung: Dr. Ellen Strittmatter
Head of Art Funding, Biennials / Leitung Kunstförderungen, Biennalen: Dorothea Grassmann
Lead Project Manager / Leitende Projektkoordination: Tuan Do Duc
Project Manager / Projektkoordination: Philipp Kind
Accounting / Buchhaltung: Tanja Spiess
Communication / Kommunikation: Hjördis Kettenbach, Miriam Kahrmann, Theresa Brüheim, Pia Roskwitalski, Bureau N
Invitation Management / Einladungsmanagement: Sophie Slade
Head of Production / Produktionsleitung: Mirja Katharina Heise
Curatorial Assistant / Kuratorische Assistenz: Anaïs Nyffeler
Curatorial Communication and Publication Management / Kuratorische Kommunikation und Publikationsmanagement: Jesi Khadivi
Visual Identity / Visuelle Identität: Dan Solbach
Design Assistance / Design Assistenz: Yewon Park
Website: Asger Behncke Jacobsen
Production Management / Produktionsmanagement: Alessandra Messali
Technical Management and Architectural Supervision / Technische Koordination und architektonische Bauleitung: Clemens F. Kusch, Martin Weigert, Andrea Giovanni Zigon
Lighting Concept / Lichtkonzept: Matthias Singer
Event Photography / Event Fotografie: Clelia Cadamuro
Installation Views / Installationsansichten: Jens Ziehe
Vermittlung / Mediation: Sara Bizai, Marco Carrino, Emma de Felice, Gaia De Santi, Fabio Lapenna, Andra Pani, Anne Rosenvold, Melanie Ruhe, Eduardo Xerex
Fundraising: ifa – Institut für Auslandsbeziehungen, Kathleen Reinhardt, sorry, not sorry—Lilli von Bodman

STUDIO HENRIKE NAUMANN

Deputy Artistic Direction / Stellvertretende künstlerische Leitung: Dr. Clemens Villinger
Project Management / Projektleitung: Alissa Dovgucic
Studio Manager / Studiomanager: Carlo Bernhardt
Consulting / Beratung: Bakri Bakhit

PRODUKTIONSTEAM / PRODUCTION TEAM HENRIKE NAUMANN

Production Management and Artistic Consulting / Produktionsleitung und künstlerische Beratung: Jonas von Ostrowski
Deputy Production Manager / Stellvertretende Produktionsleitung: Pauline Weertz

Technical Production/Technische Umsetzung: Naiv Studios (Kilien-Robinson Heiland, Simon Jenewein, Julian Kast)
Installation Assistants/Aufbauhelfer: Christian Eisenberg, Linus Schuierer, Luis Traxler
Production Team Berlin/Produktionsteam Berlin: Doreen Back, Ulrike Bernard, Julia Boxler, Shuah Brotherton, Johannes Büttner, Thomas Drerup, Markues, Bastian Hagedorn, Alice Hauck, Simone Körner, Melissa Kurt, Magdalena Loheide, Esra Nagel, Rudyard Schmidt, Inger Selck, Lee Stevens, Tobi, Theresa Tuffner, Merle Vorwald, Sebastian Warne, Elisabeth Weiß

PERFORMANCE *TRÜMMERFRAU*

Choreography/Choreographie: Il Posto Vertical Dance—Wanda Moretti
Performers/Performerinnen: Francesca D'Agostino, Isabel Rossi
Costume Design/Kostüm: Andy Besuch
Sound Design/Sounddesign: Bastian Hagedorn
Additional Editing and Mixing/Zusätzliche Bearbeitung und Abmischung: Alissa Dovgucic, Lennard Poschmann
Music Composition/Komposition: Bastian Hagedorn (featuring/mit Ben Bloodygrave, "Ich schau in dein Gesicht (Telekoma Cover)"; Milva, "Ninna Nanna 1932")

Die Performance *Trümmerfrau* wurde gefördert durch die Stiftung Kunstfonds und den Beauftragten der Bundesregierung für Kultur und Medien./The Performance *Trümmerfrau* is sponsored by Stiftung Kunstfonds and the Beauftragten der Bundesregierung für Kultur und Medien.

STUDIO SUNG TIEU

Studio Manager/Studiomanager: Silvio Saraceno
Architectural Design and Production/Architekturdesign und Produktion: Miriam Umiń
Graphic Design/Grafik: Gunar Laube
Research Assistant/Wissenschaftliche Mitarbeit: Mara Hornemann
Architectural Assistant/Assistenz Architektur: Tomi Laja
Studio Assistant/Studioassistenz: Ronald Laube
Interns/Praktikant*innen: Gena Haensel, Charlotte Mourge d'Algue, Giorgio Nigra

PRODUKTIONSTEAM / PRODUCTION TEAM SUNG TIEU

Mosaic Production/Mosaikproduktion: Ravennae Mosaico Ori e Smalti S.r.l.
Mosaic Consulting/Fachberatung Mosaik: Koko Mosaico
Exterior Install/Außenaufbau: Rio Marin S.r.l.
Interior Install/Innenaufbau: Studio Voxel
Scent/Duft: in collaboration with/in Zusammenarbeit mit Scentcommunication
Consulting/Beratung: Faraguna GmbH

PUBLICATION / PUBLIKATION

Editor/Herausgeber: Kathleen Reinhardt; ifa – Institut für Auslandsbeziehungen
Managing Editor/Redaktionsleitung: Jesi Khadivi
Project Management: DISTANZ Verlag (Charlotte Riggert, Rebecca Wilton), Anaïs Nyffeler
Design/Gestaltung: Dan Solbach
Translation/Übersetzung: soweit nicht anders angegeben, von den Autorinnen/unless otherwise noted, by the authors. Andrea Scrima (Sabeth Buchmann), Miriam Wiesel (Kathleen Reinhardt)
Copyediting/Lektorat: Jesi Khadivi (EN), Rebecca Wilton (DE), H von G/Katrin und Hans Georg Hiller von Gaertringen (Sung Tieu Chronicle), Mara Hornemann (Sung Tieu Chronicle)
Installation Views/Installationsansichten: Jens Ziehe
Lithography/Lithographie: Grafiche Veneziane
Production Mangement/Produktion: DISTANZ Verlag (Charlotte Riggert)
Printing and Binding/Druck und Verarbeitung: Grafiche Veneziane

Picture Credits/Fotocredits:
33–64 ©Jens Ziehe; 102–116 ©Henrike Naumann; 128 (top left) ©Barbara Mewis; (top right) courtesy Museum Lichtenberg; (bottom left) courtesy Weißenseer Heimatfreunde e.V./©B.Mewis; (bottom right) courtesy Weißenseer Heimatfreunde e.V./©B.Mewis; 129 (top left) courtesy Museum Lichtenberg; (top right) ©Sung Tieu; (bottom left) ©Sung Tieu; (bottom right) ©Sung Tieu; 130 (top left, top right) ©ullstein bild – EUROLUFTBILD.DE; (bottom left, bottom right) ©Studio M³ Architektur und Urbanismus/MLA+ mit Atelier Loidl; 145–146 ©Jens Ziehe

The publication was supported by the Alfried Krupp von Bohlen und Halbach Foundation./Die Publikation wurde gefördert von der Alfried Krupp von Bohlen und Halbach-Stiftung.

ISBN: 978-3-95476-826-4
Printed in Italy/Gedruckt in Italien

Published by DISTANZ Verlag
www.distanz.de
DISTANZ